D. Mullen

M y s

L

SA

SMYRNA

A

PHILADELPHIA

EPHESUS

LAODICEA

C a r i a

Phrygia

Pisidia

ATMOS

L y c i a

R E A T

S E A

SCALE

0   50   100 MILES

0   50   100 KILOMETERS

"Then is Finished The Mystery of God"

"In the days of the voice of the seventh angel, when he is about to sound, then is finished the mystery of God, according to the good tidings which he declared to his servants the prophets."
—Revelation 10:7, American Standard Version.

PUBLISHERS
WATCHTOWER BIBLE AND TRACT SOCIETY
OF NEW YORK, INC.
INTERNATIONAL BIBLE STUDENTS ASSOCIATION
Brooklyn, New York, U.S.A.

Made in the United States of America

DEDICATED
to the
"GOD OF PEACE"

Who at the Critical Time Finishes His Long-kept Sacred Secret for the Perfect Government of All Mankind

---

CONTENTS

CHAPTER 1

The Reporter of Mysteries Sees God in Vision

1

THE MYSTERY of mysteries—that is "the mystery of God." We people have a vital stake in this mystery. Just why so? Because it is tied in with the greatest issue of all times: the future rulership of our earth as well as heaven. All of us long for life and happiness, peace and prosperity. Well, all of this hangs on the settling of this crowning issue. This "mystery of God" should therefore arouse more than mere idle curiosity. It should arouse the warm interest that it so richly deserves. It should stir us to make an honest investigation that will not stop short of the goal of knowing and understanding the "mystery of God." That mystery, when finished and revealed, will win the highest admiration for its author and will result in endless good for all mankind. All the righteous desires of our hearts will be completely satisfied. This will make plain to us ever so many things that now baffle and mystify us.

2

An aged man of almost nineteen centuries ago heard the thrilling announcement of "the mystery of God." Later he saw the finishing of it, in prophetic vision. Not only that, but he also saw, in miraculous vision, the glorious God of this fascinating mystery. From this vision of God alone we have reason to believe with all our hearts that "the mystery of God" is for our eternal benefit. The man who saw that vision reported on a number of mysteries and considerately gave us the explanations of them. The man was John

7

the son of Zebedee, formerly a fisherman at the Sea of Galilee in the Middle East. At the time of the vision he was a prisoner of the Roman Empire on the penal isle of Patmos in the Aegean Sea, not far from the city of Ephesus, then the capital of the Roman province of Asia. But why was he now a prisoner? Nothing strange about why—then. It was for being a Christian, for this aged man was one of the twelve apostles of Jesus Christ.—Revelation 1:9-11.

The pagan Roman Empire might isolate him as a dangerous criminal on a forbidding penal isle and limit his free movement, but it could never limit the power of John's God from lifting him by the spirit of inspiration to realms of vision far beyond even those of scientific men in this nuclear space age. In this almost unbelievable experience John was highly honored with seeing, in miraculous vision, the Author of "the mystery of God," even God the Almighty himself, in a different setting from what earlier men such as Moses, Isaiah, Daniel and Ezekiel had seen in a vision of God. As if to photograph for us what he saw, the apostle John wrote down under inspiration the account of his awe-inspiring vision. But could the aged apostle John describe with words of human language the glorious sight so as to aid us weak-eyed humans to get some idea of what he saw?

Yes! By the spirit of inspiration John was able to do so, in simple words: "After these things I saw, and, look! an opened door in heaven, and the first voice that I heard was as of a trumpet, speaking with me, saying: 'Come on up here, and I shall show you the things that must take place.' After these things I immediately came to be in the power of the spirit: and, look! a throne was in its position in heaven, and there is one seated upon the throne. And the one seated is, in appearance, like a jasper stone and a precious red-colored stone, and round about the throne there is a rainbow like an emerald in appearance."
—Revelation 4:1-3.

The visionary "opened door in heaven" was awaiting

the entrance of someone, and that one was the apostle John. This was made certain by what was now said by a voice, possibly speaking to John in the common Greek of the first century of our Common Era, if not in John's native tongue, the Hebrew of that day. No mere human voice was it, for, without the aid of modern-day electrical loudspeakers, that first voice from heaven that John heard was "as of a trumpet." It could have reminded John of the sound of the trumpet that became continuously louder and louder, pealing forth from Mount Sinai at the time that the Ten Commandments were declared by Jehovah God there to the nation of Israel. (Exodus 19:19; 20:18, 19) And yet no one else on the island of Patmos heard that awe-inspiring voice, for only John had the vision given to him by the invisible active force or spirit of Almighty God. Thus in powerful tones that conveyed the message an invitation was given to John to enter through the door in heaven: "Come on up here, and I shall show you the things that must take place."

Only by the active force or spirit of God could the human creature John respond to an invitation such as that, one that the astronauts of this twentieth century have never received and could never fulfill in their man-made space suits. Not launched into outer space by a titanic rocket, but elevated in vision by the spirit of God, the apostle John was ushered through the "opened door in heaven" to behold a vision of the royal Ruler of heaven and earth. The setting in which this majestic Ruler throned had some features that could remind the apostle John of God's temple that once stood in old Jerusalem. For a most holy place, how fitting was all this! In the Most Holy of the temple, Jehovah God had been symbolized by the Shekinah, the miraculous light, Jehovah thus throning in the midst of ancient Jerusalem.

How could the human creature John describe God, or even the visionary picturization of God? Did John see some three-headed personage, representing the trinitarian deity of religious Christendom? No; nothing

like that idea of pagan imagination! The God whom
John saw was like the gleaming of a beautifully cut
jasper and of a precious red-colored stone (possibly
a carnelian). How appropriately John could later write,
in 1 John 1:5, these words that reflect what he had
seen in vision: "God is light and there is no darkness
at all in union with him"! God is just glorious, that
is all! The gleaming glory of his person can be compared only remotely with the dazzling gleam of precious cut gemstones that entrance the human eye.
How impossible it is, then, that he could be the source
of immoral, untrue, deceptive things that are pictured
by darkness! How worthily he is called "the Father
of the celestial lights"! (James 1:17) How suitable
that he should be the One to say, when starting the
preparation of this earth for the habitation of man:
"Let light come to be"!—Genesis 1:3.

Always master of every situation throughout all
creation, this glorious Ruler of heaven and earth
thrones in perfect sereneness and composure. See, as
a soothing, calming suggestion of this, the "rainbow
like an emerald in appearance," round about his throne.
How restful-looking that emerald-green color of the
rainbow! How a rainbow is produced is a mystery to
man, but this One on the heavenly throne knows. Over
twenty-four centuries earlier, that is to say, after the
earth had dried off from the rainfall of forty days
that caused a global deluge, God said to Noah and his
family who survived the flood in the ark: "My rainbow
I do give in the cloud, and it must serve as a sign of
the covenant between me and the earth. And it shall
occur that when I bring a cloud over the earth, then
the rainbow will certainly appear in the cloud. And
I shall certainly remember my covenant which is between me and you and every living soul among all
flesh; and no more will the waters become a deluge to
bring all flesh to ruin." (Genesis 9:13-15) How we
would like it if that rainbow about God's throne betokens the coming of endless peace for us!

God the Creator is King Supreme. This fact is illustrated by what is next disclosed to the apostle John with regard to God's throne. John says: "And round about the throne there are twenty-four thrones, and upon these thrones I saw seated twenty-four older persons dressed in white outer garments, and upon their heads golden crowns. And out of the throne there are proceeding lightnings and voices and thunders; and there are seven lamps of fire burning before the throne, and these mean the seven spirits of God. And before the throne there is, as it were, a glassy sea like crystal."—Revelation 4:4-6.

Could that part of the vision portray that God the heavenly King is surrounded by a body of twenty-four counselors or advisers with whom to consult on any problems or new purposes concerning what he should do? Not at all! The apostle Paul quotes from the prophecy of Isaiah 40:13, 14 and asks: "O the depth of God's riches and wisdom and knowledge! How unsearchable his judgments are and past tracing out his ways are! For 'who has come to know Jehovah's mind, or who has become his counselor?' Or, 'Who has first given to him, so that it must be repaid to him?' Because from him and by him and for him are all things." —Romans 11:33-36.

THE TWENTY-FOUR ENTHRONED OLDER ONES

Who, then, are those twenty-four older ones, dressed in white outer garments and with golden crowns on their heads and seated upon twenty-four thrones about God's throne?

A clue as to who they are or whom they picture is given earlier in the Revelation by John. After addressing himself to the "seven congregations" of real Christians like himself, he speaks of Jesus Christ as "The Ruler of the kings of the earth" and adds: "To him that loves us and that loosed us from our sins by means of his own blood—and he made us to be a kingdom, priests to his God and Father—yes, to him be the glory and the might forever. Amen." (Revelation 1:4-6) And just before John describes his vision of

God on his heavenly throne, he quotes Jesus Christ as saying to the "angel of the congregation in Laodicea": "To the one that conquers I will grant to sit down with me on my throne, even as I conquered and sat down with my Father on his throne." (Revelation 3:21) The twenty-four crowned and enthroned older persons must therefore be the entire body of the faithful, conquering Christians whom he finally makes priestly kings with him in the heavenly kingdom of God.—Revelation 20:4-6.

These were foreshadowed by the faithful priests of ancient Israel. Those Israelite priests were divided up into twenty-four courses or divisions for appointed terms of service at God's temple. (1 Chronicles 24:5-19; Luke 1:5) The number twenty-four would thus be appropriate for the faithful Christians in the new covenant, to whom the apostle Peter says: "You are 'a chosen race, a royal priesthood, a holy nation, a people for special possession, that you should declare abroad the excellencies' of the one that called you out of darkness into his wonderful light." (1 Peter 2:9) Besides this, the final number in the "royal priesthood" or "kingdom of priests" will be one hundred and forty-four thousand. (Exodus 19:6; Revelation 7:4-8; 14: 1, 3) And 144,000 is a multiple of twenty-four, this number being the product of 6,000 times 24. Further details, given later on in the Revelation, add to the proof that the twenty-four older persons stand for the 144,000 conquering footstep followers of Jesus Christ.

These one hundred and forty-four thousand conquerors as pictured by the twenty-four older persons were not always sitting enthroned around the heavenly throne of Jehovah God. Remember that the fulfillment of the vision of these symbolic twenty-four older persons dates from a certain time future from the apostle John's own day. Remember that the trumpetlike voice that invited John to "come on up here" added: "And I shall show you the things that must take place." Consequently, the vision of these crowned, enthroned twenty-four older persons was a prophetic preview of the arrangement that was to be set up in heaven with respect to God's throne. It was a disclosure of God's purpose to have 144,000 priestly kings associated with Jesus Christ the Chief Priest and Messianic King of God. So at the time of John's vision those who were pictured by the twenty-four older persons were not then seated on thrones around God's throne in heaven, for the faithful apostle John himself was to be among those symbolic twenty-four older ones; and certainly at the time of John's vision he was not actually among them in heaven.

Unlike the prophet Ezekiel, the apostle John did not describe God's throne as having the gleam of a "sapphire stone." (Ezekiel 1:26) Yet to John it was more awe-inspiring, for "out of the throne there are proceeding lightnings and voices and thunders." (Revelation 4:5) Flashes of dazzling enlightenment do indeed dart forth from God's heavenly throne, but his lightnings could also be employed like fiery arrows or missiles to strike his enemies dead instantly. Voices also issue out from the throne of the One who is the Creator of all speech, voices not talking meaninglessly, but conveying messages in agreement with one another and in harmony with the light of truth. Thunder follows lightning, and the peals of thunder out of God's throne pound into the senses of the people who behold and hear the meaning of the lightning flashes of divine revelation. These things proceeding out of God's heavenly throne betoken that he is on his throne at this time for a spectacular event to occur, just as when lightning flashes, thunder peals and sounds as of a horn accompanied his presence at Mount Sinai to give the Ten Commandments.—Exodus 20:18.

Necessarily God's invisible active force, his spirit, must be in heavy operation at the time his purpose is revealed. The full measure of operation of his forcefully active spirit is portrayed to us, in that "there are seven lamps of fire burning before the throne, and," says the apostle John, "these mean the seven spirits of God." (Revelation 4:5) Lamps lighted are for the purpose of giving light to persons in a room or in a certain area. The perfect number of lamps —seven of them—would shed a fullness of light, enlightenment that is due to the operation of God's spirit in a sevenfold way, in the fullness of its force. (1 Corinthians 2:10) Those seven symbolic lamps suggest that, in the fulfillment of John's vision, God is throning in his heavenly temple in behalf of pure, clean worship, inasmuch as in God's earthly tent or temple at Shiloh before King David's day there was a lampstand with seven branches, to provide seven lamps for illuminating the Holy Place.—Exodus 25:31-40; 40:1-4, 24, 25.

A further indication that the scene here presented is that of God in his heavenly temple is the fact that "before the throne there is, as it were, a glassy sea like crystal." (Revelation 4:6) In God's ancient arrangement among the Israelites there was a laver or wash basin, placed between the copper altar and the sanctuary (Exodus 30:18-21; 40:7, 11, 30, 31); and, later on in King Solomon's temple at Jerusalem, this laver or basin was so large that it was called a sea. —1 Kings 7:23-44; 1 Chronicles 18:8.

The molten sea in Solomon's temple was made of copper, but the sea seen in John's vision was glassy, "like crystal," transparent. As in ancient Israel the temple sea was for the sacrificing priests to have plenty of water to wash hands and feet, the "glassy sea like crystal" suggests purity, cleanness, on the part of those who approach God. John's fellow apostle Paul, in Ephesians 5:25, 26, speaks of the cleansing of Christ's followers "with the bath of water by means of the word." True to the picture, God keeps his "glassy sea like crystal" filled with the purifying water of his Word of truth. For those who approach God acceptably, cleansing is needed by means of his Word. —John 15:3.

THE "FOUR LIVING CREATURES"

Still another feature of John's vision suggests the temple of God and the proper surroundings of his heavenly throne. John describes this feature, saying: "And in the midst of the throne and around the throne there are four living creatures that are full of eyes in front and behind. And the first living creature is like a lion, and the second living creature is like a young bull, and the third living creature has a face like a man's, and the fourth living creature is like a flying eagle. And as for the four living creatures, each one of them respectively has six wings; round about and underneath they are full of eyes. And they have no rest day and night as they say: 'Holy, holy, holy is Jehovah* God, the Almighty, who was and who is and who is coming.'"

The "living creatures" thus described in Revelation 4:6-8 picture the cherubs of God, the first appearance of whom to human eyes is described in Genesis 3:24, after the expulsion of sinful Adam and his wife Eve from the Garden of Eden. In Ezekiel 1:6, 13, 14, 15, 19, 20, 21, 22 and 10:15, 18, 20, the cherubs that moved alongside the tremendous wheels of God's throne chariot are called "living creatures," and Ezekiel 10:1-22 directly calls the living creatures "cherubs." Whereas in Ezekiel's vision each cherubic living creature has four faces, namely, those of a man in front, of a lion to the right, of a bull (cherub) to the left, of an eagle to the rear, the cherubs seen in John's vision have each an individual face, each one having respectively one of the four faces seen in Ezekiel's vision. (Ezekiel 1:5, 6, 10, 11; 10:14, 20-22)† Thus each one of these cherubs or living creatures would give particular prominence to the special distinguishing quality that was represented by the face.

In having a man's face the third living creature in John's vision made outstanding the quality of love,

---

* The name "Jehovah" occurs here, in Revelation 4:8, instead of "Lord" (Kýrios), in nine translations of the Christian Greek Scriptures into Hebrew, from 1599 down to 1885. See footnote a on page 717 of the *New World Translation of the Christian Greek Scriptures,* edition of 1950.

† The Greek Septuagint translation (*LXX*) of Ezekiel, chapters 1 and 10, uses the same Greek expression for "living creatures" as does Revelation, chapter 4.

especially love founded, not on passion, but on principle, a love that man has in marked contrast with brute beasts. "God is love," and man, who was made in God's image and likeness, was likewise to be marked by the display of Godlike love. (1 John 4:8, 16; Genesis 1:26-28) Hence the "greatest and first commandment" of God's law given through the prophet Moses was, "You must love Jehovah your God with your whole heart and with your whole soul and with your whole mind" (Deuteronomy 6:5); and the second main commandment was, "You must love your neighbor as yourself." (Leviticus 19:18) So said the Son of God himself. (Matthew 22:36-40) Cherubs in the spirit realm, being also made in God's image, should also themselves possess the divine quality of love. In John's vision they show a love of Jehovah God as holy.

The first living creature, in being like a royal lion, gives prominence to the divine quality of justice, courageous justice. As respects courage, the Bible expression "the valiant man whose heart is as the heart of the lion" points up the fact that the lion is courageous. (2 Samuel 17:10) It takes courage to exercise impartial justice, and the combining of courage and justice is played up in Proverbs 28:1 (*Dy*): "The wicked man fleeth, when no man pursueth: but the just, bold as a lion, shall be without dread." Justice is fundamental with Jehovah God, and he rules in justice. In addressing him, the psalmist sings out: "Righteousness and judgment are the established place of your throne." (Psalm 89:14) In a song to Jehovah God the prophet Moses links the nicety of God's justice with his perfectness, saying: "The Rock, perfect is his activity, for all his ways are justice. A God of faithfulness, with whom there is no injustice; righteous and upright is he." (Deuteronomy 32:4) God's love did not set aside his justice in ransoming humankind from sin, condemnation and death. God's love provided a perfect human sacrifice that met all points of justice.

The second living creature seen in John's vision

was like a young bull, and in this respect it features the power, the dynamic energy of God. The bull, in the wild state, is fearless, because it is aware of its formidable horns and its tremendous strength. Rightly, God, who created the bull with such power, asked his pupil named Job: "Does a wild bull want to serve you, or will it spend the night by your manger? Will you bind a wild bull fast with its ropes in the furrow, or will it harrow low plains after you? Will you trust in it because its power is abundant, and will you leave your toil to it?" (Job 39:9-11) Logically, then, God would use the figure of a bull in a vision as a symbol of power, which comes from him. "Strength belongs to God."—Psalm 62:11.

In John's vision, the fourth living creature was "like a flying eagle" and thus gave due prominence to the divine quality of wisdom. (Revelation 4:7) Divine wisdom is lofty, just like the eagle in its nesting and in its flight. Proverbs 30:18, 19 speaks wonderingly of "the way of an eagle in the heavens."

God referred to how marvelously he created the eagle by asking Job: "Is it at your order that an eagle flies upward and that it builds its nest high up?" (Job 39:27) It knows where to fly for its food, for God gifted it with remarkable farsightedness. On this fact, the God of wisdom remarks: "On a crag it resides and stays during the night upon the tooth of a crag and an inaccessible place. From there it has to search for food; far into the distance its eyes keep looking. And its young ones themselves keep sipping up blood; and where the slain are, there it is." (Job 39:28-30) Jesus Christ must have had these words of God in mind when, in his prophecy on the "conclusion of the system of things," he said: "Wherever the carcass is, there the eagles will be gathered together."—Matthew 24:28; Luke 17:37.

Discerning its objective clearly, the eagle can fly swiftly and in no uncertainty to its prey, for God has given it also wings of great power. Habakkuk 1:8 makes a fine comparison when it says: "They fly like the eagle speeding to eat something." In a reference to strength of wing and lofty flying, Isaiah 40:31 remarks: "They will mount up with wings like eagles." God likens himself to an eagle as regards the way that he brought his people, whom he rescued out of Egypt, to the place that he had chosen for them, by inspiring the prophet Moses to say, in Deuteronomy 32:11-13: "Just as an eagle stirs up its nest, hovers over its fledglings, spreads out its wings, takes them, carries them on its pinions, Jehovah alone kept leading him, and there was no foreign god along with him. He kept making him ride upon earth's high places." In agreement with all this, Jehovah God possesses the quality that is symbolized by the swift, high-flying, far-seeing eagle, namely, wisdom, in its perfection.

The Most High God, who is like an eagle, not only possesses wisdom; he is the Source of all wisdom for all creation. "For Jehovah himself gives wisdom; out of his mouth there are knowledge and discernment." (Proverbs 2:6) Because he is superior in wisdom to all his intelligent creatures, the Christian apostle Paul closed his inspired letter to the congregation in Rome with the words: "To God, wise alone, be the glory through Jesus Christ forever. Amen." (Romans 16:27) Since his possession of wisdom is so prominent, wisdom's presence before God's heavenly throne is shown in that the fourth living creature "is like a flying eagle."

The apostle John observed in his vision that the four living creatures were "full of eyes in front and behind." Also, "each one of them respectively has six wings; round about and underneath they are full of eyes." (Revelation 4:6-8) Their being thus full of eyes on both body and wings, if not also denoting their being awake all the time, would denote the ability of seeing all things. How fittingly the inspired psalmist ascribes this ability to God, saying: "Look! He will not be drowsy nor go to sleep, he that is guarding Israel." (Psalm 121:4) The wisest man of ancient times says: "The eyes of Jehovah are in every place, keeping watch upon the bad ones and the good ones." (Proverbs 15:3) Over a thousand years later an inspired writer says: "There is not a creation that is not manifest to his sight, but all things are naked and openly exposed to the eyes of him with whom we have an accounting." (Hebrews 4:13) Add to this the divine ability pictured by the eye-loaded wings, six in number, or three pairs on each living creature. The number three being emphatic, in the Bible, the three pairs of wings stand for the high rate of speed to reach what is seen.

These outstanding features would make the cherubs equal to the continued service that the apostle John saw them rendering: "They have no rest day and night as they say: 'Holy, holy, holy is Jehovah God, the Almighty, who was and who is and who is coming.' " (Revelation 4:8) Their repeatedly saying "Holy" three times adds emphasis to the holiness of Jehovah God the Almighty. He is in fact the Most Holy One, no one else being so clean, pure, sacred as He is, absolutely removed from being tempted by any evil thing.

Glad we can be that holiness goes along with his being the Almighty, for it makes sure that He will never misuse or abuse his almighty power. He has ever been holy and ever will be, for he is the One "who was and who is and who is coming." Without beginning and without end is he, the God immortal, incorruptible, the Lord of all for all eternity. (1 Timothy 1:17) Since heavenly cherubic living creatures continually show regard for the holiness of the Lord God Almighty, certainly we inferior human creatures should do so.

POSITION OF THE FOUR LIVING CREATURES

As respects the four living creatures, the apostle John says that they were "in the midst of the throne and around the throne." (Revelation 4:6) How is such a thing possible when the Lord God the Almighty is himself seated upon the throne? In this way: The four living creatures were in the midst *with* the throne, for the throne occupied the central position, and the four living creatures were at the center with it. Farther out from the throne of God and all around it on four sides were seated the twenty-four older persons on their thrones. (Revelation 4:4) The expression "in the midst of the throne" could also mean that, when the throne was looked at toward each of its four sides, a living creature was at the middle of that side of the throne. In other words, the four living creatures were not at the four corners of the throne or its platform, as was the case with the four cherubic living creatures whom the prophet Ezekiel saw, one each at one of the four wheels on which the platform of God's throne chariot rode.—Ezekiel 1:15-22.

How well, then, Jehovah's position among these living creatures fits the words of Psalm 99:1! They read: "Jehovah himself has become king. . . . He is sitting upon the cherubs."

In the vision the presence of the four living creatures together with the seven lamps of fire and the glassy sea like crystal before God's throne strongly suggests that the apostle John is seeing Jehovah God enthroned in his heavenly temple some time after the setting up of his promised kingdom. Call to mind the temple that wise King Solomon was commanded to build in the capital city of Jerusalem for the worship of Jehovah God:

In its courtyard before the temple sanctuary there was the huge basin of copper that was called "the molten sea." Inside the first holy compartment of the sanctuary there were golden lampstands, ten of them, five to the north side and five to the south. But inside the second compartment of the sanctuary, its Most Holy, there were solid images of four cherubs. Two of these were of solid gold and were of one piece with the golden lid of the sacred chest, the Ark of the Covenant, over which the miraculous light, the Shekinah, hovered to represent God's presence. The other cherub images were of an olive-wood base, but were overlaid with gold, and were ten cubits (about fourteen feet seven inches) in height. With backs to the sanctuary's western walls, they faced eastward and stretched out two of their long wings toward each other, thus over-shadowing the Ark of the Covenant, which was only a cubit and a half (about two feet two inches) high and was surmounted by its two cherubs.—2 Chronicles 4:2-7, 9-22; 3:10-13; 1 Kings 6:19, 25-28; Exodus 25: 10-22.

In notable respects, then, Jehovah's envisioned throne in heaven is given a temple setting or surround-ing. This emphasizes the holiness of Jehovah God and fits in agreeably with the constantly repeated words of the four cherubic living creatures: "Holy, holy, holy is Jehovah God, the Almighty, who was and who is and who is coming." (Revelation 4:8) In themselves these four living creatures make plain why He is ex-ceptionally holy. By their distinguishing appearance, in being like a lion and like a young bull and like a man in facial features and like a flying eagle, the living creatures put into bold relief the four basic qualities of the Most High God, namely, justice, power, love and wisdom. Which of all the false gods of the religions of the world is marked by the possession and manifestation of all these four qualities in their per-fection, in perfect accord and cooperation? Not one! The one and only God of perfect justice, power, love and wisdom deserves nothing less than worship by all his intelligent creatures in heaven and on earth.

THE CREATOR OF ALL THINGS

Look further at the miraculous vision given to the apostle John and behold also how the highest-ranking ones seen at the heavenly temple are overwhelmed with the strong urge to yield to this God of perfect justice, power, love and wisdom all that is due him. John writes: "And whenever the living creatures offer glory and honor and thanksgiving to the one seated upon the throne, the one that lives forever and ever, the twenty-four older persons fall down before the one seated upon the throne and worship the one that lives forever and ever, and they cast their crowns before the throne, saying: 'You are worthy, Jehovah, even our God, to receive the glory and the honor and the power, because you created all things, and because of your will they existed and were created.' " —Revelation 4:9-11.

The apostle John himself felt that way toward the enthroned Jehovah God the Almighty. John was one of that faithful "little flock" who are called according to the divine purpose to be one of those 144,000 loyal worshipers who will be enthroned by the King of eternity, "the one that lives forever and ever," after he sets up his promised kingdom in the heavens and comes to his spiritual temple. (Revelation 1:6, 9) Jehovah God the Almighty is the one that promised and arranged to give such called and faithful worshipers a share in the heavenly kingdom; and when they come into that kingdom over the world of mankind, they will be willing to yield over their kingdom, their sovereignty, to the one Source of it, the ever-living Almighty God. They will be willing to come down off their thrones and cast their crowns before him, thus disclaiming any independent rulership. They bow and worship before him as his lowly undeserving subjects. To him belong the glory and the honor and the power. What they themselves have of these things, they accredit to him. They want him to have all these things as belonging to him, he being worthy of them all. Let all the glory, honor and power go to him!

Why do these symbolic twenty-four older persons in this way acknowledge Jehovah God the Almighty as the Universal Sovereign? It is because they recognize this ever-living One as the Creator of all things in heaven and on earth. No modern-day evolutionists are they, but with accurate knowledge and conviction they confess to him: "You created all things."

God willed for these things to come into existence and he had the ability to carry out this will. Hence they say further to him: "Because of your will they existed and were created." He is thus their Creator and the Creator of their white outer garments, their crowns and their thrones, things representing their heavenly kingship. What reason is there, then, for them to do anything else but join the four living creatures in offering to Him glory, honor and thanksgiving? This they do, in a very demonstrative way, completely unlike the human kings and rulers of mankind today. Happily these symbolic twenty-four older persons portray the kind of heavenly rulers that Jehovah God will appoint over all mankind. He created them according to his will, in evidence of what kind of God he is.

This is the God of the mystery! This is the God of whom a few men, mere human creatures such as the inspired prophets Moses, Isaiah, Ezekiel and Daniel, have had visions miraculously. When we consider just by itself the meaningful vision to the exiled Christian apostle John, the last man on earth to have a miraculous vision of Jehovah God, we are deeply impressed. We have not been dealing with human imaginations. Rather, through the authentic record of an inspired vision, written down by a truthful man who was suffering imprisonment for being a faithful apostle of Jesus Christ, we have gained a deeper, broader insight into a real divine Being, the one living and true God, the lone One responsible for all creation, including us ourselves.

Since this glorious One is the God of this greatest mystery of all, how could we be anything but benefited, blessed, comforted, revived, joyful by pursuing our investigation of this mystery to its amazing solution under the blessing and help of this God? On, then, with our investigation of "the mystery of God"!

CHAPTER 2

The Opener
of the Scroll
of Mystery

A SCROLL of mystery is being unrolled, and its contents of secrets for our days are being revealed. They are being expressed in dramatic action, made to come alive, in our marvelous twentieth century. Someone worthy has been found competent, suitable, to open this scroll of mystery and to explain its secrets to us with exciting events on the world stage of action. Who is this expert opener of the scroll, and how did he get hold of it? Why was he entrusted with its execution? The Christian apostle John of nineteen centuries ago was greatly interested in these same questions. These questions are worthy of our interest above all other interesting marvels of modern times, and we shall be hugely rewarded for making it our business to get them answered. Let us join the apostle John in learning the answers.

The vision that John was invited to come up to heaven in spirit to see did not end with merely seeing Jehovah God the Almighty on his heavenly throne, seated in glory and receiving the praises of heavenly creatures. Out of the glow of beautiful light that represented God seated upon his flashing throne there was a hand extended. It was the right hand, and it held something! The apostle John, who was put under obligation to make the revelation known to us, tells us about it, in these words: "And I saw in the right hand of the one seated upon the throne a scroll written within and on the reverse side, sealed tight with seven seals. And I saw a strong angel proclaiming with a

24

loud voice: 'Who is worthy to open the scroll and loose its seals?' But neither in heaven nor upon earth nor underneath the earth was there a single one able to open the scroll or to look into it. And I gave way to a great deal of weeping because no one was found worthy to open the scroll or to look into it."—Revelation 5:1-4.

No one could wrest that scroll forcibly out of the right hand of the Almighty God to break its seals and look inside. Only of his own accord would God's right hand, which especially symbolizes power, hand that scroll to the one whom He deemed worthy, suitable. He himself had written the contents of that scroll, inside and outside. He thus recorded exciting prophecies of events that were linked with the finishing of the mystery of God. These prophetic matters were sealed perfectly against detection by any undeserving creature in heaven and earth, the seven seals picturing that fact. But would Almighty God tantalize all who beheld the scroll by merely allowing them to see it in his right hand but never providing some worthy one to break all seven seals and make known the prophetic contents of the scroll? No! He would not have brought the mysterious scroll to the view of his creatures unless he had purposed to satisfy their proper interest and to reveal to them the sacred mystery of his will. In his due time he would reveal his mystery by his worthy one.

By proclaiming with a loud voice the gripping question, "Who is worthy to open the scroll and loose its seals?" the strong angel induced a search to be made among the persons living in heaven and on earth, and among the dead underneath the ground, for someone worthy in God's estimation. The apostle John himself was not worthy, and when it appeared to him that no other creature was worthy, he burst into tears. His great eagerness to have the mystery of the scroll solved accurately foreshadowed the intense eagerness of true Bible-studying Christians in our twentieth century to understand what was meant by the symbolic things that John saw as the seven seals were finally opened, one seal after another. Explanations given to these earnest Christian Bible students prior to the end of World War I in the year 1918 failed to satisfy them. But just as God tested out the degree of John's interest, so he tested out the degree of interest of twentieth-century Christians.

Our tears of long-tested interest and anxiety can be dried just as were John's burning tears nineteen centuries ago. But by means of whom? One of those twenty-four older persons who had cast their golden crowns at God's feet helped John, making known a vital discovery to him: "But one of the older persons says to me: 'Stop weeping. Look! The Lion that is of the tribe of Judah, the root of David, has conquered so as to open the scroll and its seven seals.' " (Revelation 5:5) The Jewish Christian apostle John well knew who is "the Lion that is of the tribe of Judah, the root of David." John recalled the prophecy that was pronounced back in 1711 B.C.E. by the dying patriarch Jacob upon his fourth son, named Judah, as recorded in Genesis 49:9, 10:

"A lion cub Judah is. From the prey, my son, you will certainly go up. He bowed down, he stretched himself out like a lion and, like a lion, who dares rouse him? The scepter will not turn aside from Judah, neither the commander's staff from between his feet, until Shiloh comes; and to him the obedience of the people will belong."

According to this uncovering of part of the mystery or sacred secret of God, "the Lion that is of the tribe of Judah" was to be a just king, a king fearless like a lion in executing divine justice. The scepter of kingly rule was at last to come to him without fail; God himself would never turn aside nor would he let be turned aside from this Lion the royal scepter of world rule, for to him the obedience of all the peoples of earth belongs. Bound to come to him is the "commander's staff," which is to rest between his knees and feet as he sits upon his throne of world rulership.

When he comes, "Shiloh" comes, this name signifying his divine right to rule, for Shiloh means (in Hebrew) "To Whom It Belongs," "The One Whose It Is." The tribe of Judah would exist from 1711 B.C.E. onward for 1743 years, or until 33 C.E., and yet, without being turned aside, the scepter and commander's staff would unerringly come into permanent possession of "the Lion that is of the tribe of Judah." God has willed it.

Out of this tribe of Judah came David the youngest son of Jesse of the town of Bethlehem-Judah. While still a shepherd boy David was anointed by the prophet Samuel at God's command to be the future king of all twelve tribes of Israel. In the year 1077 B.C.E. David was anointed at the city of Hebron to be king over the tribe of Judah. Seven and a half years later, or in 1070 B.C.E., he was finally anointed as king over all twelve tribes of Israel. He moved his capital city to Jerusalem, and there Jehovah God made a solemn covenant with him, that the kingdom of God over His chosen people should always remain in the family line of David. (2 Samuel 7:8-29) This family line of King David would end up in a permanent heir to the royal throne, and this everlasting heir would be "the Lion that is of the tribe of Judah." He would be the one whom God would use to revive the kingdom of David, which was overthrown in the year 607 B.C.E. by the pagan Babylonians. After that this final heir would become "the root of David." As a "root" he would give new life to the Davidic kingdom and keep it going forever.

To prove worthy to receive the mysterious scroll at God's hand and to open its seven seals, this "Lion that is of the tribe of Judah" first had to conquer. But conquer what, and how? His forefather David had conquered and had thus with God's help subdued all the Promised Land for the nation of Israel. How would his permanent heir conquer and prove worthy? Our making certain who this permanent heir is will help us to discern how he "has conquered so as to open the scroll and its seven seals." This worthy one has been found! The apostle John had a vision of his coming on to the heavenly scene at the tense moment. What does he look like? A lion? Tell us, John! Answering our request, John writes:

"And I saw standing in the midst of the throne [or, in the center of the throne] and of the four living creatures and in the midst of the older persons a lamb as though it had been slaughtered, having seven horns and seven eyes, which eyes mean the seven spirits of God that have been sent forth into the whole earth. And he went and at once took it out of the right hand of the one seated on the throne."—Revelation 5:6, 7.

Instead of seeing a symbolic lion, the apostle John saw, probably to his surprise, a symbolic lamb that "had been slaughtered" but that had been brought back to life by the power of the Almighty God "seated on the throne." Ah, now the identity of "the Lion that is of the tribe of Judah" becomes unmistakable. The apostle John, in the year 29 C.E., had heard the messenger, John the Baptist, say, as he pointed to the nearby Jesus, who had been baptized in water and then anointed with God's spirit from heaven: "See, the Lamb of God!" The previous day John the Baptist had said within the hearing of bystanders: "See, the Lamb of God that takes away the sin of the world! . . . I viewed the spirit coming down as a dove out of heaven, and it remained upon him. Even I did not know him, but the very One who sent me to baptize in water said to me, 'Whoever it is upon whom you see the spirit coming down and remaining, this is the one that baptizes in holy spirit.' And I have seen it, and I have borne witness that this one is the Son of God."—John 1:29-36.

THE "LAMB" THAT CONQUERED

About three and a half years later, on Nisan 14, the Passover day of the year 33 C.E., the apostle John himself saw this "Lamb of God" slaughtered, murdered, by being nailed to a torture stake outside the walls of Jerusalem to die, outwardly like a cursed criminal, but really as a symbolic passover lamb "that takes away the sin of the world." The apostle John, who stood near the torture stake of Jesus, tells us that, just as in the case of the literal passover lamb, not a bone of Jesus was broken before his dead body was taken down from the torture stake to be buried. (John 19:25-37; Exodus 12:43-46) The night before this, the apostle John had heard Jesus say to his faithful apostles: "In the world you are having tribulation, but take courage! I have conquered the world." (John 16:33) On the third day after the slaughter and burial of this world conqueror, the apostle John saw him alive again, resurrected from the dead by the power of Almighty God. On the fortieth day from then John saw this resurrected Jesus ascend from the Mount of Olives toward heaven and then disappear from sight behind a cloud.—John 20:19-25; Luke 24:36-53; Acts 1:1-12.

As a reward for his conquering the wicked world and proving faithful to the Almighty God to the death on the torture stake, this symbolic Lamb of God has become "the Lion that is of the tribe of Judah, the root of David." Almighty God has clothed him with full power, all the power that this once slaughtered Lamb needs to carry out completely God's purpose for him. This full power was symbolized by the "seven horns" that the Lamb had upon his head.

Not alone does he have fullness of power, but he has also the fullness of perfect perception, discernment and knowledge suitable to go with such a tremendous grant of power, this being symbolized by the "seven eyes" of this unusual Lamb. This fullness of perception and knowledge the Lamb received from Almighty God, for which reason the seven eyes are said to be "the seven spirits of God that have been sent forth into the whole earth." Spirit (pneúma, Greek) is active force, and the "seven eyes" or "seven spirits" stand for a fullness of active force from God. This force the Lamb can use in observing from far off in heaven all that goes on in the whole earth and discerning its meaning.—Compare Zechariah 4:10.

Beyond all dispute, this once slaughtered but world-conquering Lamb was "worthy to open the scroll and loose its seals." So past the twenty-four older persons enthroned in a circle about God's throne and past the four cherubic living creatures that were centrally located toward the four sides of the throne, yes, past the lionlike living creature, the Lamb went right up to God's throne and received out of his right hand the mysterious scroll. His being allowed to take the scroll out of God's hand meant his being commissioned to reveal to creatures in heaven and earth the things written upon the scroll. It meant also his being authorized to do whatever might be necessary to see to it that what was prophesied in writing on the scroll came true. Here is where the symbolic "seven eyes," "seven spirits," and "seven horns" of the Lamb would prove to be useful.

Thus this heavenly scene differs in certain respects from the prophet Daniel's vision as recorded in Daniel 7:13, 14. There Daniel saw in vision a heavenly person like a son of man being ushered into the presence of the Ancient of Days to be highly honored. To him the Almighty God, the Ancient of Days, gave rulership, dignity, and kingdom, not just over the twelve tribes of the nation of Israel, but over all mankind, "that the peoples, national groups and languages should all serve even him." The fulfillment of this took place in the heavens at the close of the Gentile Times, around Tishri 15 (October 4/5) in the year 1914 C.E. Since then he has been obeying the divine command, "Go subduing in the midst of your enemies." (Psalm 110:1, 2; Hebrews 10:12, 13) Daniel's vision shows all such enemies on earth being finally destroyed, to clear the way for the Son of man's kingdom to rule all peoples, national groups and languages without a rival earthly government. (Daniel 7:11, 12, 17-26) But this vision to Daniel does not show the Son of man as taking a secret scroll from God's right hand and breaking its seven seals to disclose its mysterious contents.

1 When, therefore, did the Lamb, who is also "the Lion that is of the tribe of Judah," come and take the scroll out of God's right hand and begin to open its seven seals? When, in fulfillment of John's vision, this Lamb does actually appear and take the scroll out of God's hand, it does not mean that first then Jehovah God on his heavenly throne makes his decision and shows to all creation who is worthy to take the scroll and unseal its contents. The apostle John was given his vision apparently near the close of the first century C.E., traditionally about the year 96 C.E. Well, at that time the vision disclosed that there would be such a mysterious scroll and that the honor and authority to unseal it was reserved for the symbolical Lamb, "the Lion that is of the tribe of Judah," namely, Jesus Christ, glorified in heaven. Since then Bible-studying Christians have been looking for the heavenly Jesus Christ to receive that scroll at God's hand and to reveal to their understanding the fulfillment of its prophetic contents.

2 With all that has been taking place on earth from the year 1914 C.E. onward, would it be strange or unreasonable that the breaking of the seven seals of the mysterious scroll has been taking place in this twentieth century? No, and this likelihood should lead us excitedly to examine what takes place in heaven and on earth after the breaking open of the seven seals, one by one. Why, this takes in the finishing of the "mystery of God"! But what did the apostle John see take place when the worthy Lamb got possession of the scroll in vision, and what should we expect to take place in the invisible heavens when this Lamb of God actually takes what is pictured by the scroll and stands ready to open its seals with divine approval? Tell us, John, please:

3 "And when he took the scroll, the four living creatures and the twenty-four older persons fell down before the Lamb, having each one a harp and golden bowls that were full of incense, and the incense means the prayers of the holy ones. And they sing a new song, saying: 'You are worthy to take the scroll and open its seals, because you were slaughtered and with your

blood you bought persons for God out of every tribe and tongue and people and nation, and you made them to be a kingdom and priests to our God, and they are to rule as kings over the earth.' "—Revelation 5:8-10.

Even the heavenly cherubs, pictured by the four living creatures, interrupt their continually saying, "Holy, holy, holy is Jehovah God, the Almighty, who was and who is and who is coming," to do obeisance to the Lamb and to acknowledge this Chosen One of God as worthy. (Revelation 4:8) Those who are pictured by the twenty-four older persons do not cast their crowns down before the Lamb as they did before God on his throne, but they do join in rendering obeisance to the Lamb as being God's worthy one.

According to the Greek language in which John wrote down the vision, the twenty-four older persons, and not the four cherubic living creatures, are the ones that have each a harp and a golden bowl full of incense. "Each of the elders had a harp, and they held golden bowls," is the way the *New English Bible* renders the text of verse eight in chapter five.* Later on (in Revelation 14:1-3) the 144,000 faithful footstep followers of the Lamb of God are shown as having harps and as singing a new song. They are the "holy ones," who offer up to God "prayers" like "incense" as out of golden bowls.

So the twenty-four older persons, picturing the 144,-000, are really singing the "new song" about themselves, when they acknowledge the worthiness of the Lamb and sing to him: "You were slaughtered and with your blood you bought persons for God out of every tribe and tongue and people and nation, and you made them to be a kingdom and priests to our God, and they are to rule as kings over the earth." Those followers of the Lamb who are made priests and who are to rule over the earth have part in the "first resurrection" to heavenly glory and they are called "holy." (Revelation 20:4-6; 14:4, 5) For such a glorious future the 144,000

---

* In the Greek text the word for "living creatures" is in the neuter gender, but the expression "having each" is in the masculine gender.

(of whom the apostle John was one) are greatly indebted to the once slaughtered Lamb, and most properly they ascribe worthiness to him.

ACCLAIMED AS WORTHY
BY SUPERHUMAN CREATURES

Even holy angels of heaven who were not bought for God by the blood of the Lamb are moved by unselfish appreciation to join in acknowledging the worthiness of the Lamb, "the Lion that is of the tribe of Judah." "And I saw," says the apostle John, "and I heard a voice of many angels around the throne and the living creatures and the older persons, and the number of them was myriads of myriads and thousands of thousands, saying with a loud voice: 'The Lamb that was slaughtered is worthy to receive the power and riches and wisdom and strength and honor and glory and blessing.' "—Revelation 5:11, 12.

From that scene in heaven we can imagine what kind of reception in heaven Jesus Christ received when, on the twenty-fifth day of the Jewish lunar month Iyar, 33 C.E., or the fortieth day from his resurrection from the dead, he ascended from the Mount of Olives east of the city of Jerusalem, leaving down below his watching disciples. (Luke 24:50-52; Acts 1:1-12; John 6:62; 20:17; Hebrews 1:3, 4; 1 Peter 3:22) In the heavenly scene that the apostle John beheld, Satan the Devil and his demons are not seen. This suggests that by the time John's vision is fulfilled Satan the Devil and his demons have been cast out of heaven and have been confined to the vicinity of our earth. (Revelation 12:7-13) This would locate the fulfillment of John's vision after the close of the Gentile Times in 1914 C.E. and after the war in heaven that followed and in which the Lamb, "the Lion that is of the tribe of Judah," conquered. (Revelation 5:5) Thus in the cleansed heavens all the spirit creatures acclaim the once slaughtered but now resurrected Lamb of God as deserving power, riches, wisdom, strength, honor, glory and blessing as a reward from Jehovah God.

Man is made "a little lower than angels." (Hebrews 2:5-9; Psalm 8:4, 5) Reasonably, then, if the angels who are superior to us humans hail the self-sacrificing Lamb, Jesus Christ, as worthy to receive favor and honor from God to such an extent, ought we here on earth not to show the same appreciation for the Lamb? Ought we not to join with the angels in approving and applauding the glorification of the Lamb Jesus Christ in heaven? Eventually we shall have to do so if we desire to be in the fulfillment of the further part of John's vision. This further part of John's vision looks into the distant future, yes, a thousand years into the future when all living creation in heaven and on earth will be lined up in one under the Lamb as Jehovah God's topmost representative. This will require the future final destruction of Satan the Devil and his demons and of all who wickedly choose to serve him. Giving us good promise of this desirable state of affairs, John writes:

"And every creature that is in heaven and on earth and underneath the earth and on the sea, and all the things in them, I heard saying: 'To the one sitting on the throne and to the Lamb be the blessing and the honor and the glory and the might forever and ever.' And the four living creatures went saying: 'Amen!' and the older persons fell down and worshiped."—Revelation 5:13, 14.

What a tingling sensation it gives us when John says that he saw and heard "every creature that is . . . underneath the earth" ascribing blessing, honor, glory and might to Jehovah God sitting on the heavenly throne and to the Lamb of God! Why does this stir us so much? Because such a miracle means the resurrection of the human dead from their earthly graves. On one occasion when he was a man on earth, the Lamb of God said: "Do not marvel at this, because the hour is coming in which all those in the memorial tombs will hear his voice and come out, those who did good things to a resurrection of life, those who practiced vile things to a resurrection of judgment."—John 5:28, 29.

The resurrection of the human dead under the heavenly rule of the Lamb of God and his 144,000 glorified followers will allow for all these resurrected human dead to take full advantage of God's provisions for them through his Lamb. Those resurrected ones who finally choose not to ascribe blessing, honor, glory and might forever to God and his Lamb will be destroyed with Satan the Devil and his demon angels. (Revelation 20: 7-15) These will thus prove that their resurrection was not properly taken advantage of and appreciated. They misused the glorious opportunity that this resurrection opened up to them under God's kingdom. They did so by finally going back to the practice of vile things, and for this course Jehovah God executed an adverse judgment against them, this resulting in their everlasting destruction.

The removal of all wicked ones, spirit and human, from all the realm of life and existence is a coming certainty. This will leave all heaven and all earth absolutely clean forever of wickedness. The Almighty God Jehovah is able and has promised to bring about this all-desirable condition in all creation visible and invisible. He will do so at his appointed time, thereby vindicating his word of promise and his might and power. All the cherubic living creatures around God's throne will faithfully agree to this final ascription of blessing, honor, glory and might to the enthroned Jehovah God and to his Lamb; they will say Amen to this.

The 144,000 glorified Christians, who are pictured by the twenty-four older persons and who will be alive at this victorious hour, will likewise be faithful to the universal sovereignty of Jehovah God. They will fall down and worship before the throne of Jehovah God. They will acknowledge his Lamb, "the Lion that is of the tribe of Judah," as the beloved one whom the Almighty God used in bringing about this grand, universal result, to last forever.

Overwhelming, therefore, is the heavenly approval that is given to God's choice of the Lamb, "the Lion that is of the tribe of Judah," as the one worthy of being the opener of the mysterious scroll in God's right hand. The weight of the approbation expressed by all those hundreds of millions of superhuman angels and cherubs counterbalances and outweighs all the disapproval, all the indifferent lack of support shown by the thousands of millions of perplexed, misguided humanity. Do we appreciate this true estimate of matters? Then we will join the apostle John and turn our eyes hopefully to the God-honored one, the Lamb. We will watch to see what happens when he breaks the seven seals, one at a time, to open the scroll that he has received from God's right hand. Astounding and intriguing things are due to be revealed to our spiritual vision as the prophetic scroll is gradually opened, till at last it is fully opened and the "mystery of God" is finished.

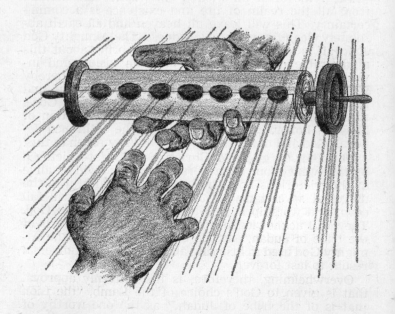

CHAPTER 3

Breaking Seals of the Mysterious Scroll

Nineteen centuries ago a prisoner on the little island of Patmos in the Aegean Sea wept, because for a moment there seemed to be nobody in heaven or on earth able to open the mysterious scroll in the right hand of Jehovah God, the Almighty.

The scroll was written on inside and on the reverse side, but it was rolled up and sealed with seven seals that could not be broken without the official approval of God. The writing on both sides of the scroll told of things to occur in the future, things that took in, not only the invisible heavens, but also the earth, our dwelling place. The handwritten scroll pictured the fixed foreknowledge and purposes of God as affecting heaven and earth. The scroll set forth what the Almighty God knew regarding the future and what he had decided to let occur and also what he himself purposed to do in the face of things that he allowed to occur. No wonder that prisoner on the Roman penal island, the Christian apostle John, wept at the desperate thought that no creature whatever could break the seven seals and reveal the secrets contained in the scroll that concerned him and us all.—Revelation 5:4.

The opening of each seal and the revealing of the corresponding part of the scroll provided only a further bit of mystery. What was revealed was in symbolic language or in images, which called for an explanation. This made it necessary for the now revealed symbolisms to be fulfilled in actual human history. Only then could they be fully understood, enabling us to see how Almighty God foreknew things accurately and how he has faithfully carried out his loving purposes. Consequently, what the apostle John wrote down in describing what he saw after the breaking of each seal did not settle the matter. The correct interpretation of the symbolic things that he saw and heard needed to be given for us to understand. This made it needful for us to wait upon the outworking of universal history for the correct interpretation to be given us by the help of God's invisible active force or spirit. This, in effect, called for the breaking of the seals of the scroll once again, in a supplementary way, in our own marvelous century so full of events of universal interest and importance.

We today are thus held spellbound, as the Christian apostle John was, as he watched God's worthy one, the Lamb, "the Lion that is of the tribe of Judah," break the seals and let the contents of the prophetic scroll be disclosed to view. The apostle John looked for the symbolisms and symbolic events to be disclosed. We today look and continue looking for the secret of these symbolisms and symbolic events to be broken, as if the seals of the scroll were being broken for the first time. What John saw was in vision. What we see is in reality, in actual human experience. With absorbed interest we listen to what John has to tell us:

"And I saw when the Lamb opened one of the seven seals, and I heard one of the four living creatures say with a voice as of thunder: 'Come!' "—Revelation 6:1.

THE OPENING OF THE FIRST SEAL

What we see take place or become known after the opening of the first seal in our modern times is important. There is no excuse for us to ignore it, for we are invited to observe it as with ear-splitting peals of thunder. "Come!" That is, come to see, is the invitation that is extended to us by what is represented by the particular "one of the four living creatures" that spoke "with a voice as of thunder" and invited John to come. This was doubtless the first of the four cherubic living creatures that the apostle John saw, namely, the one "like a lion" and representing divine justice. (Revelation 4:7) It was in the middle position before the front side of God's throne, somewhat like the throne of King Solomon of Jerusalem, who had two lion images beside the armrests of his throne and "twelve lions standing there upon the six steps, on this side and on that side." (1 Kings 10:18-20) Not only was the lionlike living creature going to call attention to something in fulfillment of divine justice, but he was about to point to someone like himself, namely, "the Lion that is of the tribe of Judah," as the heavenly king at last going into righteous action.

What did the apostle John see that was to symbolize what we today would see with our eyes of spiritual discernment? "And I saw," says John, "and, look! a white horse; and the one seated upon it had a bow; and a crown was given him, and he went forth conquering and to complete his conquest."—Revelation 6:2.

This scene did not foreshadow any invasion of the Roman Empire by the Parthians from the East. True, the Parthians were adept at using the bow from horseback. A battle ruse of their cavalrymen was to pretend to flee in retreat, but all the while shooting backward from their well-aimed bows, giving a "parting shot," as it were. While suggestive of this, the scene that the apostle John here saw foretold something far more important.

The rider of this white horse is identified for us by Psalm 45, which is an inspired poem concerning a king. Verses 4-7, in prophetic address to this king, say: "In your splendor go on to success; ride in the cause of truth and humility and righteousness, and your right hand will instruct you in fear-inspiring things. Your arrows are sharp—under you peoples keep falling—in the heart of the enemies of the king. God is your throne to time indefinite, even forever; the scepter of your kingship is a scepter of uprightness. You have loved righteousness and you hate wickedness. That is why God, your God, has anointed you

with the oil of exultation more than your partners."
The prophetic words are applied more than five hundred years later by the writer of Hebrews 1:1, 2, 8, 9 to Jesus Christ, the Son of God. In agreement with this fact, other details of the vision to John prove that the rider of the white horse is the glorified heavenly Son of God, "the Lion that is of the tribe of Judah." Thus, on opening the first seal of the scroll, the Lamb of God saw himself going into action as King.

In this preliminary vision the rider on the white horse differs in appearance from the rider of the white horse described in Revelation 19:11-16, where this same rider is pictured as having "many diadems" on his head and as having protruding out of his mouth a sharp long sword with which to smite the nations of earth, to pronounce the execution of divine judgment upon them. However, in this latter vision the rider of the white horse is riding to the "war of the great day of God the Almighty" at the "place that is called in Hebrew Har–Magedon [Armageddon]." (Revelation 16:14-16) At that "war" the foretold "time of the end" of the earthly nations closes. (Daniel 12:4) But when the rider on the white horse appears with his bow after the opening of the first seal of the scroll it is at the beginning of that "time of the end." That is when the seven Gentile Times have ended, and hence it was the early autumn of the year 1914 C.E., the same year when World War I broke out. It is therefore not on a peaceful mission that the rider on the white horse sets out.

The very fact that the heavenly rider rides a horse indicates that he is on a war errand. Back in Bible times the horse was a symbol of warfare; as Proverbs 21:31 says: "The horse is something prepared for the day of battle." (Also Job 39:19-25) The fact that the rider's horse is white confirms that it is a righteous war, a war in vindication of God's justice and righteousness. In keeping with this fact, the rider on the white horse has a bow, which is also a weapon of war. In Bible times Israelite kings were excellent bowmen.

(2 Samuel 1:22) However, the newly anointed King Jehu of Israel used his bow with deadly effect from a war chariot, not from horseback like the rider on the white horse.—2 Kings 9:20-24.

In Bible times lances used to be carried by some cavalrymen, but this required them to come to close quarters with the enemy, to jab the lance or spear into him. It was an art to shoot arrows with precision from a running horse, but in this way the rider on the white horse can pierce the hearts of his enemies with his arrow from far off.—Psalm 7:11-13.

Evidently the time had come for the Lord God in heaven to fulfill Psalm 110:1, 2 toward his Son Jesus Christ, the descendant and yet Lord of King David of Jerusalem: "Sit at my right hand until I place your enemies as a stool for your feet." "The rod of your strength Jehovah will send out of Zion, saying: 'Go subduing in the midst of your enemies.'" At the end of the Gentile Times in 1914 there were yet enemies of God and Christ even in the holy invisible heavens. So God's empowered King, Jesus Christ, would first proceed against these enemies in the heavens, as a later chapter of the Book of The Revelation shows. Hence he is, as it were, sent forth on a white horse and equipped with a bow. Any arrow that he would shoot forth from his war mount would be "Jehovah's arrow of salvation, even the arrow of salvation" against the enemies of God and of his people. (2 Kings 13:17) The symbolic arrows that he would shoot without missing their mark would be expressions of divine judgment against the enemies until their final extermination.

Fitting it is to remember here that in ancient times the land of Persia was a country of horses and that the Persians were experts with the bow. According to history this was their outstanding weapon, and largely by use of the bow they overcame the Babylonians and established themselves as the fourth of the seven world powers of human history down till now.

So the fact that the rider of the white horse is

armed with a bow suggests that he would play the role performed by King Cyrus the Great of the ancient Persian Empire, who captured Babylon on the Euphrates River in the year 539 B.C.E., overthrowing her as the third world power. Remember the white horse that was ridden by Persian kings, not to speak also of the horse ridden by Roman victors in the triumphal procession on return to the capital city. (Esther 6:8-11) This means that the rider on the white horse, Jesus Christ, would be used by Jehovah God to overthrow Babylon the Great, the world empire of false religion, and then, as the Greater Cyrus, to liberate Jehovah's people from her control. After all of God's people have got out of Babylon the Great in obedience to the divine command, this Greater Cyrus will maneuver the destruction of this wicked world empire of false Babylonish religion.—Isaiah 13:17-19; Revelation 16:12; 17:1-18; see the book *"Babylon the Great Has Fallen!" God's Kingdom Rules!*, pages 197-199.

When, though, is it that the Rider on the white horse begins to ride? First after he is crowned King! He rides forth crowned, for the Revelation (6:2) proceeds to say: "And a crown was given him, and he went forth conquering and to complete his conquest." The time is unmistakable! It is from the end of the Gentile Times in the year 1914 C.E. Then was the time for Jehovah God to place the crown upon the head of "the Lion that is of the tribe of Judah," the Permanent Heir of King David. That crown, representing active kingship, had rested on no descendant of King David since the year 607 B.C.E., when the royal city of Jerusalem was destroyed by the heathen Babylonians. Addressing himself to the last earthly king to wear that crown, namely, King Zedekiah, in whose days the Gentile Times began, Jehovah God said:

"And as for you, O deadly wounded, wicked chieftain of Israel, whose day has come in the time of the error of the end, this is what the Lord Jehovah has said, 'Remove the turban, and lift off the crown. This will not be the same. Put on high even what is low, and bring low even the high one. A ruin, a ruin, a ruin I shall make it. As for this also, it will certainly become no one's until he comes who has the legal right, and I must give it to him.' "—Ezekiel 21:25-27.

The one who has the legal right to the kingdom as represented by the crown is Jesus Christ, the Lamb of God and Permanent Heir of King David. He could not come to be crowned with this kingship at God's hands until the end of the Gentile Times in 1914 C.E. At that time he did come, as pictured in the vision of Daniel 7:13, 14. Jehovah God, the Ancient of Days, recognized his legal right to the crown and kingship, and then the divine promise was fulfilled: "And I must give it to him." (Psalm 21:1-3) This took place in the invisible heavens, and no longer was the line of kings from ancient King David the "low" one, nor were the Gentile kings on earth the "high" one. The action was the reverse of what took place 2,520 years previously, in 607 B.C.E. Now crowned with God-given royal power, the "high" Jesus Christ could proceed against all his enemies as the Rider on the white horse, armed with the bow. He must destroy the enemies of the kingdom of God.

Astride his white horse of righteous warfare, the crowned King has been riding ever since, with success. He begins conquering, he ends up conquering, with total victory fully gained. "He went forth conquering," by turning his attention to his closest enemies, Satan and his spirit demons in the invisible heavens, and these he pushed back, completely out of the heavens of intimate contact with the holy cherubim, seraphim and angels of God. The apostle John was given a vision of this ouster of Satan after the opening of the seventh seal of the mysterious scroll. (Revelation 12:1-13) Christ did not start World War I, which began on July 28, 1914, among the Gentile nations on earth, over the issue of world domination. Down here with his warring nations Satan the Devil and

his demons have been restrained, never to reenter the holy heavens.

If we judge from the appearance of things on the earth today, the crowned Rider of the white horse has not completed his conquest. The enemy Gentile nations, at present under the domination of the religious Babylon the Great, still remain. Jesus Christ could easily have destroyed them at the culmination of World War I, but it was not God's time for him to complete his conquest at that time and in that way. Other things must follow first, as disclosed by the Revelation to the apostle John. It was then not yet "the great day of God the Almighty," and the Gentile nations on earth had not yet marched to the battlefield, the "place that is called in Hebrew Har–Magedon." (Revelation 16:14, 16) There and then is the place and time for the crowned Rider to complete his conquest. He is now near the end of his victorious ride! On which side shall we be at that time?

The Rider of the white horse will not be frustrated in his purpose. His purpose is to conquer; and that is why, in the original Greek text, a purpose clause is here used: "He went forth conquering and that he might conquer." (Revelation 6:2, *Ro; Yg*) In the Greek text, the aorist tense of the verb in the subjunctive mode "here points to ultimate victory." (A. T. Robertson, in *Word Pictures in the New Testament,* Volume 6, page 340) The Rider's purpose is "to complete his conquest." (*NW*) This he will do, for he is finally declared to be "King of kings and Lord of lords." —Revelation 19:16; 17:14.

Worthy ones of this generation of mankind will see the crowned Rider of the white horse complete his conquest with the help of Jehovah God the Almighty. The apostle John saw this vision of the victorious Rider after the opening of the first seal, in the year 96 C.E., the year traditionally assigned to the Revelation. But when did any of us see the modern fulfillment of the vision?

The remnant of John's faithful fellow Christians discerned the fulfillment of the vision of the crowned Rider and his bow after the end of the Gentile Times in the year 1914 C.E. This discernment did not come to them in the summer of the year 1917. In July of that year the Watch Tower Bible & Tract Society published the book entitled "The Finished Mystery," also known as the seventh volume of the *Studies in the Scriptures*. (See the issue of August 1, 1917, of *The Watch Tower and Herald of Christ's Presence*, page 226, column 2.) This book contained a commentary on the entire Book of The Revelation, and attempted to explain, but too soon, Revelation 6:1, 2.

However, thirteen years later, or on August 11 of 1930 the Watch Tower Society released at its Brooklyn headquarters the two volumes of the book entitled "Light." Ah, at last this set forth the explanation of Revelation 6:1, 2 that was based on events since the end of the Gentile Times in 1914, which events fulfilled the thrilling Bible prophecies. By means of this publication John's fellow Christians of this twentieth century gained a discernment of the meaning of John's vision. They learned who was the armed, crowned Rider of the white horse and how he had begun his unstoppable ride to victory over all of God's enemies. Spellbound at the vision before their eyes of understanding, they watch the unconquerable Rider as he charges to triumph in the approaching "war of the great day of God the Almighty."

The Opening
of Seals Two,
Three and Four

HOW DO we humans know that "the Lion that is of the tribe of Judah" came into his heavenly kingdom in the year 1914 and that he has since been riding to ultimate conquest over all his enemies on earth at the symbolic battlefield of Armageddon? What visual evidence of this event that takes place in the invisible heavens do we have, what experiences have we had in this world, to prove these highly important things? We have the proof in the modern-day fulfillment of the things that the apostle John saw in vision at the opening of the remaining seals of the mysterious scroll. The same individual, Jesus Christ, who breaks the seven seals in heaven is also the one who, when on earth as a perfect man, provided the needed information. He foretold the visible, tangible evidences that would present themselves on earth to prove that he was invisibly present in his heavenly kingdom and was giving his attention to all his royal interests here on earth. Do the things brought to view at the opening of the other seals agree with what he foretold on earth before his sacrifice as the Lamb of God? What did he foretell back there in the year 33 C.E., about sixty-three years before sending the Revelation to John?

Four of his apostles called forth from him the prophecy of world events and conditions that were to come after the Gentile Times ended in 1914. The apostle Matthew reports the question that they put to Jesus Christ in these words: "When will these things be, and what will be the sign of your presence and of the conclusion of the system of things?" (Matthew 24:3) The disciple Mark frames the question in these words: "When will these things be, and what will be the sign when all these things are destined to come to a conclusion?" (Mark 13:1-4) The disciple Luke words the question similarly: "When will these things actually be, and what will be the sign when these things are destined to occur?" (Luke 21:7) Was there some "sign" that would immediately precede the terrible destruction that he foretold, a "sign" that also betokened his invisible arrival and presence in spirit form? He had not personally set a date for it by referring to the Bible's timetable or chronology. And so that "sign" would be just as much of an alarm clock as a fixed date, if not more so.

The apostles did not ask for the wrong thing, but they did not realize the full coverage of their question. But Jesus knew all that the question embraced in type and antitype. Hence he first gave them the prophecy that applied to the time of his sitting at the right hand of God in heaven down till the destruction of earthly Jerusalem in the year 70 C.E., to serve as a type of larger things of that kind to come. The future larger things, the antitypical things, would follow the same pattern, so that his prophecy concerning the type would also apply to the antitype. Looked at from this standpoint, the doomed unfaithful Jerusalem and province of Judea pictured Christendom, the unfaithful spiritual Israel.—Luke 21:20-24; Matthew 24:15-22; Mark 13:14-20.

Accordingly, when we make the antitypical application and keep Christendom and her worldly neighbors in view, the prophetic words of Jesus take on a twentieth-century meaning, when he said: "Nation will rise against nation, and kingdom against kingdom; and there will be great earthquakes, and in one place after another pestilences and food shortages; and there will be fearful sights and from heaven great signs." (Luke 21:10, 11) Well, now, what stage of the significant world events would those things mark? Would they mark the start of the period of time that Jesus' apostles spoke of as the "conclusion of the system of things"? The start of the "time of the end"?—Daniel 12:4.

Yes, for, according to the account in Matthew 24: 7, 8, Jesus explained what part of the world's distress those things were, when he said: "For nation will rise against nation and kingdom against kingdom, and there will be food shortages and earthquakes in one place after another. ALL THESE THINGS ARE A BE- GINNING OF PANGS OF DISTRESS." Thus the world's "pangs of distress" would first express them- selves in the form of the rising of nation against nation and of kingdom against kingdom, that is, in warfare, and famines or food shortages, earthquakes and pestilences. These things, in close combination, appear to threaten the existence of the old "system of things," and yet the complete end of that "system of things" does not occur at that point of time and at that perilous development of world affairs.

Rather, all those distressing things would be only the start, the "beginning" of the system's "pangs of distress." Viewing them from this standpoint, the dis- ciples of Jesus Christ would understand that such dis- tressing things were merely the forerunner of the complete end of the "system of things"; they were the opening phase of the "conclusion of the system of things."

It is true that a "system of things"—with special regard to the natural circumcised Jews—did end in the year 70 C.E., at the destruction of Jerusalem and her temple of worship. Jesus had just previously fore- told that disastrous event in the hearing of his dis- ciples. Hence it appears that the four apostles were directly seeking advance information with reference to this. In line with their thinking Jesus did answer their question, and in doing so he spoke of the destruc- tion of the literal city of Jerusalem, in Matthew 24: 15-20; Mark 13:14-18; Luke 21:20-24. What Jesus, in the verses preceding this, prophesied would come before Jerusalem's destruction doubtless did come true in the years from 33 C.E. down to 70 C.E., as the history of those times will show.

Yet we must remember that the unfaithful doomed Jerusalem of Jesus' day had a prophetic significance, that is, a typical meaning. What happened to this capital city of natural Israel was in itself prophetic, typical, of what was later to happen to the religious organization of unfaithful spiritual Israel, as pictured by literal Jerusalem. Accordingly, the things that Jesus predicted were to happen before Jerusalem was destroyed in 70 C.E. were also, in themselves, prophetic of what would happen on earth down till the antitypical Jerusalem, the unfaithful spiritual Israel (Christendom) is destroyed in the near future. Just as the destruction of unfaithful Jerusalem and her temple marked the end of a "system of things," so, too, the destruction of antitypical Jerusalem, unfaithful spiritual Israel (Christendom), would mark the close of a long-standing "system of things." This understanding of Jesus' prophecy is bolstered up by what the apostle John saw take place after the crowned Rider on the white horse went forth with his bow "conquering and to complete his conquest."—Revelation 6:1, 2.

What the apostle John saw after the Lamb Jesus Christ opened the first seal starts off the "conclusion of the system of things," for the vision of the first seal comes true after the end of the Gentile Times in 1914. Does the breaking of the other seals furnish the proof of this? Yes!

Let us look, now, as the apostle John watches the vision of the Lamb of God breaking the seals of the mysterious scroll: "And when he opened the second seal, I heard the second living creature say: 'Come!' And another came forth, a fiery-colored horse; and to the one seated upon it there was granted to take peace away from the earth so that they should slaugh-

ter one another; and a great sword was given him."
—Revelation 6:3, 4.

THE HORSEMAN ON THE FIERY-COLORED HORSE

The "living creature" that the apostle John heard
inviting him to come and see the next tableau was
the second living creature, the one "like a young bull,"
that one that specially displayed divine power. (Revelation 4:7) The divine power, which is all-powerful,
could have prevented what took place in fulfillment
of this vision disclosed by breaking the second seal.
But it was the purpose of Almighty God to let the
earthly nations and kingdoms show what action they
would take when the Rider on the white horse was
crowned and rode forth according to God's will. Would
they peacefully receive him or not? What did John see?

The horse that John now saw come forth was "fiery-
colored," flame-colored, red like blood. Its color suggested blood! Very appropriately so, because it fitted
in with the mission on which the horse's rider rode,
namely, "so that they should slaughter one another."
Besides this, since it was granted to the rider "to take
peace away from the earth," what could this mean
but war, bloody war? So, then, when the Gentile Times
ended in 1914 and the Rider on the white horse did
ride forth, was this event marked by bloody war?

Yes, world war, the first world war of human history! By October 5, 1914 (the middle of the seventh
Jewish lunar month, Tishri 15), the Gentile Times
had ended in that year, and by that time there were
nine nations and empires involved in war, and it was
really a world war. Many more nations entered the
war after that date, till finally twenty-eight were involved. With good reason the vision to John showed
that to the rider on the fiery-colored horse a "great
sword" (a symbol of war) was given. Indeed, the
quantity and size of carnal weapons employed in that
first world war were the largest up till that time in
all human history, airplanes and armored tanks now
coming into use in warfare.

With such a "great sword" a great slaughter could be made of humankind, making the earth run red with blood. And indeed more than 8,500,000 were killed, not to speak of the more than 21,000,000 wounded casualties and the millions of missing persons. More than 45,000,000 armed forces were mobilized, and they did "slaughter one another." And with twenty-eight nations and empires taking part in the conflict, it was truly, as Jesus Christ foretold, a case of nation arising against nation and kingdom against kingdom, and this with total mobilization of each nation. Some nations were able to remain neutral, but they were in great uncertainty, so that to that symbolic rider of the fiery-colored horse it was in real fact "granted to take peace away from the earth."

When World War I ended on November 11, 1918, world peace was not really restored to surviving mankind. The establishment of a League of Nations for world peace and security was incorporated into the peace treaty that was eventually signed. However, this League failed to preserve the peace and security indefinitely, and World War II broke out on September 1, 1939, to right the wrongs and to settle the problems that had been left by the peace agreement after World War I. If he had ever dismounted, the rider of that fiery-red horse was riding again, and his "great sword" took an unheard-of toll of 56,000,000 victims. Culminating in the explosion of the first two atomic bombs used in warfare, World War II left the world of mankind in worse fear and danger than ever before. The now dead League of Nations was replaced by a new international pact for world peace and security, namely, the United Nations, which went into force October 24, 1945. But has even this vaster organization, with 126 member nations as of this writing, restored world peace or removed the threat of world war? Let history records to date answer.

The crowned rider, with a bow, astride the white horse had nothing in common with the rider on the fiery-colored horse. The crowned rider of the white horse took no part in World War I, which was started by the second horseman armed with the "great sword." In fact, the first horseman on the white horse held back from at once following up World War I with the 'battle of Armageddon,' as many students of Bible prophecy then expected. (Revelation 16:14, 16) However, the ride of the second horseman on his fiery-colored mount was a very painful proof that the first horseman riding crowned on the white horse had truly been made king in the heavens at the close of the Gentile Times early in October of 1914.

Was this, though, the only proof that the first horseman, the Lord Jesus Christ, had been crowned king in the heavens at God's appointed time in 1914? Jesus Christ, when on earth as a man, had predicted more proofs. And there were more proofs that did come. That is why, in the apocalyptic vision to the apostle John, the Lamb of God broke more seals of the mysterious scroll. What proof, if any, did the breaking of the third seal bring to view? What did you see, John? He answers in Revelation 6:5, 6:

"And when he opened the third seal, I heard the third living creature say: 'Come!' And I saw, and, look! a black horse; and the one seated upon it had a pair of scales in his hand. And I heard a voice as if in the midst of the four living creatures say: 'A quart of wheat for a denarius, and three quarts of barley for a denarius; and do not harm the olive oil and the wine.' "

THE HORSEMAN ON THE BLACK HORSE

Whose voice was it that invited the apostle John to come and look at this tableau? The third living creature, the one that had "a face like a man's." (Revelation 4:7) Correspondingly, what it led John to see was something to stir human compassion, famine, black famine. The horseman that John now saw was on a black horse. He followed the second horseman to whom it was granted to take away peace from the earth by the "great sword" of world war.

Famine is a common aftermath of war. Repeatedly God's prophetic Word combines famine and war with its sieges of cities, its destruction of growing crops, its converting of implements of peaceful agriculture into unproductive weapons of war, its greedy appropriation of abandoned crops by invading armies. (Isaiah 51:19; Jeremiah 14:12-18; 16:4; 21:7, 9; 44:12-27; Ezekiel 6:11, 12; 12:16) Over sixty years before sending the Revelation to John, Jesus Christ had foretold famines or food shortages along with gory war. (Matthew 24:7) In the Revelation he stuck to that prophecy in its antitypical sense.

Yet, how do we know that the third horseman, the one on the black horse, represents famine, food shortage? Well, look at what he has in his hand, a pair of scales! And listen to the comment made on this that seemed to come forth from all four living creatures and that showed agreement among them, namely, "a quart of wheat for a denarius, and three quarts of barley for a denarius"! Those were really famine prices, for in the apostle John's day a Roman denarius was the day's wage for a worker who toiled for twelve hours. (Matthew 20:1-12) So the famine price meant a whole day's wage for enough wheat to sustain just one man a day, with no more for any dependents of his. Barley, a less substantial food and which was then the common food of the poor people, sold cheaper, but still at a price that compared with that of the wheat.—2 Kings 7:16, 17.

Not only were measures of staple foodstuffs to be high, but, because of the food shortage, the foodstuffs were to be weighed out, rationed, to allow for equal distribution and to prevent overconsumption of available food supplies. The black foreboding picture was enough to remind the apostle John of the famine prophecy of Ezekiel 4:10, 16: "Your food that you will eat will be by weight—twenty shekels a day. . . . and they will have to eat bread by weight and in anxious care, and it will be by measure and in horror that they will drink water itself." Necessarily the "pair of scales" of the third horseman on the black horse had to be used to control the consumption of food stocks, if any.

Not only were the poor to be affected by the famine or food shortage, but also the well-to-do people. This was suggested by the command coming from amidst the four living creatures: "And do not harm the olive oil and the wine." This might sound like a command to protect the luxuries of the rich people and discriminate in favor of them because they had the money with which to buy, even at high prices. But the command from the living creatures appears to be a control proclamation. It meant that the famine victims should not draw too heavily at a time on the available olive oil and wine, because the supplies of these also would be limited.

By drawing too heavily upon them at the start of the famine, the quantity of olive oil and wine would be 'harmed,' not leaving enough for future needs before the famine was over. The effect was that even the people with the money would be limited as to the amount of olive oil and wine they could enjoy at a time. So the famine would affect all people without regard for class distinction, social standing or financial means.

After the outbreak of World War I and the ending of the Gentile Times in 1914, this is exactly what happened. For victory at the battlefront the civilian population behind had to make their contributions and sacrifices. The nations involved in the world conflict had to be totally mobilized. With more attention on successful warfare and less attention on agriculture, and with transportation and communications being interfered with or endangered, food supplies came into high demand. Persons still living today who went through World War I do not forget the measuring out or rationing of various foods, even cows' milk for babies coming under control. In certain countries right in the theater of the war the food shortage became desperate.*

To illustrate the food situation to which peoples were reduced by World War I, let us pull out of our archives the British dispatch of March 7, 1919, which was published throughout the earth and which read: "George H. Roberts, the food minister, said today that he could state on absolutely unimpeachable authority that the situation with regard to food conditions in great areas of Europe was nothing less than tragic. 'It is not too much to say that Roumania is starving, that Serbia is starving, that Austria is starving and that Germany is starving,' he declared. 'Ever since the armistice was signed the Allies have been doing what they could to relieve the situation, and food is being sent to all the countries that I have named. But it is not enough, and the question now arises whether we shall be able to get sufficient food to those countries in time to prevent a catastrophe.'" In the following year (1920) in the famine that still persisted, there were 255,000,000 that were affected. This does not take into account the millions that were affected by food shortages in other large areas of the world, in Asia, and so forth.

At the end of World War I practically all of Europe was on the verge of starvation and calling for relief from victorious America. This famine-stricken condition in particular was part of the proof that Jesus Christ foretold, indicating that he had been crowned king in the heavens and was present in his kingdom. But he had foretold even more proof. Would his opening of further seals of the mysterious scroll corroborate this to the onlooking apostle John? Yes. There is another horseman that must ride forth.

"And," writes the apostle John, "when he opened the fourth seal, I heard the voice of the fourth living creature say: 'Come!' And I saw, and, look! a pale

---

* See in the issue of *The Watch Tower*, dated February 1, 1918, the leading article entitled "Views from the Watch Tower," paragraph 5 on page 35 down to and including the six paragraphs under the subheading "The Evil Arrows of Famine," on page 37.

horse; and the one seated upon it had the name Death. And Ha'des was closely following him. And authority was given them over the fourth part of the earth, to kill with a long sword and with food shortage and with deadly plague and by the wild beasts of the earth."—Revelation 6:7, 8.

THE HORSEMAN ON THE PALE HORSE

The fourth living creature that the apostle John had seen was "like a flying eagle." (Revelation 4:7) This cherubic living creature featured the farsighted, swiftly moving wisdom of the Almighty God Jehovah. This living creature's invitation to John at the opening of the fourth seal for John to come and see was very fitting, for God's wisdom had already, like an eagle, foreseen long previous what was prefigured when the fourth seal was broken in order to open up its section of the mysterious scroll.

A fourth figurative horseman dashes onto the scene of world affairs. His horse is yellowish pale, livid, sickly-looking in color. What a good match its color was to the name of its rider, whose name is Death! But this is not just ordinary death, which results from the sin of mankind's first earthly parents, Adam and Eve. (Romans 5:12) This is a premature death, due to a stated number of special causes, which are later named, these hastening the death of those who would have at last died of death inherited from the first Adam. It brings its victims earlier than ordinarily into the embrace of the one who is, in the Bible, a close associate with death. Who is that? What does the vision show?

Is it Gehenna? Or "the fiery lake that burns with sulphur"? Gehenna or this "fiery lake" symbolizes "the second death" or everlasting destruction out of all existence. (Matthew 10:28; Mark 9:43-47; Revelation 19:20; 20:14, 15) Ah, no, but the symbolic rider Death was accompanied by Ha'des. As the apostle John says, "its rider's name was Death, and Ha'des came close behind." (Revelation 6:8, *NEB*) Whether

Ha'des was also upon a horse or was on foot is not stated, although for Ha'des to keep up with Death on horseback a person would imagine Ha'des also to be on a horse. Says one noted Bible commentator: " . . . kept step with death, whether on the same horse or on another horse by his side or on foot John does not say."* At any rate, Ha'des overtakes those who are victimized by the fourth horseman, Death. These poor victims are not everlastingly destroyed. They go to a place for which there are keys to let the inmates out.

Even Jesus, dying on a stake outside Jerusalem, went to Ha'des, and Almighty God Jehovah used the key and let his Son out on the third day. (Acts 2: 27-32) And now the keys to Ha'des have been given to the resurrected Jesus Christ, so that he can now say triumphantly: "I became dead, but, look! I am living forever and ever, and I have the keys of death and of Ha'des."—Revelation 1:18.

What a hope these facts offer! Those brought down to Ha'des by the fourth horseman Death will, like Jesus Christ, have a resurrection from the dead. The Ha'des to which they go and to which Jesus Christ went is not the mythical Ha'des of the pagan Greeks of ancient times, but is the common grave of mankind. There they sleep in death, awaiting a resurrection that is guaranteed to them. How so? Because, as we are assured in 1 Corinthians 15:20, "now Christ has been raised up from the dead, the first fruits of those who have fallen asleep in death."—Acts 17:31.

Those brought down to Ha'des by the fourth horseman Death were to be many. Imagine people in the fourth part of the earth being killed off. That might mean the killing off of a fourth of the world's population at the time, this depending upon how thickly populated that fourth part of the earth happened to be.

Well, concerning the fourth horseman and his companion Ha'des it is stated: "And authority was given them over the fourth part of the earth." (Revelation

* Quoted from pages 342, 343 of *Word Pictures in the New Testament*, Volume 6, by A. T. Robertson, edition of 1933.

6:8) No particular "fourth part" or quarter of the earth is named, but the thought is that a population that could occupy a quarter of the earth would be threatened with Death and Ha'des. In other words, not all the world's population at the time would be killed off, nor even the larger part of it, but only a large fraction of it. There would be survivors of this ride by the fourth horseman Death accompanied by Ha'des. Yet it was to be something out of the ordinary, something that would be an added proof of the fact that the first horseman, Jesus Christ, had been crowned and had begun to ride victoriously since the close of the Gentile Times in 1914 C.E.

How, though, was the fourth horseman Death to bring down his numerous victims to Ha'des? Revelation 6:8 goes on to tell us, saying: "To kill with a long sword and with food shortage and with deadly plague and by the wild beasts of the earth."

Four disastrous means are mentioned. What a terrible corpse-strewn appearance of the earth the letting loose of those four destructive forces could produce! Those four terrors remind us of the four expressions of judgment that Jehovah God brought upon unfaithful Jerusalem in the seventh century before our Common Era. "For this is what the Lord Jehovah has said, 'So, too, it will be when there will be my four injurious acts of judgment—sword and famine and injurious wild beast and pestilence—that I shall actually send upon Jerusalem in order to cut off from it earthling man and domestic animal.'" (Ezekiel 14: 21) Some thousands of inhabitants of Jerusalem and the land of Judah survived those four expressions of divine judgment, but these were deported to far-off Babylon, and Jerusalem and Judah lay desolate without man and domestic animal for seventy years, from 607 B.C.E. to 537 B.C.E.

Back there in 607 B.C.E. after the desolation of Judah and Jerusalem the Gentile Times began. But in 1914 C.E. those Gentile Times of 2,520 years of duration ended. Then the four horsemen began to ride. To a horrifying extent the fourth horseman astride his pale horse rode up and down through the earth, laying low victims by the millions to feed Ha'des. There was (1) the "long sword" of world war, to be followed by other wars, minor ones and even a second world war. There was (2) the "food shortage," with never again an improvement in the world's food situation to follow. There was (3) the "deadly plague," or, literally, "death." Jesus had foretold "in one place after another pestilences." (Luke 21:10, 11) At the due time they came, and they spelled "death" to millions. In 1918 an influenza with great killing power was first noted in Spain, for which reason it was called "Spanish influenza." It spread, not only to the nations involved in World War I, but to all nations of the earth, even to the Eskimos of the far north. It raged through the winter of 1918-1919, and proved to be "one of the most devastating plagues of all time." In a few months it put 200,000,000 persons in beds of sickness, and in twelve months it fed 20,000,000 victims into Ha'des or Sheol, the common grave of mankind.

Not only were people to be put to death by beastly men and nations engaged in modern warfare, but they were to be set upon by (4) literal "wild beasts of the earth" and killed. To the fourth horseman and his ghastly companion Ha'des authority was to be given "to kill . . . by the wild beasts of the earth." The devastation of human communities by the widespread warfare, famine and pestilence would certainly have an effect on the wild animal life of the countries affected. (Exodus 23:29) Reasonably it would lead to the multiplication of these wild beasts so that, hunger-crazed, they would become a menace to human life in many areas. Many were reported killed by wild animal packs or by individual man-eaters. All this added to the massive harvest reaped by the fourth horseman Death at the very beginning of the "time of the end" of this human system of things.

Thus, as in the case of the four divine judgments

upon ancient Jerusalem, the four destructive elements of war (the "long sword"), famine ("food shortage"),

"deadly plague" or "pestilence" and "wild beasts of the earth" did their terrible work both before the Gentile Times began in 607 B.C.E. and immediately after they ended in 1914 C.E., just as foretold. All this latter calamity came as the result of the riding of the rider of the fiery-colored horse, the rider of the black horse, and the rider of the pale horse.

Thus far, in the vision to the apostle John, only four seals have been opened, and they have revealed incontestable evidence of the fact that the first horseman, the Rider of the white horse, is riding crowned as king and with his bow in hand, "conquering and to complete his conquest." Will the opening of the fifth seal add to the evidence of this glorious fact? Hear now what John tells us.

CHAPTER 5

The Opening
of Seals Five
and Six

Describing what "the Lamb," Jesus Christ, does with the mysterious scroll taken from God's right hand, the apostle John continues on to say: "And when he opened the fifth seal, I saw underneath the altar the souls of those slaughtered because of the word of God and because of the witness work that they used to have. And they cried with a loud voice, saying: 'Until when, Sovereign Lord holy and true, are you refraining from judging and avenging our blood upon those who dwell on the earth?' And a white robe was given to each of them; and they were told to rest a little while longer, until the number was filled also of their fellow slaves and their brothers who were about to be killed as they also had been."
—Revelation 6:9-11.

At the opening of this fifth seal none of the four living creatures invites the apostle John to come and see. What he sees is not the result of the riding of the horsemen on the fiery-colored, black and pale horses. The slaughtered souls that John saw had met death from other causes than international war, famine, deadly plague and wild beasts of the earth. They had met death for sacrificial purposes, and that was why these souls were seen underneath God's altar. These souls were no ghostly, shadowy figures or forms underneath the altar. What the apostle John saw there was really the blood of faithful Christians who died "because of the word of God and because of the witness work that they used to have." By birth John

61

was a Jew and he knew that in the animal sacrifices offered to Jehovah God in the temple at Jerusalem the blood of the victims was poured at the base of the altar, thus onto the ground. Even if splashed against the side of the altar it would run down to the ground. This was according to God's laws given to the Jews through the prophet Moses.—Leviticus 3:2, 8, 13; 4:7.

We must remember what Jehovah God said to his prophets about human blood. To the prophet Noah he said, right after the global flood: "Only flesh with its soul—its blood—you must not eat." (Genesis 9:4) To the prophet Moses in the wilderness of Sinai God said: "The soul of the flesh is in the blood, and I myself have put it upon the altar for you to make atonement for your souls, because it is the blood that makes atonement by the soul in it." (Leviticus 17:11) In the light of this, the "souls" that John saw underneath the altar picture the blood of faithful Christians who had been slaughtered because of taking up the written Word of God and preaching it, and also bearing witness to Him and to his Son Jesus Christ. For this reason their undeserved violent death was considered as a sacrifice to God for the vindication of Jehovah God as the Universal Sovereign and for the sanctification of his name. The persecutor on earth, the one chiefly responsible for the shedding of the blood of these holy ones, was Babylon the Great, who is, in reality, the world empire of false religion that was founded in ancient Babylon on the Euphrates River.

Says John: "Upon her forehead was written a name, a mystery: 'Babylon the Great, the mother of the harlots and of the disgusting things of the earth.' And I saw that the woman was drunk with the blood of the holy ones and with the blood of the witnesses of Jesus." "Yes, in her was found the blood of prophets and of holy ones and of all those who have been slaughtered on the earth."—Revelation 17:5, 6; 18:24.

The all-seeing God is aware of the blood, representing the sacrificed human souls, at the base of his altar, and he knows how the blood (their souls) got there. It calls for divine vengeance.

The blood of these innocent ones cries out loudly to Jehovah God for vengeance upon the shedders of blood. About four thousand years before John's vision the blood of God's first martyr cried out to him from the ground. It was the blood of Abel, whom his brother Cain slew over the issue of true religion. Cain tried to hide the blood of his murdered brother, but Jehovah God said to Cain: "What have you done? Listen! Your brother's blood is crying out to me from the ground. And now you are cursed in banishment from the ground, which has opened its mouth to receive your brother's blood at your hand." (Genesis 4:1-11; 1 John 3:12) In like manner the blood of the martyred Christians cried out from underneath God's sacrificial altar as long as that innocent blood of Christ's followers went unavenged. That is why the apostle John heard the souls underneath the altar cry out with a loud voice, "loud" because there were so many of them:

"Until when, Sovereign Lord holy and true, are you refraining from judging and avenging our blood upon those who dwell on the earth?"—Revelation 6:10.

These slaughtered Christian souls will not have cried out in vain. Jesus Christ assured them of that. He said: "Shall not God cause justice to be done for his chosen ones who cry out to him day and night, even though he is long-suffering toward them? I tell you, He will cause justice to be done to them speedily." (Luke 18:7, 8) Tens of thousands of these Christian souls had been slaughtered up till the end of the Gentile Times in the year 1914. But the due time for God to avenge their blood was not immediately after those Gentile Times ended in that year when World War I broke out. God's due time for such vengeance will be at his appointed time for destroying the bloodstained Babylon the Great and also at the battle of Armageddon, which promptly follows her destruction. Then the cry will ring out in heaven: "Praise Jah, you people! . . . For he has executed judgment upon the great harlot who corrupted the earth with her fornication, and he has avenged the blood of his slaves at her hand." (Revelation 19:1, 2) Her destruction is still future, but it is getting nearer.

Amid the persecutions during World War I of 1914-1918 there were anointed Christians who thought that the world war was going to lead right on into world revolution and an Armageddon of anarchy.* To their great surprise, World War I came to an abrupt end on November 11, 1918, and yet Babylon the Great still stood and the battle of Armageddon had not come. They wondered why, and saw the need to search the Holy Scriptures for an explanation. Under guidance of God's holy spirit they were led to see that there was a tremendous worldwide work yet to be done before the complete end of this wicked system of things would come in the "war of the great day of God the Almighty" at Armageddon. (Revelation 16:14-16) So the faithful remnant of anointed Christians saw that, after Jesus Christ had predicted the "beginning of pangs of distress" in the form of international war, food shortages, earthquakes and pestilences, he pointed to a worldwide work that would be done before the system of things fully ended. He said:

"And this good news of the kingdom will be preached in all the inhabited earth for a witness to all the nations; and then the end will come."—Matthew 24:14; Mark 13:10.

Certainly, then, time needed to be provided for by God in order for this foreordained work to be done. Because of taking on a worldwide scope, the work was so great, and yet the faithful anointed remnant was so small as to numbers. How much time God had allotted for this vast work to be accomplished, the anointed remnant that had survived World War I did not know. Those of this remnant were the ones

---

* See the book *The Finished Mystery,* published in July of 1917, pages 3, 4, 257. Also, *The Watch Tower,* dated November 1, 1914, pages 327, 328; also, the issue dated February 1, 1918, pages 35, 36; also February 15, 1918, page 55.

anointed with God's holy spirit to do this preaching of the "good news" of God's newly established kingdom in the hands of his crowned, enthroned King Jesus Christ. They were to do this preaching in spite of being "objects of hatred by all the nations" on account of Christ's name. (Matthew 24:9) This was certain to mean further persecution for them, and doubtless a number of these Christian brothers, anointed fellow slaves, were bound to be killed, just as their earlier Christian brothers, "fellow slaves" of Jehovah God, had been down till the end of World War I in 1918.—Revelation 6:11; 2:10.

Inasmuch as the preaching of "this good news of the kingdom" precedes the "end" of the system of things, it must be that we have been living in the "time of the end," or in the "conclusion of the system of things," since God's Messianic kingdom was established in the heavens at the close of the Gentile Times in 1914 C.E. (Daniel 12:4; Matthew 24:3) In explaining his illustration of the wheat and the weeds (tares), Jesus said: "The harvest is a conclusion of a system of things." During this harvesttime the counterfeit weedlike Christians are separated under angelic direction from the faithful wheatlike Christians, and finally the weedlike Christians are destroyed as in a fiery furnace, when Babylon the Great is destroyed. (Matthew 13:39-42) All these operations require that the "harvest" be a period of time of quite some duration after the Gentile Times ended in 1914, and particularly from the year 1918 onward. Consequently, the destruction of bloodguilty Babylon the Great was not due by the end of World War I in 1918.

The "harvest" separation of the weedlike Christians from the wheatlike Christians was to be followed by another separating work as a climax. In his prophecy on the "conclusion of the system of things" Jesus illustrated the judging of his professed Christian "brothers," and then, in a closing illustration, he said: "When the Son of man arrives in his glory, and all the angels with him, then he will sit down on his glorious throne. And all the nations will be gathered before him, and he will separate people one from another, just as a shepherd separates the sheep from the goats. And he will put the sheep on his right hand, but the goats on his left."—Matthew 25:14-33.

Before ushering the sheeplike people into the earthly blessings under God's Messianic kingdom, the enthroned Son of man, Jesus Christ, reminds them that some of his Christian or spiritual brothers had been in prison during the "conclusion of the system of things" and these sheeplike people had brought them relief. On the other hand, before sending off into everlasting destruction the cursed goatlike people, the enthroned Jesus Christ reminds them that they had failed to relieve those of his spiritual brothers who were in prison. (Matthew 25:34-46) This mention of "prison" foretold that his anointed spiritual brothers, the remnant of them on earth, would be persecuted, even to the death in some cases, during the "conclusion of the system of things." Thus, after 1918 C.E., there were to be other "brothers," "fellow slaves" of God, who would be killed for "the word of God" and for "the witness work," the same as the Christian souls whom John saw under the altar.—Revelation 6:9-11.

Hence there would have to be "a little while longer" for those slaughtered "souls" "to rest" before the Sovereign Lord Jehovah would avenge their blood upon religious Babylon the Great and her political accomplices. However, this resting would not necessarily mean their remaining dead, asleep in death. (1 Corinthians 15:17-20) Those "souls" under the altar were to rest a little while longer as to the satisfaction of justice in their case. For "a little while longer" they were not to press for the avenging of their blood. They were to refrain from insisting that their blood be avenged there in 1918. They should "rest" by letting the account against the bloody slaughterers go unsettled for "a little while longer," until God's own chosen time to settle accounts.

A WHITE ROBE GIVEN TO EACH

However, though they were asked to wait until the time interval of "a little while longer" was ended, something was done for them in 1918. What? Revelation 6:11 says that "a white robe was given to each of them." This doubtless refers to their resurrection from the dead at that time and their entrance into the heavenly kingdom of Christ which had already been born or established. It would hardly be fitting for those slaughtered souls to receive these white robes while still remaining under the altar. White robes would be most inappropriate down there in such a place as "underneath the altar" of sacrifice. How could long flowing robes be kept "white" down there? Jesus Christ had promised white robes as a reward for faithfulness in overcoming this wicked world. (Revelation 3:4, 5) Such an outer garment as a white robe would be a mark of honor and a symbol of their innocence, of God's favorable judgment toward them. It would be appropriate to wear such white robes in the heavenly throne after their resurrection from the dead. (Revelation 4:4) But, although resurrected back there in 1918, they would still rest as to being avenged.

What, though, was to happen to their spiritual brothers yet alive on earth during that "little while longer" that they were to rest until being avenged? Revelation 6:11 indicates this by saying "a little while longer, until the number was filled also of their fellow slaves and their brothers who were about to be killed as they also had been." That meant more persecution upon faithful Christians. That meant more slaughtering of true Christians on earth in addition to the number of Christian souls that had been slaughtered down till 1918 by Babylon the Great and her political paramours. The full number of 144,000 who taste of a sacrificial death with Jesus Christ had not been filled by the year 1918. There was yet a remnant that needed to be added to complete the required number of 144,000 heirs of God's kingdom.

Many of this remnant "were about to be killed" as

earlier ones of "their fellow slaves and their brothers" had been down till 1918. The persecution of Christ's true footstep followers was not to be ended by 1918; there was more to follow after the close of World War I in that year. Was this not also what Jesus Christ foretold in his prophecy on the "conclusion of the system of things" as another of the evidences that he was present in his heavenly kingdom? Yes. He said, right after predicting international war, famine and pestilences:

"Then people will deliver you up to tribulation and will kill you, and you will be objects of hatred by all the nations on account of my name. Then, also, many will be stumbled and will betray one another and will hate one another. And many false prophets will arise and mislead many; and because of the increasing of lawlessness the love of the greater number will cool off. But he that has endured to the end is the one that will be saved. And this good news of the kingdom will be preached in all the inhabited earth for a witness to all the nations; and then the end will come." —Matthew 24:9-14; Luke 21:12-19.

Those prophetic words of Jesus Christ have been fulfilled, as history shows, since the end of the Gentile Times in 1914 and down till today. Thus down till the close of World War I in 1918 there had been the unrighteous shedding of the blood of genuine Christians who were "slaughtered because of the word of God and because of the witness work that they used to have," and after 1918 a faithful surviving remnant of "fellow slaves" have taken up the word of God and have been giving the witness in all the inhabited earth, preaching the good news of God's newborn kingdom to all the nations. Some of these have been slaughtered because of this, and others will yet be slaughtered before "the end" of this system of things comes. Till the full number have been slaughtered and thus till Babylon the Great and her political accomplices have filled up the measure of their bloodguiltiness, God will refrain from avenging the blood of his

Christian slaves. When God finally executes his vengeance, it will be for all the Christian blood that has been shed, all at one time. Till then the souls that John saw under the altar must rest in hope.

SIXTH SEAL BROKEN

The breaking of the fifth seal revealed further proof that the Rider of the white horse had been crowned King and was riding victoriously with his bow to the completing of his conquest. What will take place when he completes his conquest in the not distant future? This is disclosed when the Lamb Jesus Christ breaks the sixth seal of the mysterious scroll that he took from the right hand of Jehovah God. What did the Christian apostle John see?

"And I saw when he opened the sixth seal, and a great earthquake occurred; and the sun became black as sackcloth of hair, and the entire moon became as blood, and the stars of heaven fell to the earth, as when a fig tree shaken by a high wind casts its unripe figs. And the heaven departed as a scroll that is being rolled up, and every mountain and every island were removed from their places. And the kings of the earth and the top-ranking ones and the military commanders and the rich and the strong ones and every slave and every free person hid themselves in the caves and in the rock-masses of the mountains. And they keep saying to the mountains and to the rock-masses: 'Fall over us and hide us from the face of the one seated on the throne and from the wrath of the Lamb, because the great day of their wrath has come, and who is able to stand?' "—Revelation 6:12-17.

The "great earthquake" that the apostle John witnessed was not a mere local one. It shook the whole earth. Back in the year 33 C.E. John had heard Jesus predict the occurrence of literal earthquakes as something to mark the opening part of the "conclusion of the system of things," saying: "earthquakes in one place after another. All these things are a beginning of pangs of distress." (Matthew 24:7, 8; Mark 13:8) But the "great earthquake" occurring in the vision after the opening of the sixth seal is evidently a symbolic earthquake. It symbolizes a great upheaval in the human earthly system of things, everything man-made not having God's approval and blessing being terribly shaken, yes, shaken down, flattened, all around our terrestrial globe. Hence any man-made thing out of harmony with God and the Lamb would provide no proper covering for men, such not being habitable, not providing the comforts of home, nor being safe to live in. The whole earthly system becomes uninhabitable; men are forced to move out, seeking safety.

Oftentimes when there are great earthquakes there are also celestial and atmospheric phenomena. When a literal earthquake occurs, many persons cry heavenward, appealing to God, even if they have never called upon him before. When that "great day" for the executing of divine wrath upon disobedient mankind arrives, men will look skyward. But will there be any indication of heaven's favor toward them in their direst distress? Says the prophetic vision: "The sun became black as sackcloth of hair, and the entire moon became as blood, and the stars of heaven fell to the earth, as when a fig tree shaken by a high wind casts its unripe figs." (Revelation 6:12, 13) What could such heavenly phenomena symbolize?

As a whole, the people under God's wrath would have nothing from heaven to brighten the situation for them. The daytime would be dismal, mournful, as if the sun had been blacked out, not by a tremendous cloud of dust particles in outer space, but as if cloaked over by black sackcloth made of the hair of black goats and worn in times of grief and mourning. Having refused the spiritual light from God's inspired Word, the Bible, people would mourn during the daytime. And at night? No silvery moon to shine down benignly upon them! Not silvery rays, but bloody rays, with no life-giving light. Bloodshed will be rife throughout the earth by night, if not also by day.

Blood will mark the night. But certainly the billions of stars will offset this bloodstained appearance of the moon! No! Have you ever seen a fig tree caught in a high wind and whipping down its unripe winter-grown figs? That is the way the stars will drop from the skies. Drop where? Not down to the earth, but out of sight. They will give no glimmer of heavenly light or serve as guides to travelers in the night. So by day or by night men will have nothing to brighten the scene.

Symbolically speaking, would not those heavenly bodies all disappear when the further part of the vision as released by the sixth broken seal takes place? Yes! "And the heaven departed as a scroll that is being rolled up." Men have used the heat and light rays from the sun in power projects. They have harnessed the tides that are caused by the gravitational pull of the moon, and have used that same gravitational pull in order to bring a manned spacecraft from the earth into orbiting around the moon. They have used the stars as guides to travel at night. They have cast astrological horoscopes by reference to stars and planets and zodiacal signs. More than that, they have worshiped star gods and planetary gods. They have worshiped the moon as a god or a goddess. They have worshiped the sun as a companion god or goddess.

In this manner the "heaven" with its bodies in outer space has represented powers higher than man and wielding controlling influence over man. The real heavenly forces, or forces higher than man, are invisible to him. They are Satan the Devil, who has been worshiped as the sun, and also all his demon angels, who have been worshiped as stars or constellations, lesser deities. These must now go!

For millenniums these unseen demon rulers of mankind have written their record on the pages of human history. Now it is time for a new page to be written in human affairs. Hence those symbolic heavens must depart, their page in human history disappearing as when a papyrus or calfskin scroll is rolled up around its central stick, hiding what has been written within the scroll. (Luke 4:20; Daniel 12:4) At the day of divine wrath the time has come for new and righteous heavenly powers to take control over human affairs. Those new righteous heavens established by Almighty God will never be rolled up like a scroll and put away in a bin. They will remain forever for the blessing of God-fearing men.

3 -17   VISIBLE EARTHLY CHANGES DUE

Not alone will there be changes in the invisible heavenly realm, but there will be necessary changes in the visible earthly scene. Revelation 6:14 continues on to say: "And every mountain and every island were removed from their places." This betokens something for the political governments of this system of things, for, in the Holy Scriptures, mountains are used to picture ruling governments. In the coming day for executing God's wrath neither the height of prestige and power nor the isolation of any government as on an island surrounded by water will be of any protective use. As parts of the present system of things they will all be removed because of being no part of God's kingdom. They will not be transformed from despotic, dictatorial, autocratic forms of governmental rule to popular, democratic forms of government, thus merely undergoing a change of structure, but remaining selfishly human. They will be removed into destruction.

Such things were also foretold in the Revelation to occur at the time when the seventh plague is poured out by God's angel. The account of this is given in Revelation 16:18-21, in these words: "And lightnings and voices and thunders occurred, and a great earthquake occurred such as had not occurred since men came to be on the earth, so extensive an earthquake, so great. And the great city split into three parts, and the cities of the nations fell; and Babylon the great was remembered in the sight of God, to give her the cup of the wine of the anger of his wrath.

Also, every island fled, and mountains were not found. And a great hail with every stone about the weight of a talent descended out of heaven upon the men, and the men blasphemed God due to the plague of hail, because the plague of it was unusually great." This prophetic vision is a confirmation of what is due to take place as a result of the opening of the sixth seal of the mysterious scroll.

All classes of persons who are a part of this system of things will be affected, "the kings of the earth and the top-ranking ones and the military commanders and the rich and the strong ones and every slave and every free person." Then they will all realize that they have come to the end of this system of things. The continual failure of their selfish schemes to preserve this old wicked system will force them to see that they do not have heaven's favor upon them, the favor of the enthroned God of the universe nor the favor of the Lamb of God, Jesus Christ, whom Christendom has claimed to serve and follow. The time will then have come for the prayer of Psalm 83:18 to be answered: "That people may know that you, whose name is Jehovah, you alone are the Most High over all the earth." Yes, the time will have come for this Most High God to carry out his declaration repeatedly made through his prophet Ezekiel: "People will have to know that I am Jehovah. . . . and the nations will have to know that I am Jehovah."—Ezekiel 39:6, 7; 6:7, 10, 13, 14; 7:4, 9, 27.

To preserve their lives through the greatest tribulation of all human history men will run for cover. But where? They may make desperate cries to God for help, but they will still put their real trust in their own organizations, and not in God's Word and in his heavenly kingdom. They have all along trusted in their governments and political organizations, which dominate the earth like lofty mountains, as backbones of the present system of things. So Revelation 6:15, 16 tells us in figurative language that they "hid themselves in the caves and in the rock-masses of the mountains. And they keep saying to the mountains and to the rock-masses: 'Fall over us and hide us from the face of the one seated on the throne and from the wrath of the Lamb, because the great day of their wrath has come, and who is able to stand?'"

Men will want then, not to die, but to be buried out of sight. Jesus Christ foretold such human behavior when he predicted the destruction and desolation of Jerusalem and Judea during the years 66 to 73 C.E. On his way to death on a stake at Calvary, he stopped and said to tenderhearted women who bewailed him: "Stop weeping for me. On the contrary, weep for yourselves and for your children; because, look! days are coming in which people will say, 'Happy are the barren women, and the wombs that did not give birth and the breasts that did not nurse!' Then they will start to say to the mountains, 'Fall over us!' and to the hills, 'Cover us over!'" (Luke 23:26-30) The Jewish historian Josephus describes in great detail what the inhabitants of Judea and Jerusalem, in fulfillment of Jesus' prophecy, did in 63-73 C.E. Judea's last stronghold, Masada, fell in 73 C.E.

Among the events that are due to take place during "the final part of the days" the prophet Isaiah was inspired to say: "And the haughtiness of the earthling man must bow down, and the loftiness of men must become low; and Jehovah alone must be put on high in that day. And the valueless gods themselves will pass away completely. And people will enter into the caves of the rocks and into the holes of the dust because of the dreadfulness of Jehovah and from his splendid superiority, when he rises up for the earth to suffer shocks. In that day the earthling man will throw his worthless gods of silver and his valueless gods of gold that they had made for him to bow before to the shrewmice and to the bats, in order to enter into the holes in the rocks and into the clefts of the crags, because of the dreadfulness of Jehovah and from his splendid superiority, when he rises up for the earth to suffer shocks." "Enter into the rock

and hide yourself in the dust because of the dreadfulness of Jehovah, and from his splendid superiority."
—Isaiah 2:1, 2, 17-21, 10.

Divine prophecy will inevitably be fulfilled. We are fast approaching the day for the final expression of the wrath of God and of his Lamb Jesus Christ to be made against this system of things. Already the political rulers of this earth are dismayed because the prayers of the religious leaders of Babylon the Great fail to gain heaven's help for the preservation of their national governments and commercial, social, and peace-keeping institutions. The "great day of their wrath" will come shortly when the preaching of "this good news of the kingdom" has been done earth wide to the extent that God wants the witness to be given to all the nations. (Matthew 24:14) Then the vital question to be answered by those who are not on the side of the kingdom of God but who are part of this doomed system of things will be: "Who is able to stand?" (Revelation 6:17) These people will then know they will not be able to stand; otherwise, why would they seek to hide from God and the Lamb rather than joyfully welcome them and the promised heavenly kingdom? One's standing approved means being spared from destruction and entering into God's perfect new order.

Heart-gripping, therefore, are the once mysterious things revealed by the opening of the first six of the seven seals that had locked up the contents of the scroll in the right hand of the One seated on the throne of the universe. What the apostle John revealed in cryptic symbols we see in understandable modern-day fulfillment. Especially from the year 1930, when, in September, the Bible-study aid entitled "Light," in two volumes, was published generally, have dedicated Christian witnesses of Jehovah God come to an understanding of prophetic symbols disclosed by the Lamb's breaking those six seals that kept secret the contents of the scroll. No longer do we weep with the apostle John, but we rejoice with him at the disclosure of the sealed-in things. We exult with unspeakable joy at the pictures that were acted out after the breaking of the first five seals proving that God's Messianic kingdom has been born in the heavens, that its King rides to final conquest.

We are grateful that we today can discern the modern fulfillments of those prophetic tableaus seen by the apostle John. Wisely we prepare ourselves to be found worthy "to stand" when the "day of their wrath" arrives to remove forever this wicked system of things in the foretold "great tribulation." Till then we continue on, despite persecution, in preaching "this good news of the kingdom" in "all the inhabited earth for a witness to all the nations."—Matthew 24:14; Mark 13:10.

The 144,000
Sealed Ones

3-31

SIX SEALS of the mysterious scroll from God's hand had been broken before the wondering gaze of the Christian apostle John. They had been broken in steady succession, and at last the frantic fears of ungodly men at the coming of the great day of God's wrath against them had been portrayed. But here, at this stage of uncovering the divine secrets, the Lamb of God, Jesus Christ, did not at once proceed to break the mystifying seventh seal of the scroll. Evidently everything in connection with the sixth seal has not been revealed by simply portraying the mad scramble of the ungodly people for protective cover at the coming of the "great day" of the wrath of Jehovah God and of his Lamb Jesus Christ. There is something more to be revealed, and it has to do with the saving of godly persons before the outburst of that wrath from heaven on the approaching "great day." That "great day" of wrathful destruction of the ungodly people cannot come until this work for the saving of the godly persons has been fully accomplished. See now what John saw in this regard. Says he:

"After this I saw four angels standing upon the four corners of the earth, holding tight the four winds of the earth, that no wind might blow upon the earth or upon the sea or upon any tree. And I saw another angel ascending from the sunrising, having a seal of the living God; and he cried with a loud voice to the four angels to whom it was granted to harm the

77

earth and the sea, saying: 'Do not harm the earth or the sea or the trees, until after we have sealed the slaves of our God in their foreheads.' "—Revelation 7:1-3.

Here the apostle John sees something that has never been photographed and radioed to the earth by any weather satellite launched into orbit above the earth by the Weather Department to study cloud formations or the origination and movement of hurricanes. No astronaut or cosmonaut, hurled into outer space in a rocket capsule and orbiting the earth for days at a time, or even orbiting the moon, has ever seen what John saw by the illuminating power of God's spirit, namely, four angels standing upon the four corners of the earth and holding back the four winds of the earth. This evidently indicates that a violent windstorm or whirlwind is about to be let loose. But no worldwide chain of weather forecasting stations has been able to predict this extraordinary storm and the direction from which it comes and when it will reach any area and with what velocity. Yet what John saw is an infallible storm signal to us.

These "four angels" do not picture just four individual angels but rather picture four bands of angels. The Revelation speaks of an angel having "authority over the fire" (14:18) and an "angel over the waters." (16:5) But here these four angels at the four corners of the earth have authority over the "four winds of the earth." They are not like humans who cannot shelter the wind in the right hand (Proverbs 27:15, 16), but they are superhuman and have been commissioned by the Creator of heaven and earth, who "has gathered the wind in the hollow of both hands." (Proverbs 30:4; Jeremiah 10:13) These angels are holding the winds prisoner, waiting for God's signal to release them at the time for the expression of his wrath against his enemies upon the earth.

Their being said to stand at the four corners of the earth does not say that the earth is flat and literally has four corners; for the Bible definitely speaks of the earth as being spherical and suspended by invisible forces in space. (Isaiah 40:22; Job 26:7) But, standing not directly north, south, east or west, but at the corners or angles, the four angels would let loose the winds obliquely from diagonal directions, such as the "tempestuous wind called Euroaquilo" mentioned in Acts 27:14, which led to the wreck of the ship carrying the Christian apostle Paul. Thus, too, no quarter of the earth would be spared from the disastrous blowing of the winds, converging at the center to produce a global whirlwind. Long before this oncoming storm a devastating storm was used to illustrate execution of the vengeance of Jehovah God upon enemy nations in the seventh and sixth centuries B.C.E. Here is the description, in Jeremiah 25:32, 33:

"Look! A calamity is going forth from nation to nation, and a great tempest itself will be roused up from the remotest parts of the earth. And those slain by Jehovah will certainly come to be in that day from one end of the earth clear to the other end of the earth. They will not be bewailed, neither will they be gathered up or be buried. As manure on the surface of the ground they will become."

For the moment, it looked to the apostle John as if the four angels were about to let loose the four winds to blow upon the earth and sea and against every tree, wreaking havoc everywhere. This was the appearance of things in the final year of World War I, in 1918, when the modern-day spiritual brothers of the apostle John thought that the then raging war and revolution would lead right on into the expected 'battle of Armageddon,' that is, "the war of the great day of God the Almighty" at the symbolic place called Armageddon in Hebrew. But No! Look! See what the apostle John now sees at this critical point of time. What?

A fifth angel, "another angel ascending from the sunrising, having a seal of the living God." He comes upon the scene, not from any corner of the earth, but from the sunrising or the east. He comes from the

same direction as do the "kings from the rising of
the sun." For these kings the way is prepared by the
drying up of the waters of the great river Euphrates
after the pouring out of the sixth bowl of God's anger.
Likewise, figuratively, the ancient kings Darius the
Mede and Cyrus the Persian came from the sunrising
in their victorious movement against ancient Babylon
on the Euphrates River back in 539 B.C.E., thus
opening the way for the freeing of the exiled people
of Jehovah God who were held captive in the Babylonian Empire. (Revelation 16:12; Isaiah 46:11; 44:28
to 45:7; Daniel 5:30 to 6:3) So, not unexpectedly,
but quite agreeably, something good should come from
or through this angel ascending from the sunrising.
Ah, yes!

In confirmation of this, note what the angel carries
—a "seal of the living God." He evidently has a work
to do, and this requires time, time extending beyond
World War I. Not yet is it the time for the anticipated
'battle of Armageddon.' Babylon the Great must yet
be destroyed. True it is that after World War I she
experienced a fall from religious power due to the
invisible heavenly "kings from the rising of the sun."
But she must yet be destroyed, and first after that
there comes the "war of the great day of God the
Almighty." (Revelation 16:12-16) Hence, as in the
nick of time, the fifth angel, the one from the sunrising, gets ahead of any premature action on the
part of the four angels who till then were holding
back the threatening "four winds of the earth." He
has greater authority than those four angels, and so
with a loud voice he cries out to those four angels:
"Do not harm the earth or the sea or the trees, until
after we have sealed the slaves of our God in their
foreheads."—Revelation 7:3.

THE SEALING IN THE FOREHEAD

The ride of the four horsemen who had been disclosed by the breaking of the first four seals of the
scroll had begun, and their ride had been made evi-

dent by World War I. But now there must be first
a finishing of the sealing of the foreordained number of God's chosen ones, his elect ones. (Revelation 6:1-8; Matthew 24:30, 31) For that reason
he had not appointed the "four winds of the earth"
to be let loose in 1918 to bring about immediately the destruction of religious Babylon the Great
and thereafter to bring the "war of the great day
of God the Almighty." During this gracious interval of time before the "four winds of the earth" are
to be let loose the sealing of the "slaves of our God
in their foreheads" must be completed.

The sealing of those "slaves of our God" had begun
in the first century of our Common Era. The apostle
John himself was one of those sealed ones. The apostle
Paul was also one of those sealed ones, and he wrote
about this sealing work. When writing his second
letter to the Christian congregation in ancient Corinth
about the year 55 C.E., Paul said: "But he who guar-
antees that you and we belong to Christ and he who
has anointed us is God. He has also put his seal upon
us and has given us the token of what is to come,
that is, the spirit, in our hearts." (2 Corinthians 1:
21, 22) From this it is clear that the sealing is done
by means of the spirit of God, that is, by his holy
invisible active force. This is substantiated also by
what Paul wrote to the Christian congregation in ancient Ephesus, Asia Minor, about the year 60 or
61 C.E. Associating the spirit with the sealing, Paul
wrote:

"We who have been first to hope in the Christ.
But you also hoped in him after you heard the word
of truth, the good news about your salvation. By
means of him also, after you believed, you were sealed
with the promised holy spirit, which is a token in
advance of our inheritance, for the purpose of releasing by a ransom God's own possession, to his glorious praise."—Ephesians 1:12-14.

The sealing with God's spirit is a token of what is
to come. It is an indication that the believing, dedi-

cated, baptized Christian has become part of God's possession, with the hope of at last becoming his everlasting possession for his glorious praise. For this reason such an anointed Christian who has the token of the spirit must preserve that seal faithfully to the end of his earthly course. He must not grieve that holy spirit of God with which he has been sealed by acting contrary to the way that this invisible active force tends to activate him in God's worship and service. If he persists in thus grieving God's spirit or active force in its proper holy operation, he will lose God's spirit and so have the seal of God's spirit wiped out, removed. The right thing for the sealed Christian to do is to live in harmony with God's spirit till at last he makes sure that he is entitled to God's deliverance of him into the heavenly inheritance, the Kingdom. Exhorting the Ephesian Christians on this matter, Paul wrote:

"Do not be grieving God's holy spirit, with which you have been sealed for a day of releasing by ransom."—Ephesians 4:30.

That a seal marks a person as having a certain possession, the apostle Paul illustrates in his letter to the Romans, chapter four, verse eleven, in which he says: "He [that is, Abraham] received [from Jehovah God] a sign, namely, circumcision, as a seal of the righteousness by the faith he had while in his uncircumcised state." Also, that a seal is an authoritative mark to show that a person is the real, genuine, authentic thing that he claims to be, the apostle Paul illustrates in his first letter to the Corinthians, chapter nine, verses one and two, where he says, in defense of his apostleship: "Am I not an apostle? Have I not seen Jesus our Lord [since his resurrection from the dead]? Are not you my work in the Lord? If I am not an apostle to others, I most certainly am to you [to whom I brought Christianity], for you are the seal confirming my apostleship in relation to the Lord." Not only did Paul have such a seal of his Christian apostleship, but he also had the seal of his being in line for the heavenly inheritance, namely, God's holy spirit, the token from God of what is to come.

In the year 1918 C.E., when the fifth angel ascended from the sunrising and called out to the four other angels at the four corners of the earth, the final, irremovable sealing of the full number of dedicated, baptized, anointed Christians, "the slaves of our God," had not been completed. This was indicated at the time of the breaking of the fifth seal of the scroll, when the apostle John saw souls under God's altar who were crying out for the avenging of their blood upon earth's inhabitants who had shed their blood. What were they told? "To rest a little while longer, until the number was filled also of their fellow slaves and their brothers who were about to be killed as they also had been." (Revelation 6:9-11) Consequently, in 1918 C.E., as the actual facts since then show, the full number had not been made complete of those who kept the "seal of the living God" upon their foreheads until their final and decisive test, till a martyr's death, if necessary. Almighty God, who does the sealing by means of his spirit, knew that. Hence he sent this fifth angel to call out to the other four angels not to let loose the winds.

Well, now, what is the full number of permanently sealed ones? How many from among mankind will go to heaven to be with Jesus Christ in the heavenly kingdom? Apparently down to the time of the Revelation to the apostle John, about the year 96 C.E., he himself did not know. How glad he must have been to have this mystery or sacred secret opened up as to how many the "living God" had foreordained or predestinated to be associated with his Son Jesus Christ in the heavenly kingdom! How glad we are, also, that John did not keep the secret to himself! Under God's command he wrote:

"And I heard the number of those who were sealed, a hundred and forty-four thousand, sealed out of every tribe of the sons of Israel: Out of the tribe of Judah

twelve thousand sealed; out of the tribe of Reuben twelve thousand; out of the tribe of Gad twelve thousand; out of the tribe of Asher twelve thousand; out of the tribe of Naphtali twelve thousand; out of the tribe of Manasseh twelve thousand; out of the tribe of Simeon twelve thousand; out of the tribe of Levi twelve thousand; out of the tribe of Issachar twelve thousand; out of the tribe of Zebulun twelve thousand; out of the tribe of Joseph twelve thousand; out of the tribe of Benjamin twelve thousand sealed."
—Revelation 7:4-8.

Twelve tribes with twelve thousand sealed out of each tribe produced one hundred and forty-four thousand sealed ones. Judah, Reuben, Gad, Asher, Naphtali, Manasseh, Simeon, Levi, Issachar, Zebulun, Joseph, Benjamin—those twelve names were well known to the apostle John. He could Scripturally figure out why the two patriarchal names of Dan and Ephraim were omitted from among the list. The patriarch Levi was one of the original sons of the patriarch Jacob the son of Isaac the son of Abraham. Jehovah God separated the tribe of Levi from the rest of the nation of Israel after their deliverance from slavery in the land of Egypt in 1513 B.C.E. He made the Levites a tribe of sanctified religious servants of his house of worship. This left a vacancy among the tribes that were to inherit the Promised Land in the Middle East. How was it to be filled? By means of Joseph, the firstborn son to Rachel, a wife of Jacob (or Israel). Because of his faithfulness to God, Joseph came into possession of the birthright from his father Israel. Down in Egypt, Joseph became the father of two sons, Manasseh the firstborn and Ephraim.

Because of attaining to the birthright (1 Chronicles 5:1, 2), faithful Joseph was due to have two parts in the nation of Israel. Hence he deserved to be responsible for the existence of two tribes in the structure of the nation. Accordingly, in ancient Israel none of the tribes of Israel was named after Joseph himself, but he had two parts in the nation nonetheless, for the tribes of his two sons Manasseh and Ephraim were made legally recognized tribes of Israel. However, in the listing of the twelve tribes in Revelation 7:4-8, the name of Ephraim is left out. Instead, the name of his father Joseph is assigned to a tribe, and Ephraim his second son would be understood to be included in his father Joseph. This let Joseph take over the responsibility for the tribe of his son Ephraim. Thus, even in the list of twelve tribes of sealed servants of the living God, Joseph had two parts, like the firstborn son in Israel.

We note also that the name of Levi was not omitted from the list of twelve tribal names in Revelation 7:4-8. In this listing of 144,000 sealed ones, the name of Levi would not mark a tribe specially separated to be the temple servants for God's whole nation. Why not? Because all of the 144,000 sealed ones become "priests of God and of the Christ." (Revelation 20:6) This inclusion of the name of Levi in the number of tribal names would therefore call for the name of Dan, one of Israel's original twelve sons, to be left out. His name was not left out because of any special prejudice against the ancient tribe of Dan, for Samson the son of Manoah, one of the judges of ancient Israel, was of the tribe of Dan. (Judges, chapters 13-16; Hebrews 11:32) In proof of that, in the naming of the twelve tribes of Israel whose names appear on the twelve gates of the prophetic city of Jehovah-shammah ("Jehovah Himself Is There") the name of Dan appears, in the listing in Ezekiel 48:30-35. Thus, although the name of this tribe is not found among the 144,000 sealed ones, it will have an honorable application in Jehovah's new system of things.

When the apostle John received the Revelation, about 96 C.E., it was sixty-three years since the nation of natural, circumcised Israel had been rejected by Jehovah God through Jesus Christ, back in 33 C.E. It was also sixty years since the Christian good news and the opportunity to enter into the kingdom of the heavens had gone to the non-Jews, or Gentiles, in 36 C.E., at the conversion of the Italian centurion, Cornelius of Caesarea, to Christianity. He and fellow believing Gentiles received at that time the holy spirit with which the "chosen ones" of God are sealed. (Matthew 23:37-39; Acts 10:1 to 11:18; Romans 11:5-25) This was because only a "remnant" of the natural, circumcised Jews or Israelites received the seal of God's holy spirit. So the remainder of the number of the sealed ones has to be made up by faithful ones chosen from among the Gentiles. Since the admission of the uncircumcised Gentiles to the ranks of the sealed ones in 36 C.E., Jehovah God has had no fleshly nation of natural Israel. Instead, there has been a spiritual "Israel of God." Its members are spiritual Israelites.—Galatians 6:15, 16.

Because a person is a natural, circumcised Israelite or Jew, it does not mean that he is automatically a member of the spiritual "Israel of God." With regard to this spiritual Israel of God the fact stated by the apostle Paul back in 56 C.E. or so in his letter to the Roman Christians holds true: "Not all who spring from Israel are really 'Israel.' Neither because they are Abraham's seed are they all children, but: 'What will be called "your seed" will be through Isaac.' That is, the children in the flesh are not really the children of God, but the children by the promise are counted as the seed." (Romans 9:6-8; Genesis 21:12) Since the year 36 C.E., what an individual is naturally according to the flesh does not determine the matter with Jehovah God as to becoming a member of the 144,000 sealed ones. He can make a spiritual Israelite even out of a non-Jew or uncircumcised Gentile. It is just as he inspired the apostle Paul to write to the Roman Christians, a number of whom were uncircumcised Gentiles:

"He is not a Jew who is one on the outside, nor is circumcision that which is on the outside upon the flesh. But he is a Jew who is one on the inside, and his circumcision is that of the heart by spirit, and not by a written code."—Romans 2:28, 29.

From this standpoint, even a natural circumcised Jew or Israelite who is not a member of the spiritual "Israel of God" is, spiritually speaking, a Gentile or non-Jew. On this basis the apostle John could be instructed to write to the congregation of spiritual Israelites in the ancient city of Philadelphia in Asia Minor: "Look! I will give those from the synagogue of Satan who say they are Jews, and yet they are not but are lying—look! I will make them come and do obeisance before your feet and make them know I have loved you." (Revelation 3:9) Because such a sharp distinction is made between one who is a Jew or Israelite merely in name and according to the circumcised flesh, it helps us to appreciate that the twelve tribes of the 144,000 sealed ones are the spiritual "Israel of God," and not 144,000 who were originally natural circumcised Israelites or Jews.

THEIR PLACE IN GOD'S FINAL ARRANGEMENT

In Revelation 7:4-8, aside from the fact that they are sealed with the "seal of the living God," nothing is there said about the purpose or place of these 144,000 spiritual Israelites in the final arrangement of Jehovah God. However, this can be determined by what is said farther on in the Revelation to the apostle John. In chapter twenty-one John is given a vision of the Bride of Christ, "the Lamb's wife." She is pictured as a radiant city that descends out of heaven from God and bears the name New Jerusalem. In describing this glorious heavenly city, John proceeds to say: "It had a great and lofty wall and had twelve gates, and at the gates twelve angels, and names were inscribed which are those of the twelve tribes of the sons of Israel. . . . The wall of the city also had twelve foundation stones, and on them the twelve names of the twelve apostles of the Lamb."—Revelation 21:2, 9-14.

Thus the gates of this bridal city of New Jerusalem

were for the entry of the twelve tribes of the sons of Israel. Since this is not an earthly old Jerusalem, but a heavenly New Jerusalem, these twelve tribes of the sons of Israel who gain access into this symbolic city must be the twelve tribes of Israel named in Revelation 7:4-8. From this it is evident that the purpose of the twelve tribes there named is to make up a heavenly government that will, as a whole, serve as "the bride, the Lamb's wife."

Furthermore, the official position held by those who enter into those pearly gates guarded by angels is plainly stated. John says: "Also, the twelve gates were twelve pearls; each one of the gates was made of one pearl. . . . And the nations will walk by means of its light, and the kings of the earth will bring their glory into it. And its gates will not be closed at all by day, for night will not exist there." (Revelation 21:21, 24, 25) Ah, yes, the 144,000 sealed ones of the twelve tribes of spiritual Israel will all be "kings of the earth," and they will be the only ones from the nations of the earth who will enter into that heavenly government, New Jerusalem, by means of a spiritual resurrection from the dead to immortal life in heaven. (1 Corinthians 15:22-53) Having such a royal position, they can, all together, make up a "bride" of suitable station for the Lamb, Jesus Christ, who is himself a heavenly King, seated at the right hand of Jehovah God.

It must be remembered, also, that these 144,000 sealed ones were called "the slaves of our God" by the angel that had the seal of the living God. (Revelation 7:3) That they are to serve as kings in the heavenly New Jerusalem is expressly stated when the apostle John closes his description of the holy city. Unlike the unfaithful earthly Jerusalem, it will never become a cursed city but will forever be a blessed city and a blessing to all mankind. "And no more will there be any curse," writes John. "But the throne of God and of the Lamb will be in the city, and his slaves will render him sacred service; and they will see his face, and his name will be on their foreheads. Also, night will be no more, and they have no need of lamplight nor do they have sunlight, because Jehovah God will shed light upon them, and they will rule as kings forever and ever." (Revelation 22:3-5) The 144,000 sealed slaves of the living God become the "kings of the earth" who alone enter the heavenly New Jerusalem by means of the pearly twelve gates on which are the names of the twelve tribes of Israel.

The fact that they are called the twelve "tribes of the sons of Israel" thus has helped us to make out what is the purpose that Jehovah God has for them, their place in his new system of things after the battle of Armageddon and the binding and abyssing of Satan the Devil and his demons. However, the number of them, that is, 144,000, also aids us in fixing upon God's purpose toward them, that his purpose is to have them be kings with his Lamb Jesus Christ in the heavenly New Jerusalem. Only in Revelation, chapter fourteen, is that number again stated. There we are informed of what position this foreordained number of spiritual Israelites will occupy in God's realm. In Revelation 14:1-5, John writes:

"And I saw, and, look! the Lamb standing upon the Mount Zion, and with him a hundred and forty-four thousand having his name and the name of his Father written on their foreheads. And I heard a sound out of heaven as the sound of many waters and as the sound of loud thunder; and the sound that I heard was as of singers who accompany themselves on the harp playing on their harps. And they are singing as if a new song before the throne and before the four living creatures and the older persons; and no one was able to master that song but the hundred and forty-four thousand, who have been bought from the earth. These are the ones that did not defile themselves with women; in fact, they are virgins. These are the ones that keep following the Lamb no matter where he goes. These were bought from among mankind as first fruits to God and to the Lamb, and no falsehood was found in their mouths; they are without blemish."*

4-14

With the Lamb Jesus Christ, these followers of his who have been bought from among mankind as a firstfruits to God and to the Lamb make up a company of 144,001. Where is it that they are seen standing together? "Upon the Mount Zion." Not upon the earthly Mount Zion in the Middle East, for that small hill and its neighboring hills would be too small an area for "the holy city, New Jerusalem" into which these twelve tribes of spiritual Israel and their Leader, the Lamb of God, enter through the twelve pearly gates. The square base of that holy city is described as being three thousand furlongs (375 miles) to each side and thus having a circumference of twelve thousand furlongs or 1,500 miles. Earthly Mount Zion, on which a part of ancient Jerusalem stood, would be

* See "Babylon the Great Has Fallen!" God's Kingdom Rules!, chapter 21, pages 454-462.

just a tiny feature of such a large land area 375 miles square. (Revelation 21:2, 10-17) Logically, then, the Mount Zion upon which the 144,000 spiritual Israelites stand with the Lamb of God is the heavenly Mount Zion, upon which the heavenly Jerusalem stands.

To the Hebrew Christians, about nine years before earthly Jerusalem was destroyed in the year 70 C.E. by the Roman armies, it was written: "You have not approached that which can be felt and which has been set aflame with fire . . . But you have approached a Mount Zion and a city of the living God, heavenly Jerusalem, and myriads of angels." (Hebrews 12:18-22) On this heavenly Mount Zion the 144,000 sealed spiritual Israelites stand with the Lamb. As regards a seal of the living God on their foreheads, it is said that they have the name of the Lamb Jesus Christ and the name of his heavenly Father, Jehovah God, written on their foreheads. Like a seal, these two names distinguish the 144,000 as belonging to God inasmuch as he has bought them by the sacrifice of the Lamb Jesus Christ his Son.

Since the heavenly Mount Zion is the location of the "city of the living God, heavenly Jerusalem," the fact that the 144,000 stand there with the Lamb of God indicates that they are at the heavenly seat of government. It indicates that they rule there as the "kings of the earth," and "they will rule as kings forever and ever." (Revelation 21:24; 22:5) So, once again, God's purpose in sealing twelve tribes of twelve thousand each of spiritual Israelites is made clear in the Revelation to the apostle John. In view of such a sublime purpose we can appreciate why it was so urgent to finish the sealing of these 144,000 spiritual Israelites with the seal of the living God before the four winds of the earth were let loose by the four angels at the four corners of the earth. Loosing those winds would produce a violent storm that would destroy religious Babylon the Great and then bring an Armageddon of defeat and annihilation upon all the political nations of the earth.

In Revelation 7:4-8 the smallest units into which the 144,000 sealed ones are broken up are tribes, each tribe of this spiritual Israel being made up of 12,000 members. This partitioning of the spiritual Israel into twelve equally large tribes represents the final arrangement of them in the heavenly kingdom. It denotes a balanced organization, in which no favoritism plays a part. In the Holy Bible twelve is a number representing organization. Not without purposeful design did Jehovah God bless the ancient patriarch Jacob with twelve sons, who could become the patriarchal heads of twelve tribes. What Jehovah God prefigured in the twelve tribes of Israel he has fulfilled and preserved in these twelve equal tribes of spiritual Israel, all sealed as being the special possession of the living God, his holy nation. However, while the members of this spiritual Israel are being prepared here on earth, being sealed with God's holy spirit, they are generally divided up into congregations of varying size throughout the whole earth.

Eight or more years before earthly Jerusalem and its Herodian temple were wiped out by the pagan Romans in 70 C.E., the disciple James likened the Christian congregations of his day to a spiritual Israel, when he opened up his general letter by writing: "James, a slave of God and of the Lord Jesus Christ, to the twelve tribes that are scattered about: Greetings!" (James 1:1) More than thirty years afterward the apostle John was favored with the fascinating Revelation and in it special recognition was given to seven congregations still in existence near the end of the first century of our Common Era. He was commanded to write distinctive messages to these seven nearby congregations. Because of the great significance of these messages to us in this critical time of the twentieth century C.E., heavenly wisdom urges upon us the making of an examination of what was written under divine inspiration to those seven congregations of the first century C.E.

Congregations Producing 144,000 Sealed Ones

LOVERS of good government for the peoples of earth hail the cheering fact that the slaves of God, who are sealed in their foreheads with the "seal of the living God," 144,000 of them, will rule as "kings of the earth" together with the resurrected Son of God, Jesus Christ, in the heavens. (Revelation 7:4-8) On earth while undergoing training, discipline and proving, these prospective heavenly rulers who gain the divine seal of approval have been grouped together in congregations.

That these congregations of sealed slaves of God were being prepared for their part in the heavenly kingdom after the end of today's wicked system of things is plainly pointed out by the apostle John toward the close of the first century of our Common Era. After identifying himself as the favored slave who received the marvelous Revelation from God through Jesus Christ, John writes these words of salutation to certain named congregations, saying:

"John to the seven congregations that are in the district of Asia: May you have undeserved kindness and peace from 'The One who is and who was and who is coming,' and from the seven spirits that are before his throne, and from Jesus Christ, 'The Faithful Witness,' 'The first-born from the dead,' and 'The Ruler of the kings of the earth.' To him that loves us and that loosed us from our sins by means of his own blood—and he made us to be a kingdom, priests to his God and Father—yes, to him be the glory and the might forever. Amen."—Revelation 1:1-6.

It is the "seven congregations that are in the district of Asia" to whom the inspired apostle John says: "He [that is, Jesus Christ] made us to be a kingdom, priests to his God and Father." This proves that some members of the 144,000 sealed ones of spiritual Israel were to be found among those seven particular churches. Why so? Because the 144,000 spiritual Israelites are to rule as kings with Jesus Christ the Lamb on the heavenly Mount Zion, in the "holy city, New Jerusalem." What was specially written to those seven congregations would therefore be of interest and spiritual benefit to the remnant of spiritual Israelites on earth today. These are being sealed with the "seal of the living God" in this shortening time before Jehovah God signals to the four angels at the four corners of the earth to let loose the "four winds of the earth" and bring the greatest storm of trouble that has ever struck the human family since the creation of man almost six thousand years ago.—Revelation 7:1-3; 14:1-3.

Those seven congregations in Asia Minor were not far from where the apostle John wrote down the Revelation, that is, within a radius of 175 miles from the island of Patmos that hugs the coast of Asia Minor along the Aegean Sea. Because of his Christian activity as an apostle of Jesus Christ, the aged John was a prisoner on this penal island, suffering persecution by the Roman Empire. First of all, in the Revelation given him here on this island, he has a vision of the one who is the principal caretaker of the seven Asian congregations and who is also the one whom God delegated to give the Revelation to John. In opening up his account John writes: "A revelation by Jesus Christ, which God gave him, to show his slaves the things that must shortly take place. And he sent forth his angel and presented it in signs through him to his slave John, who bore witness to the word God gave and to the witness Jesus

Christ gave, even to all the things he saw. Happy is he who reads aloud and those who hear the words of this prophecy, and who observe the things written in it; for the appointed time is near."—Revelation 1:1-3.

Being the principal caretaker appointed by Jehovah God over the congregations of those whom he loosed from their sins by means of his own blood, Jesus Christ would send this Revelation from God for the benefit of these congregations. Though the Revelation was sent first directly to the seven Asian congregations named, all the other congregations from that first apostolic century down to our twentieth century have benefited from it. They have been made happy by hearing the words of that marvelous prophecy of the Revelation and by observing obediently the things written in it. And this is very important to us today, for certainly now, so late in this twentieth century, it must necessarily be true that "the appointed time is near."

The glorified Jesus Christ did not materialize to the apostle John on Patmos in order to reveal himself as he did to his disciples during the forty days after he was raised from the dead, as "The first-born from the dead," on Nisan 16 of 33 C.E. Instead, he appeared in a glorious vision, picturing him as the High Priestly Caretaker among the congregations on earth of his faithful followers who are sealed with the holy spirit of God. John was careful to note all the distinguishing features about his glorious appearance, and we should likewise be careful to do the same. So John writes:

"I John, your brother and a sharer with you in the tribulation and kingdom and endurance in company with Jesus, came to be in the isle that is called Patmos for speaking about God and bearing witness to Jesus. By inspiration I came to be in the Lord's day, and I heard behind me a strong voice like that of a trumpet, saying: 'What you see write in a scroll and send it to the seven congregations, in Ephesus and in Smyrna and in Pergamum and in Thyatira and in Sardis and in Philadelphia and in Laodicea.'"—Revelation 1:9-11.

This command to write down the message from heaven was given, not to any Christian apostle in earthly Jerusalem, for Jerusalem in the Middle East was then out of existence if, as the second-century Christian Irenaeus expressly says, the Revelation to John was written at the close of the reign of the Roman emperor Domitian, who died in 96 C.E., twenty-six years after Jerusalem's destruction by the Romans. Neither was the command to write down the Revelation given to any Christian apostle in the imperial capital of Rome. It was given to the aged apostle John on the penal island of Patmos, nine hundred miles southeast of Rome.

There, "by inspiration," John was transported out of the first century down to this twentieth century of our Common Era, for he "came to be in the Lord's day." That "day" must begin when the crowned rider on the white horse, described in Revelation 6:2, begins to ride forth with his bow, "conquering." As all the evidence bearing upon the matter proves, this began in the year 1914 C.E., the year marked by the outbreak of World War I. The Lord, whose "day" it is, is the crowned and installed Jesus Christ; and his "day" must continue on till he completes his conquest at "Armageddon" and binds and abysses Satan the Devil and on to the end of his thousand years of reigning with his 144,000 faithful followers over all mankind. (Revelation 19:11 to 20:7) What the apostle John describes as an eyewitness and records in the Revelation spans for the most part this "day" or special time period of activity of the Lord Jesus Christ.

What appearance did the glorified Lord Jesus Christ have here in the vision to John? It was nothing of the modern psychedelic style of coloration induced by the drug LSD, but was a radiant appearance having a definite form and describable features. John was able to describe it in these words:

"And I turned to see the voice that was speaking with me, and, having turned, I saw seven golden lampstands, and in the midst of the lampstands someone like a son of man, clothed with a garment that reached down to the feet, and girded at the breasts with a golden girdle. Moreover, his head and his hair were white as white wool, as snow, and his eyes as a fiery flame; and his feet were like fine copper when glowing in a furnace; and his voice was as the sound of many waters. And he had in his right hand seven stars, and out of his mouth a sharp, long two-edged sword was protruding, and his countenance was as the sun when it shines in its power. And when I saw him, I fell as dead at his feet."—Revelation 1:12-17a.

In this vision the glorified Lord Jesus Christ appeared to be barefooted, like the high priest when ministering in Jehovah's ancient temple in earthly Jerusalem. However, he wore no bonnet or headgear like that of the ancient high priest, his head being crowned with beauty of hair that had grown snow-white in the way of righteousness. (Proverbs 16:31) He was not clad in sacrificial garments, for he was girded at the breast with a golden girdle, betokening glorious divine service. His face, not sad or humiliated, shone like the enlightening sun at midday, but his eyes were ablaze, either with searching, testing power or with indignation against disapproved persons. His voice was resonant, resounding like many waters in motion. Such vocal power would add to the pronouncing of adverse judgment to be executed, as symbolized by the sharp, long two-edged sword that protruded out of his mouth. In his right hand he controlled seven stars or what they symbolized. The Lord Jesus Christ later mentions some of these distinguishing features in referring to his identity when speaking to the seven congregations.

Little cause for amazement that at such a glorious appearance the apostle John should fall as if dead to the ground before the feet of the Lord Jesus Christ! But the realism of the vision was very powerful, and it had the effect of reality, so much so that John was reacting to it in both speaking and acting as if to reality. John saw seven lighted lampstands and the glorified Lord Jesus Christ standing in among them. In ancient Israel, in the temple at Jerusalem as constructed by wise King Solomon, the high priest served in the midst of ten golden lampstands in the Holy of the temple. (1 Kings 7:48, 49; 2 Chronicles 4:7, 19, 20) In the vision that John saw there was a special reason for there being just seven lampstands, aside from the fact that seven is the Bible number denoting spiritual completeness or perfectness. When writing to the congregation in Ephesus, John was told to refer to the one who holds the seven stars in his right hand as well as "who walks in the midst of the seven golden lampstands." (Revelation 2:1) Stars, lampstands and the Lord's glorious appearance—everything was brightness.

Before being told what to write specifically to the seven congregations in the Roman province of Asia, the apostle John was revived from his deathlike condition and calmed. As he tells us: "And he laid his right hand upon me and said: 'Do not be fearful. I am the First and the Last, and the living one; and I became dead, but, look! I am living forever and ever, and I have the keys of death and of Ha'des. Therefore write down the things you saw, and the things that are and the things that will take place after these. As for the sacred secret [the mystery, *AS; RS;* the secret meaning, *NEB*] of the seven stars that you saw upon my right hand, and of the seven golden lampstands: The seven stars mean the angels of the seven congregations, and the seven lampstands mean seven congregations.' "—Revelation 1:17b-20.

"THE FIRST AND THE LAST"

"The First and the Last"! In the prophecy of Isaiah 44:6 Jehovah God says: "I am the first and I am the last, and besides me there is no God." And in Isaiah 48:12, 13 he says: "I am the same One. I am the first.

Moreover, I am the last. Moreover, my own hand laid the foundation of the earth, and my own right hand extended out the heavens." Also, in the Greek alphabet the first letter is called Alpha and the last letter Omega (Great O); and so Jehovah God again emphasizes his being "the First and the Last" by saying, in Revelation 1:8: " 'I am the Alpha and the Omega,' says Jehovah God, 'the One who is and who was and who is coming, the Almighty.' " And in Revelation 22:13 he says: "I am the Alpha and the Omega, the first and the last, the beginning and the end." Hence, in speaking of himself as "the First and the Last," is the Lord Jesus Christ claiming to be Jehovah God the Almighty? Not at all, but he is referring to himself as "the First and the Last" in another sense, in another connection. How is that?

This was in connection with death and life. The glorified Jesus Christ in heaven was then, as he says, "the living one." But what about before then? "I became dead," he says. That was when he became a man and lived for thirty-three and a half years down here on earth. His enemies then put him to death by impaling him on a stake outside Jerusalem. But on the third day "the King of eternity, incorruptible, invisible, the only God," resurrected Jesus Christ from the dead. (1 Timothy 1:17) From then on the resurrected Lord Jesus Christ could say: "Look! I am living forever and ever." (Revelation 1:17, 18) At his resurrection he was clothed upon with immortality in the heavenly spirit realm, and thus can die no more. (1 Peter 3:18, AS; RS; 1 Corinthians 15:45-54; Romans 6:9) At his death Jesus Christ on earth went to Ha'des, which is the common grave of mankind. On the third day Jehovah God used the 'key of Ha'des' and let his faithful Son out and restored him to life, to live forever, immortal.—Acts 2:22-36; 13:33-37; 26:23.

Can we see now how, in this connection, Jesus Christ could speak of himself as "the First and the Last"? He was the first one whom Jehovah God the

Almighty raised directly, without another agency, from the dead, not to live a little while longer and then die once more, but to live forever. That is why the apostle John could speak of him as "Jesus Christ, 'the Faithful Witness,' 'The first-born from the dead.' " (Revelation 1:5) Furthermore, he was the first one to be resurrected from human death to life as a spirit in the heavenly realm. The purpose of Jehovah God the Almighty is to raise no others from the dead directly, without some agency, not even from human death to spiritual, heavenly life. For that reason Jesus Christ is also "the Last" to have this direct divine intervention. Will there, then, be no other resurrection from the dead but that of Jesus Christ? No, but thereafter God will use his resurrected Son in raising all others for whom he laid down his perfect human life in sacrifice.—John 5:21-29.

This explains why Jesus, after saying, "Look! I am living forever and ever," added the words: "And I have the keys of death and of Ha'des." Jehovah God has committed to Jesus the use henceforth of that key of death and that key of Ha'des.* He is the one whom Jehovah God will use to release mankind from the death that they inherited from their sinful first human father Adam and also from the common grave of mankind, that is to say, Ha'des, to which the general mass of mankind goes at death.

Very fittingly Jesus could say: "I am the resurrection and the life. He that exercises faith in me, even though he dies, will come to life; and everyone that is living and exercises faith in me will never die at all." (John 11:25, 26) Jesus, when on earth as a flesh-and-blood man, also said: "Unless you eat the flesh of the Son of man and drink his blood, you have no life in yourselves. He that feeds on my flesh and

---

* In six (6) Hebrew translations of the Revelation the word "Ha'des" in Revelation 1:18 is rendered as "She·ol'"; and in the Syriac (Philox-enian Harkleian) Version it is rendered as "Shi·ul'." Hence the Ha'des of the pagan Greeks is not meant here, but the Sheol of the inspired Hebrew Bible, namely, the common grave of mankind.

drinks my blood has everlasting life, and I shall resurrect him at the last day; for my flesh is true food, and my blood is true drink. . . . Just as the living Father sent me forth and I live because of the Father, he also that feeds on me, even that one will live because of me. This is the bread that came down from heaven. . . . He that feeds on this bread will live forever."—John 6:53-58.

Because the glorified Jesus Christ is alive from the dead forevermore and has the power to wipe out the death and the grave to which sinful mankind is subject, there was solid basis for him to tell the apostle John: "Therefore write down the things you saw, and the things that are and the things that will take place after these." (Revelation 1:19) The ever-living, mightily empowered Jesus Christ will see to it that all the things that are due to take place according to the purpose of Jehovah God "will take place after these." Now among the things that John saw in the vision were the seven stars in the right hand of the glorified Jesus Christ and also the seven golden lampstands. What is the mystery, the sacred secret, about

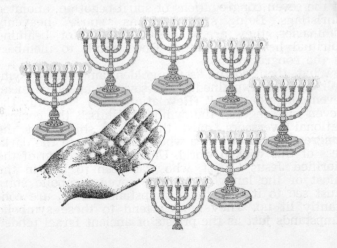

these? What do they symbolize? The Lord Jesus Christ himself explains their meaning.

THE MYSTERY OF THE STARS AND THE LAMPSTANDS

The seven stars upon the right hand of the Lord Jesus are symbolic of the "angels of the seven congregations" in the ancient Roman province of Asia (now part of modern Turkey). Are such "angels" invisible ones? No. The apostle John received the entire Revelation from Jesus Christ by means of a heavenly angel, and it would be unreasonable for him to be writing back to angels in heaven, in invisible realms. They do not need the messages written to the seven congregations in Asia. The basic meaning of the title "angel" is "messenger; message bearer." The "stars" of the seven congregations are seven human messengers sent forth by Jehovah God to be in charge of those seven congregations. As these seven symbolic stars are seen to be upon Jesus' right hand, they are in his care and charge and under his direction, his "right hand" of applied power being able to direct and protect them. So they correspond with the presiding minister or overseer, superintendent, in each of the seven congregations of spirit-begotten, anointed Christians. Being symbolized as "stars," heavenly luminaries, they are means, agencies, for beaming spiritual heavenly light of God's truth to members of the congregations.

What, then, do the "seven golden lampstands" symbolize? Jesus explained: "The seven lampstands mean seven congregations." (Revelation 1:20) Not only the 'seven messengers,' the symbolic "stars," the congregational overseers, must themselves shine, but the congregations must as a whole also shine in the darkness of this wicked world. Under the direction of the glorified Jesus Christ, who was seen to be "in the midst of the lampstands," the seven symbolic stars must see to it that these lampstands shine, are constantly lit up. They must attend to these symbolic lampstands just as the priests of ancient Israel tended to the lampstands in the Holy of Jehovah's temple at Jerusalem. The human "angels," the symbolic stars, set the example for the congregations by themselves shining, with power greater than that of any lamp on a lampstand. They must remember and act on the words of Jesus in his Sermon on the Mount, when he said to his followers:

"You are the light of the world. A city cannot be hid when situated upon a mountain. People light a lamp and set it, not under the measuring basket, but upon the lampstand, and it shines upon all those in the house. Likewise let your light shine before men, that they may see your fine works and give glory to your Father."—Matthew 5:14-16.

The apostle John addressed the written Revelation to "the seven congregations that are in the district of Asia." The glorified Jesus Christ told him to do so. (Revelation 1:4, 10, 11) The apostle Paul had earlier written letters to the congregations in Ephesus and Laodicea. (Ephesians 1:1, 2; Colossians 2:1; 4:16) It is possible that the apostle John made seven copies of the Revelation and sent a separate copy to each of the seven congregations named by the glorified Jesus Christ, at Ephesus, Smyrna, Pergamum, Thyatira, Sardis, Philadelphia and Laodicea.

However, the information contained in the entire Revelation was of benefit to all the true Christian congregations, the allness being indicated by the number of the congregations directly addressed, namely, seven, this number symbolizing spiritual perfection, completeness. So, doubtless, in course of time copies were made from the original seven manuscripts of the Revelation and sent to all other congregations or circulated among them, translations being made thereof into other languages as needed.

None of those seven original Asian congregations remains till today, but we have copies and translations of the Revelation that was sent to them in the first century C.E. In the vision of the Revelation the apostle John found himself by divine inspiration "in the Lord's day." (Revelation 1:10, 11) To a limited degree the congregations in that first century needed the Revelation, but those who specially and immediately need the Revelation in its final application are the true Christian congregations of spirit-begotten, anointed Christians actually in existence "in the Lord's day." That would mean the symbolic "seven congregations," or all such congregations, in existence since the year 1914 C.E., when the "day" of the Lord Jesus Christ began. Such congregations will not continue on earth till the end of "the Lord's day" at the close of the thousand years of Christ's reign over mankind. Yet they urgently need the Revelation and the unraveling of its mysteries for as long as any members of such spiritual congregations are in the flesh on this earth, that is, till their glorification in the heavens with Jesus Christ the reigning King.

As the "seven lampstands" in the visionary "Lord's day" pictured all the true Christian congregations in this present, real "Lord's day" since 1914 C.E., so the "seven stars" symbolize all the spirit-begotten, anointed angellike overseers of such congregations of today. These human "angels," in being compared to "stars," are reminded that, as the apostle Paul wrote to the congregation in Ephesus, God "raised us up together and seated us together in the heavenly places in union with Christ Jesus." (Ephesians 2:4-6) Such symbolic stars of today need to take note of what the apostle John wrote to the "seven stars" of his day and make a present-day application thereof. The first-century Asian congregations did not exist in any succession to one another, like links in a chain, but they all existed at the same time. So the conditions described in what was written to those seven congregations exist in the spirit-begotten, anointed congregations contemporaneously (at the same time) in the present "Lord's day," since 1914 C.E.

Therefore all members of such congregations are vitally affected and should take serious heed to what is written.

CHAPTER 8

To the Angel
in Ephesus

EPHESUS was the metropolis of the ancient province of Asia, and was about sixty miles from the Isle of Patmos where John was. In fitness with this fact the glorified Jesus Christ directed the apostle John to write to the human overseer of the congregation there first. "To the angel of the congregation in Ephesus write: These are the things that he says who holds the seven stars in his right hand, he who walks in the midst of the seven golden lampstands, 'I know your deeds, and your labor and endurance, and that you cannot bear bad men, and that you put those to the test who say they are apostles, but they are not, and you found them liars. You are also showing endurance, and you have borne up for my name's sake and have not grown weary. Nevertheless, I hold this against you, that you have left the love you had at first.

" 'Therefore remember from what you have fallen, and repent and do the former deeds. If you do not, I am coming to you, and I will remove your lampstand from its place, unless you repent. Still, you do have this, that you hate the deeds of the sect of Nicolaus, which I also hate. Let the one who has an ear hear what the spirit says to the congregations: To him that conquers I will grant to eat of the tree [Greek, *xylon*] of life, which is in the paradise of God.' "—Revelation 2:1-7.

Years previous to the giving of the Revelation, the apostle Paul had spoken of the presence of false apos-

105

tles in the congregation at Corinth, Greece. Later he warned the overseers from the city of Ephesus that false apostles would arise among the Christians in their city, the city that had the famous temple of Artemis (Diana), the moon goddess. (2 Corinthians 11:12-15; Acts 20:17-31) Before the apostle John died this had already occurred. But in loyalty to Christ's true apostles, the Ephesian congregation put to the test these false claimants to apostleship and Scripturally found them to be liars. Likewise today!

When "the Lord's day" broke upon the world in the year 1914, it found many religious leaders in Christendom claiming to be apostles of Christ or "apostolic successors." In fact, the Pontiff of the Roman Catholic Church at the Vatican in Italy had been hailed as "Heir of the Apostles; Peter in Power," and as "Apostolic Lord and Father of Fathers." But the fully dedicated, baptized Bible students, who held to the "twelve apostles of the Lamb" (Revelation 21:14), studied the written Word of Jehovah God and found these modern claimants to apostleship to be false and would have nothing to do with them. This was one of the reasons why they came out of Christendom, which is the dominant part of Babylon the Great, the world empire of false religion. (Revelation 18:4; 17: 1-5) They did not tolerate such religious liars among themselves.

One thing that the glorified Jesus Christ mentioned as having against the congregation in Ephesus toward the end of the first century was that it had left its first love: "You have left the love you had at first." (Revelation 2:4) It did not have that fervor of Christian love for Jehovah God that it had at its beginning, as referred to in the apostle Paul's letter to the Ephesians and as described in Acts 19:1 to 20:1, 17-38.

This reminds us of the case of the nation of Israel, which, in its youth as a nation had fervent love for its God, like that of a youthful bride for her newly married husband: "This is what Jehovah has said: 'I well remember, on your part, the loving-kindness of your youth, the love during your being engaged to marry, your walking after me in the wilderness, in a land not sown with seed. Israel was something holy to Jehovah, the first yield to Him.' " (Jeremiah 2: 1, 2) So, too, at its beginning the congregation of Ephesus had a consuming love for Jehovah God in response to his own love for them. The apostle John himself describes this responsive love springing from appreciation, when he writes:

"The love is in this respect, not that we have loved God, but that he loved us and sent forth his Son as a propitiatory sacrifice for our sins. As for us, we love, because he first loved us."—1 John 4:10, 19.

In a striking likeness, at the beginning of "the Lord's day" in 1914, even the dedicated, baptized Bible students who had come out of religious Christendom had left the love that characterized the Christian congregation in the first century. In what way? More attention, more expressed love, was being heaped upon the Son of God than upon Jehovah God himself. This, of course, was measurably due to the use in Bible study of translations of the Holy Scriptures in which the translators of Christendom and Jewry rarely used God's name Jehovah or did not use it at all.

For example, the King James or Authorized Version Bible renders the name Jehovah only four times, and the Jewish Isaac Leeser translation of The Twenty-four Books of the Holy Scriptures does not use the divine name at all, using "the LORD" and "God" instead. But after World War I the dedicated, baptized Bible students awoke to the unsuitableness of this, and in correction of this, in the issue dated January 1, 1926, of their official magazine *The Watch Tower and Herald of Christ's Presence*, the leading article bore the challenging title "Who Will Honor Jehovah?"

In the course of the years these Christian Bible students gave more and more attention to bearing witness to God's name, and as a climax on Sunday, July 26, 1931, at their international convention in

Columbus, Ohio, a resolution was adopted by which the name "Jehovah's witnesses" was embraced as the designation by which they chose to be identified and distinguished from Christendom. Thereafter this name was embraced by the congregations of these dedicated Christians throughout the earth. In its issue of March 1, 1939, the title of their official magazine was altered to *The Watchtower Announcing Jehovah's Kingdom.* They wanted to be like Jesus Christ, whom the apostle John calls "the Faithful Witness," that is, Witness of Jehovah God his heavenly Father. (Revelation 1:5) This was indeed a sincere effort to get back to that first love, the love that the Christian congregation of the first century "had at first." This love moves them today, and they have proved that they remembered from what those professing to be Christians have fallen. Their repentance at this oversight of Jehovah God, the Universal Sovereign, was genuine.

So they returned to their obligation to "do the former deeds," namely, to bear witness to the name and Messianic kingdom of the Most High God. (Isaiah 43:10-12; Acts 1:8) They came to appreciate that the vindicating of Jehovah's universal sovereignty by means of his Messianic kingdom is the prime purpose of Jehovah and is the primary teaching of the Holy Bible. The salvation of human creatures through the ransom sacrifice of Jesus Christ was merely secondary, although it was a prominent and inseparable part of the general purpose of Jehovah God. Galvanized into action by appreciation of this, they set themselves to the worldwide work of preaching Jehovah's Messianic kingdom by which his universal sovereignty and name are to be vindicated and by means of which also mankind is to be saved.—Matthew 24:14; Mark 13:10.

In Christ's instructions to the "angel of the congregation in Ephesus" these spiritual Israelites were warned that, if they did not do this carrying out of the "former deeds" in this "the Lord's day," then the one "who walks in the midst of the seven golden lampstands" would remove their "lampstand from its place." In their case the heavenly lampstand Caretaker has not had to do this, for since the close of World War I they have been striving to shine as "the light of the world." Down till now the rays of this symbolic lampstand have reached into as many as 200 lands and island groups. Christendom has claimed to be "the light of the world" in that she had made nominal converts to her type of Christianity of more than 977,383,000 all around the globe. But do her millions of members of many races and nationalities display the "first love," such as the true Christians of the apostolic first century had? (Revelation 2: 4, *AV*) It is her millions of members who have fought the two world wars, who have supported the Fascist, Nazi and Communist dictators, who have taken part in the political revolutions and other disturbances of the nations.

Is Christendom fulfilling Jesus' prophecy of Matthew 24:14 in this "the Lord's day" by preaching "this good news of the kingdom" in all the inhabited earth for a witness to the nations? No, but in her choice of the kingdoms of this world and her setting up of the League of Nations and its successor, the United Nations, Christendom has left this earth-wide preaching to the Christian witnesses of Jehovah to do. Even if, as Christendom claims, she had a symbolic lampstand or was one in God's Christian arrangement, the glorified Jesus Christ has removed her "lampstand from its place." From the facts of history since 1914 C.E. it is manifest that Christendom is not the light-bearing congregation (symbolic lampstand) of God; she has no light-bearing organization. Her light has gone out, and she herself is enshrouded in the darkness that covers the earth and in the thick gloom that covers the national groups. She is too far gone for repentance. She cannot arise and shine.—Isaiah 60:1, 2.

SECTARIANISM HATED

Christendom has been fragmented into a thousand or more religious sects, the number of which she is trying to reduce by church mergers or by the ecumenism promulgated by the second Vatican Council in 1962-1965. To Christendom the commendatory words of Christ to the congregation of Ephesus cannot be applied: "Still, you do have this, that you hate the deeds of the sect of Nicolaus, which I also hate." (Revelation 2:6) Back in the first century, as the apostle Paul made clear, the true Christian congregation had to fight against the tendency to form religious sects, such as the Nicolaitans. (1 Corinthians 1:12-15; 3:1-5) He warned the very overseers of the congregation of Ephesus that after his going away men would arise among the disciples there and would "speak twisted things to draw away the disciples after themselves." (Acts 20:29, 30) Not strange, then, that at the beginning of this "the Lord's day" there was a tendency to establish a religious sect among those today known as the Christian witnesses of Jehovah.

Charles Taze Russell, the president of the Watch Tower Bible & Tract Society from 1884 to 1916, did not try to set up a religious sect among the members of the Society and members of the related organization, International Bible Students Association. Rather, he expected the heavenly glorification of the true Christian congregation around the end of the "times of the Gentiles" in 1914. (Luke 21:24, *AV*) Nevertheless, after his death on October 31, 1916, in the midst of World War I, there was a tendency to form a religious sect around his teachings and organizational structure, although it was not intended to do so. In July of 1917 the book "The Finished Mystery," the seventh volume of the *Studies in the Scriptures,* was published in English and it was called the "posthumous work of Pastor Russell," on page 2, the Publishers page. This book treated C. T. Russell as having been "the faithful and wise servant" foretold in Matthew 24:45-47, *AV.* In its commentary on the book of Revelation it presented C. T. Russell as being the "seventh messenger," that is, "the angel of the church of the Laodiceans," the seventh and last congregation mentioned in the list. (Revelation 3:14, *AV*) In its commentary on the prophecy of Ezekiel, the book presented C. T. Russell as having been the foretold 'man clothed in linen with the writer's inkhorn by his side.' (Ezekiel 9:4-11; 10:1-7, *AV*) Naturally, those accepting such interpretations felt a sense of loyalty to a marvelously used servant of Jehovah God. They felt it obligatory upon them to adhere to him as an earthly instrument of the Most High God in what was called "the Laodicean period."

BETHEL, 122-124 COLUMBIA HEIGHTS, BROOKLYN, NEW YORK

C. T. RUSSELL

However, this tendency toward the formation of a sect among his faithful followers was displeasing to the one "who holds the seven stars in his right hand." Under his guidance this tendency toward the founding of a religious sect like the sects of Christendom out of which they had come was fought against by those who hate unchristian sectarianism. Those who chose to follow a dead man left the ranks. Those who believed that the light of Bible truth did not stop advancing with the death of the first president of the Watch Tower Bible & Tract Society held to God's visible organization and continued searching the Holy Scriptures in the advancing light.

In 1927, in the issue of February 15, the *Watch Tower* magazine published the leading article "Servant—Good and Evil," based on the theme text of Matthew 24:45, 46, *AV*. Faithfully and courageously this explained that the "faithful and wise servant" there mentioned was, not any individual man, but a class, a servant body, the whole congregation of Christ's faithful spiritual followers at the time. It was as in the case of the nation of ancient Israel, which was called Jehovah's servant, and to whom it was said: " 'You are my witnesses,' is the utterance of Jehovah, 'even my servant whom I have chosen.' " (Isaiah 43:10) One "servant," but many "witnesses." Likewise, in the case of Matthew 24:45-47, one "servant" (or slave), and many component members, all together forming one servant or slave body charged with the care of the Lord's goods or belongings. This weakened any basis for forming a sect around Russell.

Working farther in that direction, in September of 1930 the book *Light,* in two volumes, was published, giving a commentary on the whole book of the Revelation. This book gave an understanding of the "seven stars" and the 'seven angels' of the congregations different from that presented in *The Finished Mystery*. So it did not identify Charles T. Russell as the "seventh messenger," or, "the angel of the church of the Laodiceans." (See *Light,* Book One, page 13;

and pages 44-52 under "Laodicea.") Furthermore, years before this, the book *The Finished Mystery* was allowed to go out of circulation.

Finally, on July 30, 1931, the book *Vindication,* Volume One, was published. This volume set forth that the 'man clothed with linen and with the writer's inkhorn by his side' was not an individual man in the fulfillment of the prophecy of Ezekiel, chapter nine. On pages 99, 100, under the subheading "Man with Inkhorn," this volume said: " 'The man with the writer's inkhorn by his side,' therefore, clearly represented the anointed 'servant' class of the Lord on earth, which class is a part of God's organization."

Thus, finally, on three essential points of argument, the basis was totally taken away for building any religious sect around Charles T. Russell. These Christian spiritual Israelites had insultingly been dubbed "Russellites" by the disdainful clergy of Christendom; but these faithful Christians, like those in the first-century congregation in Ephesus, hated sectarianism and refused to accept this contemptible nickname. Hence, on July 26, 1931, at the same international convention in Columbus, Ohio, at which the book *Vindication,* Volume One, was released, they embraced, by resolution, the Scriptural designation "Jehovah's witnesses."

For this anti-sectarian action the glorified Lord Jesus Christ could commend these Christian witnesses of Jehovah of today just as he commended the congregation at Ephesus for their stand against the "deeds of the sect of Nicolaus."

TREE OF LIFE IN GOD'S PARADISE

In closing the message to the congregation in ancient Ephesus the glorified Jesus Christ said: "Let the one who has an ear hear what the spirit says to the congregations: To him that conquers I will grant to eat of the tree [Greek, *xylon*] of life, which is in the paradise of God."—Revelation 2:7.

Here all seven of the "congregations that are in the district of Asia" are alerted. Every spiritual Israelite "who has an ear" in all those congregations is called upon, not to stop up his ear, but to prick up his ear and "hear what the spirit says" to all seven congregations, for what the spirit says applies to them all. "The spirit"—what spirit? We remember that in his salutation to the seven congregations the apostle John prayed that they might have undeserved kindness and peace "from the seven spirits" that are before the throne of Jehovah God. (Revelation 1:4) Later, in John's marvelous vision of God on his heavenly throne, the "seven spirits of God" are pictured by "seven lamps of fire burning before the throne." (Revelation 4:5) Interestingly, in each of the messages to the seven Asian congregations the invitation is given to each one having an ear to "hear what the spirit says to the congregations," or seven times in all. This does not mean that one individual spirit of these "seven spirits" addresses one congregation, and the other six address each one a congregation, each one its own congregation, in succession.

Evidently, "the spirit" speaks through the glorified Lord Jesus Christ in all seven cases, and it is the spirit of God, the active force of God, that is with the Lord Jesus Christ. This means that Jesus here is not speaking of his own initiative or on his own authority. What he speaks in all seven cases to the Asian congregations is by the authority of God. Hence each one with an ear who hears can be sure that what Jesus here says has the approval and backing of God and is certain of fulfillment.

Since what the spirit says it says "to the congregations," then what it says to the congregation in Ephesus applies also to all the other congregations, not to just the Ephesian congregation. Likewise, what it says in the message to any of the other Asian congregations applies to all the seven congregations. Thus the glorious promises that God's spirit in Jesus makes in all seven messages apply to all the congregations and are shared by them all.—Revelation 2:7, 11, 17, 29; 3:6, 13, 22.

All members of the congregations are encouraged to conquer, with the promise of a reward bestowed by Jehovah God through his Son Jesus Christ. Jesus Christ himself is an example of conquering or overcoming. In his speech to his eleven faithful apostles before he was betrayed by Judas Iscariot, Jesus said: "In the world you are having tribulation, but take courage! I have conquered the world." (John 16:33) By his faith in Jehovah God and by his faithfulness to Him Jesus Christ conquered the world, despite the tribulation he had to endure. Years later, even after receiving the Revelation, the apostle John wrote: "Everything that has been born from God conquers the world. And this is the conquest that has conquered the world, our faith." (1 John 5:4) To the spirit-begotten Christians who thus conquer the promises are given.

The first promise given points to "the paradise of God." (Revelation 2:7) This is, of course, not the "garden of Eden," "the paradise of pleasure," out of which Adam and Eve were driven after disobeying God their Creator. (Genesis 2:8; 3:24, *NW; Dy*) In a comparison with that original earthly paradise, the district of the Jordan River in Abraham's day was said to be like "the paradise of the Lord." (Genesis 13:10, *Dy*) Because of the beauty of his location the king of ancient Tyre in the days of the prophet Ezekiel was said to be "in the pleasures of the paradise of God." (Ezechiel 28:13, *Dy*) That original "paradise of pleasure" passed out of existence. So Revelation 2:7 does not refer to it. Neither does it refer to paradise restored to earth during the thousand-year reign of Christ. Jesus Christ, when hanging on the stake at Calvary, referred to that earthly paradise when he said to the sympathetic evildoer hanging on a stake alongside him: "Truly I tell you today, You will be with me in Paradise."—Luke 23:39-43.

That evildoer had not conquered the world so as to entitle himself to eat from the tree of life in the paradise of God. That evildoer was not a baptized member of the "congregation of God," for it was first founded on the day of Pentecost of the year 33 C.E., or fifty-one days after the evildoer died alongside Jesus. (Acts 2:1-42) Also, since the holy spirit was first poured out upon Christ's disciples on that day of Pentecost, this evildoer was not begotten of the spirit of God, which is one of the requirements of anyone who would see and enter into the heavenly kingdom of God. (John 3:3, 5; 7:39) The Paradise into which this evildoer will come by means of a resurrection from the dead must be the coming earthly Paradise under God's kingdom. This differs from the paradise of God mentioned in Revelation 2:7, which is a heavenly, spiritual paradise promised to the conquering church or congregation.

The "tree of life, which is in the paradise of God," is not necessarily a symbol of Jehovah God, the Source of life and of immortality. It symbolizes, rather, the divine provision for sustained life; and the conquerors' partaking of that "tree of life" would signify their partaking of that divine provision for the particular life here indicated. The Greek word that John used here was *xylon* and literally means "wood," and so it could mean "trees," as in an orchard. Continually eating of that "tree of life" would mean continually living in that place where the tree is located, namely, "in the paradise of God." How grand to think that this means to live and dwell under paradisaic conditions in the very presence of Jehovah God himself and in association with him! This would require that in their resurrection they be raised from the dead as heavenly, spirit creatures. (1 Corinthians 15:43-50) What a grand reward for conquering! Today it is indeed worth while for a spiritual Israelite who has an ear capable of taking in spiritual things to hear this promise that God's spirit in his Son Jesus Christ says to the congregation of spirit-begotten ones.

CHAPTER 9

To the Angel
in Smyrna

THE SECOND congregation to which the glorified Jesus Christ addresses himself is the one in Smyrna in the ancient Roman province of Asia. This city was located on a gulf of the Aegean Sea, about thirty miles north of Ephesus, and thus farther away from the Isle of Patmos, where the apostle John was then a prisoner. Smyrna had a temple of Tiberius Caesar and thus promoted emperor worship. It also had a considerable population of natural, circumcised Jews, who were opposed to apostolic Christianity. What is John told to write for the congregation in Smyrna? Let us read:

"And to the angel of the congregation in Smyrna write: These are the things that he says, 'the First and the Last,' who became dead and came to life again, 'I know your tribulation and poverty—but you are rich—and the blasphemy by those who say they themselves are Jews, and yet they are not but are a synagogue of Satan. Do not be afraid of the things you are about to suffer. Look! The Devil will keep on throwing some of you into prison that you may be fully put to the test, and that you may have tribulation ten days. Prove yourself faithful even to death, and I will give you the crown of life. Let the one who has an ear hear what the spirit says to the congregations: He that conquers will by no means be harmed by the second death.'"

These words, in Revelation 2:8-11, are without a word of faultfinding against the congregation in

117

Smyrna, not even because of its "poverty," its being materially poor. This material poverty was counterbalanced by their being spiritually rich. Better was it for the Smyrna congregation to be in such a condition than for them to be materially rich but spiritually poor, as was the case with the congregation in Laodicea. (Revelation 3:17) Jesus himself on earth as a man was materially poor; and his fleshly half brother James wrote to the spiritual Israelites of his day this corrective reminder: "Listen, my beloved brothers. God chose the ones who are poor respecting the world to be rich in faith and heirs of the kingdom, which he promised to those who love him, did he not?" (James 2:5) Yes! And according to Jesus' words, the Smyrna congregation was rich in faith and in good works toward God. For this they continued to be heirs of the heavenly kingdom of God. It is therefore without point that the religious clergy of Christendom today reproach the remnant of spiritual Israelites among Jehovah's witnesses for being poor.

In what way the natural, circumcised unbelieving Jews of Smyrna blasphemed the Christian congregation there is not explained. Probably it was like the abusive blasphemy against the apostle Paul at Antioch of Pisidia and in Corinth. (Acts 13:45; 18:6) These blasphemers prided themselves on being Jews by fleshly birth and circumcision; but they had ceased to be real Jews. Why? Because they did not prove to be Jews inwardly, circumcised in heart; they had not become spiritual Israelites like the Smyrna congregation. Such unbelieving Jews attended the local synagogue, but they were not the synagogue of Jehovah God but the "synagogue of Satan"; their blasphemy bore out this fact. They resisted Jehovah God and his Messiah Jesus, and thus put themselves in a class with Satan, for the name Satan means "Resister." They were not in the new covenant that had been mediated by Jesus Christ over the sacrifice of his own perfect human life. (Jeremiah 31:31-34; Matthew 26:27, 28; Luke 22:20; 1 Timothy 2:5, 6) Likewise today, the remnant of spiritual Israelites need not mind being blasphemed by clergymen who merely claim to be spiritual Jews.

By the end of the first century the ancient congregation in Smyrna had undergone a great deal of "tribulation," doubtless in the form of persecution, this making their state of material poverty worse. But they were to go through still more. Yet, said the glorified Jesus, "do not be afraid of the things you are about to suffer." How were they to suffer still more? "Look! The Devil will keep on throwing some of you into prison." This would fully put them to the test. Especially so since the purpose of this was "that you may have tribulation ten days." (Revelation 2: 10) Ten literal days of tribulation or persecution, if concentrated, could be very severe and, apparently, enough for a lifetime; but likely "ten days" is to be understood figuratively, especially in its modern-day application. "Ten" being used in seven other places in the Revelation as a symbol of allness or completeness in an earthly way, "ten days" could symbolize all the days of the congregation on earth. At the longest, till the Devil is bound.

IMPRISONMENT

Since the apostle John was himself writing as a prisoner from the Isle of Patmos, the Smyrna congregation could well accept through him this exhortation not to be afraid of suffering further imprisonments at the hands of the Devil. Of course, the Devil would use human agencies to do the imprisoning, and those humans whom he used to cast them into prison and keep them there would be servants of the Devil. The Christians would be imprisoned, not for moral or political wrongdoing, but under false charges. Their being falsely accused is indicated by its being said that they are thrown into prison by the Devil. The name Devil means "Slanderer; False Accuser." Thus the members of the Smyrna congregation would be imprisoned in Christian innocence and would therefore have a clean conscience, just like all the apostles when they were imprisoned on various occasions.

Imprisonments have featured prominently in the modern experiences of the remnant of spiritual Israelites among Jehovah's witnesses. In the year 1919 many members of the anointed remnant of spiritual Israelites emerged from the prisons into which they had unjustly been thrown during the course of World War I from 1914 to 1918. This included the then president of the Watch Tower Bible & Tract Society, J. F. Rutherford, the secretary-treasurer of the same Society and two other members of the editorial committee of the Society, and three other responsible members of the Society, all of whom were involved in preparing and publishing the famous book *The Finished Mystery,* which was a religious commentary on the two Bible prophecies of the Revelation and of Ezekiel. All seven having been sentenced on June 21, 1918, on the false charges of political sedition and obstruction of the American military draft, for twenty years of imprisonment on each of four counts, they were denied the right to bail and were finally committed to the Federal penitentiary in Atlanta, Georgia. Along with them went an eighth well-known member of the Society, who was sentenced for ten years.

Belatedly, in March of 1919, bail was granted pending their appeal for a retrial by a higher court, and they were released. The United States government never did bring the case to trial again, and these eight members of the Watch Tower Bible & Tract Society were exonerated. Also, in 1920 the book *The Finished Mystery* was released from under ban and again began to be circulated in the United States and Canada.

However, the Smyrna congregation of the first century had been warned by the glorified Jesus Christ: "Look! The Devil will keep on throwing some of you into prison that you may be fully put to the test." (Revelation 2:10) Conformable to this, the imprisonment of members of the remnant of spiritual Israelites among Jehovah's witnesses did not cease after the release of many of them in 1919. Rather, it increased on a grand scale, especially with the spread of Russian Communism, Fascism, Catholic Action, Hitlerite Nazism, and nationalism.

Already in the year 1926, in Germany, cases were brought into court against 897 active members of Jehovah's devoted people, this resulting in many of these being fined. During the year 1927 the number of these worshipers of Jehovah who were arrested in Germany rose to 1,169; and out of 353 of these legal actions that were disposed of there were punishments meted out to forty. The Watch Tower Bible & Tract Society found it necessary to establish its own legal department in its German branch to take care of all this legal work, for the arresting of these Christian witnesses of the Most High continued, by the hundreds.

This was all preliminary to the dictatorship of Adolf Hitler, which began in 1933. During the spring of that year there were 19,268 Christian witnesses of Jehovah active in the field in Germany. They refused to follow the Nazi dictator as their Fuehrer, their Leader, and to have any share in his political and military aggressions. Because of such absolute, undivided devotion to Jehovah God and his kingdom by Christ they were thrown into prisons and concentration camps by the thousands. Despite World War II (1939-1945) they maintained their Christian neutrality, many of them even to the death. When World War II ended, two thousand of them had perished in their places of confinement, and of those 8,000 who came forth from concentration camps two thousand were incapacitated. In many cases, shortly after these faithful witnesses of Jehovah got out of Nazi concentration camps they were put into Communist prisons and concentration camps in East Germany.

Imprisonments of Jehovah's Christian witnesses took place in other lands during this period. As never before these witnesses came out boldly for Christian neutrality toward worldly political and military con-

flics. In Great Britain during the course of World War II, 1,593 youthful Witnesses were imprisoned for refusing to violate their Christian neutrality. Since military conscription in Britain then applied to young women as well as young men, 344 of those thus imprisoned for Christian neutrality were women. Imagine the total amount of their prison terms, over six centuries in length of time!

And what as to the United States of North America? In the early 1930's the persecution of Jehovah's witnesses began to get more intense. Pursuant to this fact, J. F. Rutherford, president of the Watch Tower Bible & Tract Society, spoke over a chain of radio stations, with WBBR as the key station, on the subject "Jehovah's Witnesses: Why Persecuted." This was on Sunday, May 1, 1932. Shortly afterward, on Sunday, May 22, 1932, an organized band of Jehovah's witnesses invaded the persecution "hot spot" of Bergenfield, New Jersey, to carry on their Kingdom witnessing work from house to house. If and when arrested, they were instructed to say they were Jehovah's witnesses, refusing to give their personal names until the due time came in the courtroom before the judge. This course was courageously followed.

At first, it not being foreseen how numerous the cases would at last become in the United States, statistics were not kept of the number of arrests and imprisonments. However, in the year 1934 the number increased to 340; in 1935 to 478; in 1936 to 1,149; and so on. As in Germany, it finally became necessary for the Watch Tower Society to establish a legal department at its Brooklyn (N.Y.) headquarters to handle all these cases of arrest and imprisonment, for preaching "this good news of the kingdom," from house to house on all days of the week including Sunday.

Military conscription in peacetime was instituted in September of 1940 in the United States, and on Sunday, December 7, 1941, the country was plunged into the vortex of World War II. This called upon the American witnesses of Jehovah who were subject to the draft to maintain their stand for absolute Christian neutrality. Their faithfully doing so resulted in the imprisonment of thousands of them for terms of several years each. Since military conscription has never been revoked in the United States, the matter of Christian neutrality has continued to be an issue. To this day there are hundreds of Christian witnesses of Jehovah who are serving prison terms because of holding fast to their Christlike neutrality respecting the military conflicts of this bellicose world.

Statistics could be produced here with regard to imprisonments of these Christian witnesses of Jehovah both before and after World War II. Truly the victorious Lord Jesus Christ did not say pointlessly to the congregation in ancient Smyrna that the Devil would keep on throwing some of them into prison and that they would have tribulation ten days. (Revelation 2:10) Particularly from the year 1935 C.E. onward the modern-day remnant of anointed members of God's spiritual congregation began to be joined by a "great crowd" of persons who dedicated themselves to God and got baptized but whose hopes are not heavenly, but simply to dwell forever in the coming earthly paradise under God's Messianic kingdom. All these, too, have faithfully met the issues of the times and have suffered being thrown by the Devil's agents into prison, and undergoing much tribulation. From the standpoint expressed in Hebrews 10:32-34 the anointed remnant have suffered sympathetically with these imprisoned ones of the "great crowd."

"Keep on remembering the former days in which, after you were enlightened, you endured a great contest under sufferings, sometimes while you were being exposed as in a theater both to reproaches and tribulations, and sometimes while you became sharers with those who were having such an experience. For you both expressed sympathy for those in prison and joyfully took the plundering of your belongings, knowing you yourselves have a better and an abiding possession."—Hebrews 10:32-34.

"THE CROWN OF LIFE"

Under such sufferings great is the reward for faithfulness, even to the death if necessary. The faithful "great crowd" will get its appropriate reward on earth, but, in order to strengthen the anointed remnant of his Kingdom joint heirs, the Lord Jesus Christ said to the Smyrna congregation in the face of its tribulation: "Prove yourself faithful even to death, and I will give you the crown of life."—Revelation 2:10.

Many of the anointed remnant have proved faithful to Christian principles under tribulation even to violent death. Although not all will suffer finally such a violent death, they must prove faithful to the end of their earthly days. For doing so, they are sure to receive "the crown of life." The word "crown" here does not mean "topmost" as if to refer to the highest form of life in heaven, immortality with the divine nature, but refers to a prize as a reward for Christlike faithfulness. They are in a contest for victory over this world. Even though in this fierce contest they may lose their earthly life violently at the hands of the Devil's agents, their Devilish enemies will not wipe out their lives forever. In due time God through Christ will crown them with heavenly life. So they have no reason to fear death.

Deathlessness, immortality will be their reward. This is to be understood from the closing words of the glorified Jesus Christ to the Smyrna congregation: "Let the one who has an ear hear what the spirit says to the congregations: He that conquers will by no means be harmed by the second death."—Revelation 2:11.

Only in the Revelation to John is this expression "second death" used. It denotes an everlasting death without any possibility of a resurrection. In Revelation 20:14, 15; 21:8 it is given a symbol, in these words: "And death [inherited from sinner Adam] and Hades were hurled into the lake of fire. This means the second death, the lake of fire. Furthermore, whoever was not found written in the book of life was hurled into the lake of fire." "But as for the cowards and those without faith and those who are disgusting in their filth and murderers and fornicators and those practicing spiritism and idolaters and all the liars, their portion will be in the lake that burns with fire and sulphur. This means the second death."

One's being written in the book of life means everlasting life for that one. One's being hurled into the symbolic lake of fire means everlasting death, "second death," for that one. Satan the Devil will be punished with everlasting death, for he is subject to the second death and will be "harmed by the second death." And so too will his demon angels.—Revelation 20:10.

Those who are unable to be "harmed by the second death" are unmistakably pointed out to us. After the account of the binding and abyssing of Satan the Devil and his demons, in Revelation 20:1-3, we read: "This is the first resurrection. Happy and holy is anyone having part in the first resurrection; over these the second death has no authority, but they will be priests of God and of the Christ, and will rule as kings with him for the thousand years." (Revelation 20:5, 6) Hence those described in Revelation 20:4 can be called happy and holy, for of them the apostle John writes: "And I saw thrones, and there were those who sat down on them, and power of judging was given them. Yes, I saw the souls of those executed with the ax for the witness they bore to Jesus and for speaking about God, and those who had worshiped neither the wild beast nor its image and who had not received the mark upon their forehead and upon their hand. And they came to life and ruled as kings with the Christ for a thousand years."

It is because these Christian conquerors are faithful even to death and are not "harmed by the second death" that they have a resurrection from the dead. By God's power exercised through Christ they come to life again in the resurrection, in "the first resurrection." It is a resurrection to life in heaven as spirit creatures, that thus they may be able to be heavenly priests of God and of the Christ and may reign with Christ for a thousand years. Concerning their resurrection and as respects the body with which they will be brought back to life it is written:

"So also is the resurrection of the dead. It is sown in corruption, it is raised up in incorruption. It is sown in dishonor, it is raised up in glory. It is sown in weakness, it is raised up in power. It is sown a physical body, it is raised up a spiritual body. If there is a physical body, there is also a spiritual one. It is even so written: 'The first man Adam became a living soul.' The last Adam [that is, Jesus Christ] became a life-giving spirit."—1 Corinthians 15:42-45.

A person's being a spirit creature does not in itself mean that he is not liable to the "second death," everlasting destruction. Satan the Devil and his demons are spirit creatures, but they will experience the "second death" by being hurled into the symbolic "lake of fire." (Revelation 20:10; Matthew 25:41) Consequently, the Christian conquerors will not only be resurrected from the dead as spirit creatures but will also be clothed upon with incorruption and immortality in their resurrection. In proof of this the apostle Paul describes further their resurrection by adding:

"The trumpet will sound, and the dead will be raised up incorruptible, and we [the apostle Paul and fellow Christians] shall be changed. For this which is corruptible must put on incorruption, and this which is mortal must put on immortality. But when this which is corruptible puts on incorruption and this which is mortal puts on immortality, then the saying will take place that is written: 'Death is swallowed up forever.' "—1 Corinthians 15:52b-54.

Because of being clothed with incorruption and immortality, they will never be able to be "harmed by the second death."

Thus this wonderful promise of Revelation 2:11 signifies that the Christian conquerors who listen to what the spirit says to the congregations will take part in the "first resurrection," the resurrection that is "first" in time of occurrence, in quality and in importance. Since they will also be granted to "eat of the tree of life, which is in the paradise of God," they will be privileged to enjoy this total immunity to the "second death" in the heavenly "paradise of God," for all eternity to come. What a grand reward for being a conqueror faithful even to death!

To the Angel
in Pergamum

ABOUT one hundred and thirty miles
to the north-northeast of the Isle of Patmos and about
fifty miles north of Smyrna lay Pergamum, a Mysian
city near the northern border of the Roman province
of Asia. It had a 1,000-foot-high acropolis and also a
shrine to Aesculapius, the god of medicine, together
with a university for medical study. Parchment, such
as the Christian apostles used, gets its name from
Pergamum, namely, *charta Pergamena*. (2 Timothy
4:13) Pergamum brought itself into line with the
cult of emperor worship and had a temple for the
worship of Caesar Augustus, the first emperor of the
Roman Empire. The Christian congregation that was
established in Pergamum was one of the seven congregations to whom the book of Revelation was directed. To this congregation John was instructed to
write the following:

"And to the angel of the congregation in Pergamum write: These are the things that he says who
has the sharp, long two-edged sword, 'I know where
you are dwelling, that is, where the throne of Satan
is; and yet you keep on holding fast my name, and
you did not deny your faith in me even in the days
of Antipas, my witness, the faithful one, who was
killed by your side, where Satan is dwelling.

" 'Nevertheless, I have a few things against you,
that you have there those holding fast the teaching
of Balaam, who went teaching Balak to put a stumbling block before the sons of Israel, to eat things

128

sacrificed to idols and to commit fornication. So you, also, have those holding fast the teaching of the sect of Nicolaus likewise. Therefore repent. If you do not, I am coming to you quickly, and I will war with them with the long sword of my mouth.

" 'Let the one who has an ear hear what the spirit says to the congregations: To him that conquers I will give some of the hidden manna, and I will give him a white pebble, and upon the pebble a new name written which no one knows except the one receiving it.' "—Revelation 2:12-17.

Since the speaker here warns of his having the sharp two-edged sword protruding out of his mouth, it identifies him as being the glorified Jesus Christ. (Revelation 1:16) With it he threatens to fight against the offensive ones if they are not cleared out of the Pergamum congregation or if these do not repent. With judicial decisions that proceed out of his mouth like a sharp, two-edged long sword he fights to keep the congregation of his true followers clean, free from sectarian divisions.

The glorified Jesus Christ knew the difficult situation in which the Pergamum congregation found itself back there in the first century C.E., just as he knows the trialsome situation in which the remnant of his anointed followers find themselves today since the close of World War I in 1918 C.E. He denominated Pergamum where this Christian congregation dwelt as the place "where the throne of Satan is," the place "where Satan is dwelling." (Revelation 2:13) The "throne of Satan" would be where he sits as political ruler and as judge. (Compare Revelation 20:4 and Matthew 19:28; Luke 22:30.) Where he sits pictures that on which he bases his rulership, that which serves as his justification and support for ruling and judging. On what basis, then, does he seat himself in power?

The basis is indicated in his very name, namely, Satan, which means "Resister; Adversary." At the Garden of Eden shortly after the creation of Adam and Eve, this mighty spirit creature Satan set out to resist Jehovah God as the Universal Sovereign, the Sovereign of heaven and earth. He adopted the view that Jehovah as God and Ruler does not and cannot command the loving, unselfish loyalty of his creatures as his subjects and worshipers, and that his creatures are not absolutely dependent upon Jehovah. On this basis Satan made himself a resister of God and set up his own throne to extend his rule over all these creatures who, as Satan insisted, were not really loyal worshipers of Jehovah at heart. The right to prove his ability to capture these as his subjects was the basis that Satan laid for setting up a throne rivaling that of Jehovah God. Satan claimed that Jehovah could not maintain himself as a God and Ruler who is exacting exclusive devotion and absolute obedience.

At ancient Pergamum Satan especially set up conditions to put the Christian congregation to the test in this regard. Here he caused to be established a temple of Zeus or Jupiter, the chief god among all the pagan gods and goddesses. Also, out of the rock of the Pergamum Acropolis he had a throne altar cut to Zeus or Jupiter. Although thus magnified, this Zeus or Jupiter did not insist on exclusive devotion to himself, but allowed other gods as well as goddesses to be worshiped, but as subordinate to him. Satan wanted to force Jehovah God into a position like that of Zeus or Jupiter, a position in which Jehovah God would have to give up his claim to exclusive devotion and universal sovereignty.

Here also in Pergamum Satan caused a temple to be set up for the worship of the Roman emperor, Augustus or Octavius Caesar, who died in the year 14 C.E. The setting up of the worship of the Roman emperor was really a political move, one meant to weld all the various conquered countries in the Roman Empire together by the worship of a god common to them all, namely, the Roman emperor. In this matter the Roman emperor did not demand the exclusive religious devotion of his imperial subjects; they still could worship their local or national gods and goddesses, but they must also include him in their worship so as thus to have a common imperial worship and be held together by common religious ties. The worship of the Roman emperor as well as of Zeus or Jupiter is really the worship of the great Resister of Jehovah God, and for this reason Pergamum could be said to be "where the throne of Satan is" and "where Satan is dwelling."

This being in such close touch with Satan's throne and presence imposed a severe test upon the exclusive devotion of the Christian congregation to Jehovah God, nineteen centuries ago. Today a like test is imposed upon the remnant of anointed Christians who are in line for reigning with Christ in the heavens. How so? In that since the end of World War I in 1918 self-determination of peoples has been glorified and nationalism is therefore sweeping the world, with many new nations being born as a result. All these political nations demand the exclusive devotion of their subjects even to the extent of one's sacrificing life for the nation, and really the political State is put above God. But despite this crucial test the anointed remnant of today, like the Pergamum Christians, "keep on holding fast my [Christ's] name." They persist in openly declaring "Jesus is Lord." They refuse to say, under any pressure, "Jesus is accursed," and the political State ("Caesar") is Lord.—1 Corinthians 12:3.

"ANTIPAS, MY WITNESS"

To this anointed remnant of today the glorified Jesus Christ can say: "You did not deny your faith in me even in the days of Antipas, my witness, the faithful one, who was killed by your side, where Satan is dwelling." (Revelation 2:13) Antipas must have been killed on the issue of imperialism, refusing to worship Caesar, the deified head of the Roman Empire, as god, and choosing to continue worshiping Jehovah as the divine Head of all the living universe and as the only living and true God. He continued holding fast to Jesus Christ as the one whom Jehovah God had appointed to be Lord, *Kýrios*. And so in this regard the Lord Jesus Christ could speak of Antipas as "my witness, the faithful one."—Matthew 23:9, 10; 1 Corinthians 8:5, 6; Ephesians 4:5, 6; Acts 2:36.

Today, nineteen centuries later, the issue is in essence the same, especially since Jehovah God enthroned his Son Jesus Christ as reigning King in the heavens in the year 1914 C.E. Particularly since 1920 C.E. the anointed remnant have been proclaiming world wide the established Messianic kingdom of God, in fulfillment of Jesus' prophecy recorded in Matthew 24:14. And in the year 1941 C.E., on August 6, the opening day of the national assembly of Jehovah's witnesses at St. Louis, Missouri, J. F. Rutherford as president of the Watch Tower Bible & Tract Society imparted a larger view of the issue. In his keynote speech on "Integrity" he announced that the great issue before heaven and earth was that of "universal sovereignty" on God's part. He said:

"The primary issue raised by Satan's defiant challenge was and is that of UNIVERSAL DOMINATION" or sovereignty.—Par. 19.

And in the third last paragraph of his speech he said to his assembly audience of 64,000:

"We must and will be entirely, wholly, unreservedly and completely devoted to The THEOCRATIC GOVERNMENT by Christ Jesus. We can have no part in and nothing in common with Satan's organization. We are wholly and steadfastly for The THEOCRATIC GOVERNMENT, and here, by God's grace, we will remain. We know it shall vindicate JEHOVAH's name and bring deliverance to all who love righteousness and who serve Jehovah under his righteous government."

J. F. RUTHERFORD

The next day, August 7, 1941, the issue of *The Watchtower* of August 15, 1941, containing this keynote speech on "Integrity" was released for circulation among the now 70,000 attending the St. Louis assembly. For keeping their integrity toward Jehovah God on the burning issue of UNIVERSAL SOVEREIGNTY a number of the anointed remnant have been killed by the political, military and religious powers of Satan's world, since the year 1919, just like the Christian martyr Antipas of the first century C.E.

TEMPTATION TO SEXUAL IMMORALITY

Satan, however, was trying to undermine the integrity of the Pergamum congregation by another means, of a very subtle sort. The glorified Jesus Christ called attention to this when he said: "Nevertheless, I have a few things against you, that you have there those holding fast the teaching of Balaam, who went teaching Balak to put a stumbling block before the sons of Israel, to eat things sacrificed to idols and to commit fornication." (Revelation 2:14) Ah, yes, sexual immorality, to be used as an inducement to committing idolatry! Back in the year 1473 B.C.E. the Mesopotamian prophet Balaam hired himself out to King Balak of Moab in order to pronounce curses upon the sons of Israel. These were encamped on the plains of Moab just before their crossing the Jordan River to take possession of the Promised Land. But Jehovah the God of Israel foiled this conspiracy by turning the curses of Balaam into a blessing for the sons of Israel. (Numbers 22:1 to 24:25) So now Balaam suggested to King Balak another way to bring about Israel's downfall. What? Sex, along with idolatry!

Women who were associated with idolatrous worship were used as lures to draw male Israelites away from the worship of Jehovah God to the lewd worship of pagan gods and to offering sacrifices to such gods. This scheme succeeded with 24,000 Israelites. (Numbers 25:1-18; 1 Corinthians 10:8) Those Israelites who fell victim to this scheme of mixing sexual immorality with idolatry and did not keep their integrity to Jehovah God never did enter the Promised Land right across the Jordan River. Consequently, those in the Christian congregation in Pergamum who were "holding fast the teaching of Balaam" could not be tolerated.

Evidently these taught that God is merciful and the power of Christ's blood is very effective, so that Christians who now and then or regularly pleased their fallen flesh by committing fornication and even pagan idolatry along with it could be forgiven and have their willful sins washed away and thus they could continue in membership in the Pergamum congregation. Such Balaam-like teachers were "ungodly men, turning the undeserved kindness of our God into an excuse for loose conduct and proving false to our only Owner and Lord, Jesus Christ."—Jude 4, 11; 2 Peter 2:14, 15.

Such corrupters of Christian morals and faith were not to be allowed to remain in the Pergamum congregation. Neither are they to be allowed to mix in freely with the Christian congregation of the anointed remnant. This is especially so since Jehovah God, accompanied by his Messenger of the covenant, Jesus Christ, came to the spiritual temple for inspection and cleansing work in the spring of the year 1918 C.E. —Malachi 3:1-5.

Not only must the morals of the Christian congregation be preserved pure, but the unity of organization was likewise to be safeguarded. No religious sectarianism was to be allowed to divide the anointed remnant of the spiritual body of Christ. Christ, as represented by his anointed congregation, may not be divided; it cannot exist as a house divided. (1 Corinthians 1:10-13) The congregation at ancient Pergamum did not get the commendation that the glorified Jesus Christ gave to the Ephesus congregation, saying: "You hate the deeds of the sect of Nicolaus, which I also hate." (Revelation 2:6) Rather, one of the critical things that he had against the Pergamum congregation was religious sectarianism, just as he said: "So you, also, have those holding fast the teaching of the sect of Nicolaus likewise."

Religious sectarianism was dangerous and was condemnable back there, and it is so today. Its existence in any section of the general congregation of anointed Christians is something to repent over, followed by diligent efforts to root it out, for Jehovah's appointed Inspector, Jesus Christ, warns:

"Therefore repent. If you do not, I am coming to you quickly, and I will war with them with the long sword of my mouth."—Revelation 2:16, 12; 1:16.

Since coming to the spiritual temple in company with the Supreme Judge Jehovah God in 1918, the Inspector Jesus Christ has been warring with the symbolic long sword out of his mouth. He wars against those with any sectarian inclinations in the general congregation of his anointed remnant. Through the publications of the Watch Tower Bible & Tract Society he has pronounced plainspoken disapproval of all religious sectarianism as well as any interfaith movements of Christendom. It has been purged out from the ranks of the anointed remnant of Jehovah's witnesses.

Like a sharp, two-edged, long sword proceeding out of the mouth of the Lord Jesus, the pronouncement of judgment has proceeded forth against any promoters of sectarianism, either the "sect of Nicolaus" or that of any other man or religious movement. As Jesus said in his prophecy in which he foretold that he would find such an "evil slave" class at his second coming: He "will punish him with the greatest severity and will assign him his part with the hypocrites. There is where his weeping and the gnashing of his teeth will be." (Matthew 24:48-51) No sect established by the "evil slave" class since 1918 C.E. is recognized as Scriptural.

Thus the glorified Jesus Christ brings to reality the prayer that he offered to God on the last night with his apostles in the flesh: "I make request, not concerning these only, but also concerning those putting faith in me through their word; in order that they may all be one, just as you, Father, are in union with me and I am in union with you, that they also may be in union with us, in order that the world may believe that you sent me forth. Also, I have given them the glory that you have given me, in order that they may be one just as we are one. I in union with them and you in union with me, in order that they may be perfected into one, that the world may have the knowledge that you sent me forth and that you loved them just as you loved me." (John 17:20-23) With his "long sword" Jesus now wars for this unity.

"HIDDEN MANNA" AND A NAME-BEARING "PEBBLE"

There are faithful and obedient ones that conquer these wrong conditions inside the congregation and conquer this wicked world. For the encouragement of these the glorified Lord Jesus gives final words to the Pergamum congregation: "Let the one who has an ear hear what the spirit says to the congregations: To him that conquers I will give some of the hidden manna, and I will give him a white pebble, and upon the pebble a new name written which no one knows except the one receiving it."—Revelation 2:17.

"Manna"? a person might ask. "What is that?" This is just what the Israelites said when they first saw it in the wilderness of Sinai away back in the year 1513 B.C.E. It was food that Jehovah God miraculously provided for the wandering Israelites under the leadership of the prophet Moses. When the dew fell at night, this manna would form, and the next morning the Israelites would gather enough for the day's needs of each one. On the sixth day God provided them the double amount for them to collect, because none would fall or form on the sabbath day. Only that portion collected for the sabbath day would not spoil by the next morning. According to God's will the prophet Moses said to his brother Aaron, who later became high priest of Israel: "Take a jar and put in it an omerful of manna and deposit it before Jehovah as something to be kept throughout your generations." Not much later, when the golden Ark of the Covenant was constructed for Jehovah's tabernacle of worship, a golden jar of this manna was put inside this sacred chest, along with the stone tablets containing the Ten Commandments.—Exodus 16:13-33; Hebrews 9:4.

6-23

However, when the golden Ark of the Covenant was transferred from the tabernacle to the magnificent temple that King Solomon built for it in Jerusalem, the golden jar of manna was missing, for some reason. (1 Kings 8:9) But from when the manna was put into the Ark of the Covenant by Moses (1512 B.C.E.) to King Solomon's dedication of the completed temple (1027 B.C.E.) was 485 years. So for most of this time this omer of manna, which ordinarily spoiled overnight, did not perish, but was imperishable. In a literal sense this was "hidden manna," and in his message to the Pergamum congregation the glorified Jesus Christ used it as a symbol of an imperishable food supply, or that which results from such a food supply, namely, endless life. In the case of the faithful congregation of anointed Christians this life is immortality in the spirit realm, hidden from the eyes of fleshly mankind. (1 Corinthians 15:50-54) The hope of receiving such a reward is enough to spur on an anointed Christian to be a conqueror in imitation of Jesus Christ himself.

In addition to the "hidden manna," a white pebble with a new name written thereon is promised. This promised "white pebble" is symbolic of much. The original Greek word used here and translated into English as "pebble" is *pséphos*. It is the Greek that the apostle Paul used when making his Christian apology before King Agrippa in Caesarea and when describing his persecution of Christians before his own conversion. He said: "Many of the holy ones I locked up in prisons, as I had received authority from the chief priests; and when they were to be executed,

I cast my vote [*pséphos;* literally, voting pebble] against them." (Acts 26:10) This notifies us of the fact that back there pebbles were used in courts of justice in rendering judgment or voicing an opinion of either innocent or guilty. White pebbles were used for pronouncing innocence, acquittal; black ones for pronouncing guilt, condemnation. The whiteness of the pebble that the heavenly Jesus gives to the anointed conquerors means his judgment of them as innocent, pure, clean. They pass his approval as disciples.

Note, though, that this "white pebble" has on it a name, "a new name written which no one knows except the one receiving it." Such a name stone was anciently used like a modern-day ticket to an event; it was the thing that must be shown or deposited for gaining admittance to an entertainment or spectacle. The symbolic "white pebble" would accordingly picture the privilege of admittance into certain private, intimate association with Jesus Christ.

Are not just 144,000 conquering disciples the only ones to be admitted into the heavenly kingship and priesthood with him, to reign with him for a thousand years for the blessing of all mankind? (Revelation 20:4-6; 2 Timothy 2:11, 12) Are not just 144,000 conquering disciples the only ones to make up the "chaste virgin" class, the spiritual "bride," "the Lamb's wife"? Did not the apostle John later hear a voice from heaven say: "Let us rejoice and be overjoyed, and let us give him the glory, because the marriage of the Lamb has arrived and his wife has prepared herself"? Yes; and John then reports: "And he tells me: 'Write: Happy are those invited to the evening meal of the Lamb's marriage.'" (2 Corinthians 11:2; John 3:29; Revelation 21:9-15; 19:7-9) For admission into all these unique privileges the symbolic "white pebble" may have to be shown to Jehovah God. There are just 144,000 of such 'white pebbles,' and highly favored indeed are the receivers of them.

The "new name written" on each stone, is it a new personal, individual name that all others of the group of 144,000 will never learn to know? Will it entitle the pebble holder to a special individual relationship to the Lord Jesus Christ that none of the others in the group of 144,000 will enjoy? Not likely! Rather, this "new name" may stand for a name that is new to them but that will be common to them all but unknown to all other creatures in heaven and earth. So the "new name" written on the "white pebble" may mean sharing together the newly bestowed heavenly name of the Lord Jesus Christ.

This harmonizes with the message that he gave to the faithful congregation in Philadelphia, in which he says: "The one that conquers . . . I will write upon him . . . that new name of mine." (Revelation 3:12) And after the seventh angel blows his trumpet and certain tableaus appear, the apostle John says: "I saw, and, look! the Lamb standing upon the Mount Zion, and with him a hundred and forty-four thousand having his name and the name of his Father written on their foreheads." (Revelation 11:15; 14:1) Finally, after the seventh angel pours out his bowl of God's wrath and certain other tableaus follow, John says that he saw the heavenly Lord Jesus Christ riding to the "war of the great day of God the Almighty" at Armageddon, and he notes this feature about him: "Upon his head are many diadems. He has a name written that no one knows but he himself."—Revelation 16:17; 19:11, 12.

Since, now, the 144,000 receivers of the "white pebble" with the "new name" written thereon are to be joint heirs with Christ as well as his "wife," the "new name" on the symbolic "white pebble" may mean their sharing in common certain intimate privileges with their heavenly Bridegroom in connection with his own name. But whichever thing it actually is, it is sure to be a 'good name,' one that "is to be chosen rather than abundant riches," and "better than good oil." (Proverbs 22:1; Ecclesiastes 7:1) It is a worthy prize for all of the 144,000 anointed conquerors.

To the Angel
in Thyatira

UNLIKE Pergamum, the city of Thyatira had no emperor worship but had as its chief god Apollo, the sun-god and brother of the goddess Diana or Artemis. This city lay some forty miles southeast of Pergamum and was therefore farther away from the Isle of Patmos on which the apostle John was a prisoner. In the first century of our Common Era there was a congregation of true Christians in Thyatira. To its "angel," who shone like a star with heavenly spiritual light, John was directed to turn his attention with the following words:

"And to the angel of the congregation in Thyatira write: These are the things that the Son of God says, he who has his eyes like a fiery flame, and his feet are like fine copper, 'I know your deeds, and your love and faith and ministry and endurance, and that your deeds of late are more than those formerly.

" 'Nevertheless, I do hold this against you, that you tolerate that woman Jezebel, who calls herself a prophetess, and she teaches and misleads my slaves to commit fornication and to eat things sacrificed to idols. And I gave her time to repent, but she is not willing to repent of her fornication. Look! I am about to throw her into a sickbed, and those committing adultery with her into great tribulation, unless they repent of her deeds. And her children I will kill with deadly plague, so that all the congregations will know that I am he who searches the inmost thoughts and hearts, and I will give to you individually according to your deeds.

140

" 'However, I say to the rest of you who are in Thyatira, all those who do not have this teaching, the very ones who did not get to know the "deep things of Satan," as they say: I am not putting upon you any other burden. Just the same, hold fast what you have until I come. And to him that conquers and observes my deeds down to the end I will give authority over the nations, and he shall shepherd the people with an iron rod so that they will be broken to pieces like clay vessels, the same as I have received from my Father, and I will give him the morning star. Let the one who has an ear hear what the spirit says to the congregations.' "—Revelation 2:18-29.

The Sender of this message by John identifies himself as being the Son of God and, in keeping with this fact, he speaks of God as "my Father," from whom he has received something to share with his conquering followers, "my slaves." About two years later the apostle John was inspired to write his Evangel or Gospel account to prove this identification to be true, "that Jesus is the Christ the Son of God, and that, because of believing, you may have life by means of his name." (John 20:31) About sixty-three years before this, John had seen the resurrected Jesus, not like in this Revelation vision, but materialized in flesh in order to become visible to his disciples. But here in this glorious vision the Son of God appears as having "eyes as a fiery flame," this symbolizing well that he has more than human visual power, the ability to search "inmost thoughts [literally, kidneys] and hearts," to know what his disciples really are within themselves. He also appears with feet "like fine copper," in fact, "like fine copper when glowing in a furnace." (Revelation 1:14, 15) How brilliantly this pictures his clean standing in God's sight!

The message that comes from the resurrected Son of God to the congregation claiming to be Christian is therefore not to be taken lightly, indifferently. Nothing in the congregation escapes his vision, from the starlike overseer down to the least of the "slaves" of Christ. As in the case of the congregation in Thyatira, this glorious Son of God well knows the deeds, the love, the faith, the ministry and the endurance of the congregation of the remnant of his anointed followers on earth today. We need not detail these things about the congregation as they were being manifested down till the year 1919 C.E. But the congregation may have all these commendable things to its credit, and its "deeds of late" may be "more than those formerly," and yet the standing of the congregation and its angellike overseer may be tarnished by the existence of something unclean within the congregation as a whole. This may be sexual immorality, together with false teaching and idolatry, the sad part of the matter being that all of this is tolerated, not ferreted out, nor purged out.

Sadly this was true of the first-century congregation in Thyatira. For persons familiar with the Holy Bible few names are more odious than that of Jezebel the wife of King Ahab of ancient Israel. Over a thousand years after the historical Jezebel was pitched by her eunuchs out of the window at Jezreel and devoured by street dogs (905 B.C.E.) there was a counterpart of her in the Thyatira congregation. That is why the glorified Jesus Christ with blazing eyes chose to call her, not by her real name, but by the reproachful expression "that woman Jezebel." She called herself "a prophetess." But was she? If at all, a false prophetess at most, not filled with the inspiring spirit of Jehovah God. Usurping the position of the male person in the congregation, "that woman Jezebel" was teaching and misleading the slaves of the Son of God "to commit fornication and to eat things sacrificed to idols." This certainly was not the conduct of a true prophetess of God, the only One worthy to be worshiped.

The pre-Christian Jezebel was the daughter of Ethbaal, the king of Sidon in pagan Phoenicia and priest of the false goddess Astarte, the consort of Baal. (1 Kings 16:31) She induced her husband, King Ahab, to introduce Baal worship in the northern kingdom of Israel and to build a temple to his worship. She entertained four hundred false prophets at her royal table, besides which there then were four hundred and fifty prophets of Baal officially recognized in Ahab's kingdom. (1 Kings 18:19 to 19:2) Queen Jezebel was also notorious for practicing fornications and sorcery in the kingdom of Israel. (2 Kings 9:22-37)

Her ambitious daughter Athaliah murderously usurped the throne of the kingdom of Judah and reigned for about seven years. (2 Kings 11:1-20) Odious as Queen Jezebel was in ancient apostate Israel, her first-century counterpart whom Jesus Christ called "that woman Jezebel" was still more odious, because she played a like immoral, idolatrous role as a false prophetess in the Christian congregation.

THE CASE OF "THAT WOMAN JEZEBEL"

Because "that woman Jezebel" was being tolerated, even by the "angel of the congregation in Thyatira," the glorified Jesus Christ had been giving her time to repent of her subtle method of using her sex appeal to further her wicked course in the congregation. Likely, because the later works of the congregation were more than those formerly, she was persuading some "slaves" of Christ to believe that it was all right for them to commit fornication with her and to commit idolatry indirectly by eating things sacrificed to idols, seeing that they had such a good service record in trying to spread Christianity; their record of activities in the preaching of Christianity counterbalanced any moral violations and compromises with idolatry. Just as the unfaithful prophet Balaam taught King Balak of Moab how to seduce the ancient Israelites into fornication and idolatry by means of the female sex appeal, so "that woman Jezebel" coupled up her sex appeal with her false doctrine and prophesying and seduced Christians in Thyatira to indulge in fornication and idolatry. (Revelation 2: 14) She taught them how to salve their consciences.

Likewise in the twentieth-century congregation of Christ's anointed remnant Satan the Devil has tried to corrupt the Christian by means of female sex appeal, even under innocent guises. There has been no particular individual woman thus far during this century who outstandingly could be styled "that woman Jezebel," for now we are not dealing with one particular congregation like that of ancient Thyatira. Nevertheless, the records show that Satan the Devil has not been backward about using woman influence with effect in the wrong direction in the true Christian congregation, since he has been so effective with it throughout Christendom. Sad results have followed for those who have not repented of their immoral, idolatrous wrongdoing.

The glorified Christ abominates today those like "that woman Jezebel" just as much as he did that false, immoral, idolatrous prophetess of the Thyatira congregation nineteen centuries ago. His eyes, "as a fiery flame," blaze against such professing Christians. Since his coming to the spiritual temple with his heavenly Father in the spring of 1918, he has taken part in the fulfillment of the prophecy of Malachi 3:1-5, by becoming a "speedy witness against the sorcerers, and against the adulterers, and against those swearing falsely." He has alerted the congregation of his anointed remnant against professed Christian women of the Jezebel type. He has made their consciences very tender against the sly inroads of seductive women who by sex appeal lure men into wrong thinking about immorality and forms of idolatry. As a safeguard he has caused increasing emphasis to be laid upon the rightness of the apostle Paul's inspired position: "I do not permit a woman to teach [inside the congregation], or to exercise authority over a man, but to be in silence."—1 Timothy 2:12.

Leading up to an instance of the tenderizing of the Christian conscience on this issue, in the year 1905* a book entitled "Daily Heavenly Manna for the Household of Faith" was published by a Christian woman. This was distributed by the Watch Tower Bible & Tract Society and was used by the International Bible Students for years in their morning

---

* See announcement on page 346 of *The Watch Tower* of November 15, 1905.

religious devotions and especially at the Wednesday-night prayer, praise and testimony meetings. The book was used for keeping a record of birthdays and collecting signatures and addresses of fellow Bible students. About 1926 the offer was made by the book's compiler to revise the *Manna* book and bring it up to date. This offer was refused, in the light of 1 Timothy 2:12. Instead, in that year the first *Year Book* of the International Bible Students Association with Daily Texts and Comments was prepared by the president of the Watch Tower Bible & Tract Society and the Society's writing staff, and was introduced to the congregations world wide for their use during the year 1927. Each succeeding year a new *Yearbook* has thus been published till now.

We have no record in the Bible or in Church history to show that "that woman Jezebel" of the Thyatira congregation repented. If she actually did not, we do not know how and when the glorified "Son of God" did what he spoke in warning to her, saying: "She is not willing to repent of her fornication. Look! I am about to throw her into a sickbed, and those committing adultery with her into great tribulation, unless they repent of her deeds. And her children I will kill with deadly plague, so that all the congregations will know that I am he who searches the inmost thoughts and hearts, and I will give to you individually according to your deeds." (Revelation 2: 21-23) That was no idle threat!

That warning really stands as a prophecy for our day, concerning "the things that must shortly take place." (Revelation 1:1) No less than in the case of congregations of nineteen centuries ago, "all the congregations" today must know that the glorified "Son of God" at the spiritual temple since 1918 is one who "searches the inmost thoughts [kidneys] and hearts" and gives to you Christians "individually according to your deeds." So it has come about that professed Christian women of the Jezebel type have been thrown by the heavenly Son of God, not into a bed of illicit sexual lovemaking with the ecstasies of sensuous passion, but "into a sickbed," because of not repenting. Till now this has been done by the disfellowshiping of such immoral, idolatrous women from the true Christian congregation. This has been no happy religious bed for them to lie in, for it betokens spiritual death, the forerunner of absolute annihilation at one's bodily death in this disfellowshiped state. If, before then, they are overtaken by the destruction of religious Babylon the Great or the "war of the great day of God the Almighty," it will bring their everlasting execution at His hands.

Those professed Christian males who become guilty of "committing adultery with her" are properly thrown "into great tribulation" for not repenting "of her deeds." No less than the immoral, idolatrous women, those who have yielded to their sex appeal and seductive reasoning have been excommunicated from the congregation, thus to remove reproach and pollution from the congregation. (1 Corinthians 5:1-13) Spiritually this has meant "great tribulation" for them. But worse may lie just ahead of them. If the war of Almighty God at Armageddon overtakes them, it will spell their inescapable destruction by execution at His hands. (Revelation 16:14-16) They face doom at the outbreak of the "great tribulation such as has not occurred since the world's beginning until now," for they do not prove themselves to be permanently of God's "chosen ones" for whose sake the days of tribulation are to be shortened. (Matthew 24:21, 22) Even those who may be lured by such professed Christian women of the Jezebel type into immoral relations with this unclean world will be destroyed at Armageddon, at the latest, because of being friends of the world and enemies of God. —James 4:4.

"Her children," the children of her fornication, have a poor outlook for life, since they are to be killed "with deadly plague." (Revelation 2:23) This may be a spiritual death-dealing plague. Certainly children literally born to such illicit, unchristian sexual unions receive a poor spiritual heritage and poor prospects of being brought up as true Christians with hope of eternal life. Remaining in a spiritually diseased condition, such children will at last die spiritually and be in danger of everlasting destruction. This also bodes no good for persons who are "her children" in the sense of being religious disciples of that false prophetess, "that woman Jezebel." The way of the fornicatrix and adulteress leads down to death and destruction.—Proverbs 7:6-27.

ANTI-JEZEBEL

As back in the days of the Thyatira congregation, it is evident today that there are "those who do not have this teaching [of that woman Jezebel], the very ones who did not get to know the 'deep things of Satan.'" Satanic reasonings that lead to self-deception with pious salving of one's conscience, the faithful ones of the anointed remnant do not recognize. They do not enter into a knowledge of the "deep things of Satan" by trying them out for the sake of personal experience. Rather, they interest themselves in the "deep things of God," which God reveals to them through his holy spirit.—Revelation 2:24; 1 Corinthians 2:10-13.

To such faithful anointed disciples since 1919 the glorified Son of God says: "I am not putting upon you any other burden." So they dare not fall for the enticing argument of "that woman Jezebel" that it is not spiritually harmful for a dedicated Christian to indulge at times in sexual immorality and forms of idolatry provided that one has a fine-showing record for doing outwardly Christian works such as preaching Christian teachings to others. The "burden" or obligation to resist such spiritual enticement rests upon the faithful ones. It comes within the instructions given to Gentile Christians as contained in the decree of the Jerusalem Council of the first century, which read (in part):

"The apostles and the older brothers to those brothers . . . from the nations: Greetings! . . . the holy spirit and we ourselves have favored adding no further burden to you, except these necessary things, to keep yourselves free from things sacrificed to idols and from blood and from things strangled and from fornication. If you carefully keep yourselves from these things, you will prosper."—Acts 15:23-29.

For these vital reasons we can never go along with the clergymen of Christendom who today ignore the plain statements of the Jerusalem Council's decree. These men ignore also that warning word of the Son of God when they publicly say that there can be something beautiful in a life of homosexuality between adults who willingly consent to it, and that it is useful and not morally improper for engaged or betrothed couples to indulge in sex relations before marriage or for single persons to undertake trial marriages. Such clergymen, regardless of their religious denomination or sect, are adopting the immoral position of "that woman Jezebel" in the Thyatira congregation of nineteen centuries ago. We do not choose to suffer any execution of divine judgment like that of "that woman Jezebel" at the coming destruction of the world empire of false religion, Babylon the Great. Rather, we will bear the "burden" that the Son of God imposes upon us as his faithful followers. With a hearing ear we will listen to what the spirit says to all the congregations. We will hold fast to Christlike purity and righteousness. This we will do, as Jesus says, "until I come."

SHEPHERDING THE PEOPLE WITH AN IRON ROD

In the special message to the Thyatira congregation all those who are members of the anointed remnant are encouraged to be conquerors: "And to him that conquers and observes my deeds down to the end I will give authority over the nations, and he shall shepherd the people with an iron rod so that they will be broken to pieces like clay vessels, the same as I have received from my Father, and I will give him the morning star." (Revelation 2:26-28) While yet on earth in the flesh the faithful anointed ones gain a spiritual conquest over the enemy world and its wicked system of things. But for such conquerors another conquest lies still ahead, one that will mean destruction literally to the present system of things, in the "war of the great day of God the Almighty," at Armageddon. (Revelation 16:14, 16) How is this? By means of a resurrection from the dead before war begins.

Those members of the anointed remnant of Christ's followers who prove faithful and die since his invisible presence at the spiritual temple began in the spring of 1918 will not sleep in death. They will have an instantaneous resurrection in the spirit immediately after their death in the flesh, to join the heavenly Son of God at the temple. In this way they will be "happy" in a sense that was not true of the faithful anointed disciples who died prior to the presence of the Son of God at the temple and who therefore had to sleep in death waiting to hear his voice from the temple bidding them to arise from the dead to heavenly life. (John 5:28, 29) Even though they rest from their earthly labors, the "things they did go right with them" into the heavenly realm. (Revelation 14:13) In their earthly labors they proclaimed to the nations "the day of vengeance on the part of our God," but now in their resurrected spirit estate they will share in the executing of that divine vengeance. (Isaiah 61:1, 2) To them the Son of God "will give authority over the nations." This they never had on earth.

Thus the Son of God will give them a share in his authority. From his heavenly Father he received the privilege to fulfill the prophetic words of Psalm 2: 7-9: "Let me refer to the decree of Jehovah; he has said to me: 'You are my son; I, today, I have become your father. Ask of me, that I may give nations as your inheritance and the ends of the earth as your own possession. You will break them with an iron scepter, as though a potter's vessel you will dash them to pieces.' " In agreement with that, the apostle John says concerning the newborn kingdom of God that this newborn kingdom "is to shepherd all the nations with an iron rod." (Revelation 12:5) The nations of this world have preyed like wild beasts upon the little flock of Christ's sheep, his Kingdom joint heirs. Now, in a reversal of matters, each one of that "little flock" who is resurrected before the war at Armageddon shall, with Christ, "shepherd the people with an iron rod so that they will be broken to pieces like clay vessels." This breaking of the nations to pieces will work for the glorious fulfillment of the Kingdom prophecy of Daniel 2:44.

The small portion of the anointed remnant who will be protected on earth through the battle of Armageddon will not take part in any physical violence in order to speed up or further the destruction of the Devil's visible organization on earth. Down till when the Son of God and his resurrected faithful followers begin shepherding the nations with an iron rod and dashing them to pieces like mere clay vessels of a potter, these preserved ones on earth will persist in declaring the impending execution of God's judgments upon the earthly enemies of His Messianic kingdom. Then, when the destruction begins from the invisible heavens, they will do like what the prophet Moses told the frightened Israelites when about to cross the Red Sea with the pursuing Egyptian military forces hot on their heels: "Do not be afraid. Stand firm and see the salvation of Jehovah, which he will perform for you today." (Exodus 14:13) They will take to heart the words of Jehovah's prophet to his worshipers in Jerusalem when it was threatened by the combined enemies in the days of faithful King Jehoshaphat, as recorded in 2 Chronicles 20:14-17:

"Do not be afraid or be terrified because of this large crowd; for the battle is not yours, but God's. . . . You will not need to fight in this instance. Take your position, stand still and see the salvation of Jehovah in your behalf."

Their witnessing safely on earth the brandishing of the "iron rod" from heaven for the destruction of the wicked nations at Armageddon will be equivalent to the preserved remnant themselves having a direct part in 'shepherding the people with an iron rod.' They will thus feel that the promise of Revelation 2:27 has been fulfilled toward them. They will be satisfied and rejoice.—Psalm 149:5-9.

THE GIFT OF THE MORNING STAR

In due time the preserved remnant that will have survived the breaking of the vessel-like nations to pieces will finish their earthly course faithfully and will enjoy with all the previously resurrected Kingdom heirs the fulfillment of the further promise made by the resurrected Son of God to each of his conquering followers: "And I will give him the morning star." (Revelation 2:28) They know that this symbolic "morning star" is the glorified Son of God himself, for he said to the apostle John near the close of the marvelous Revelation: "I, Jesus, sent my angel to bear witness to you people of these things for the congregations. I am the root and the offspring of David, and the bright morning star." (Revelation 22:16) In Bible prophecy the kings of God's chosen people were likened to heavenly stars, even as the angellike overseers of the seven congregations of Asia were likened to seven stars in the right hand of the Son of God. (Revelation 1:16, 20) Fifteen centuries before this it had been prophesied concerning Jesus as the royal "offspring of David":

"A star will certainly step forth out of Jacob, and a scepter will indeed rise out of Israel. . . . And out of Jacob one will go subduing, and he must destroy any survivor from the city."—Numbers 24:17-19.

Above this "bright morning star" Satan the Devil, who was typified by the king of ancient Babylon, wanted to fix his own heavenly throne. He recalled that the king of Babylon fixed his earthly throne above the starlike kings of Jerusalem in the years 617-607 B.C.E. In doing this the king of Babylon took two kings of Jerusalem into exile in Babylon and destroyed their royal throne-city, Jerusalem, all this in carrying out his expressed determination: "Above the stars of God I shall lift up my throne, and I shall sit down upon the mountain of meeting [at Jerusalem], in the remotest parts of the north." (Isaiah 14:4, 13; 2 Kings 24:10 to 25:21) The opposite of this has happened to Satan the Devil already since 1914 C.E., for he has been cast out of heaven and down to the neighborhood of our earth. After the destruction of his visible earthly organization at Armageddon he and his demons will be sealed up, chained, in an abyss. There they will await their destruction after the successful reign of the "bright morning star" for a thousand years over liberated mankind. (Revelation 12:3-13; 20:1-10) O how the "morning star" will shine then!

In view of all this, how will the glorified Son of God give to each faithful conqueror of his congregation "the morning star"? Evidently by giving them his own self, by taking them into the closest relationship with himself, to have an intimacy with him that none of the other heavenly creatures will enjoy. In this way they will share with him in the many privileges that are foretold for this "morning star" in the prophecies of God's Word, the Holy Bible. With him his fellow conquerors will shine forever to Jehovah's glory.—Daniel 12:3; Matthew 13:43.

In view of such grand promises it was most appropriate for the "Son of God" to close his message to the angel of the congregation in Thyatira with these words of wisdom: "Let the one who has an ear hear what the spirit says to the congregations." —Revelation 2:29.

To the Angel
in Sardis

7-21

1

SOME thirty miles south of the city of Thyatira and about one hundred and fifteen miles northeast of the island of Patmos lay the city of Sardis, the onetime wealthy capital of Lydia. Along with Phrygia and Mysia, Lydia was one of the early centers of the worship of the nature goddess Cybele, the so-called mother of the false god Zeus or Jupiter. Her pagan worship was licentious. Toward the end of the first century of our Common Era the Christian congregation in Sardis had fallen into a bad spiritual condition. For this reason the apostle John in exile on the Isle of Patmos was told to send the following message to the starlike overseer of the Sardis congregation:

2

"And to the angel of the congregation in Sardis write: These are the things that he says who has the seven spirits of God and the seven stars, 'I know your deeds, that you have the name that you are alive, but you are dead. Become watchful, and strengthen the things remaining that were ready to die, for I have not found your deeds fully performed before my God. Therefore, continue mindful of how you have received and how you heard, and go on keeping it, and repent. Certainly unless you wake up, I shall come as a thief, and you will not know at all at what hour I shall come upon you.

3

" 'Nevertheless, you do have a few names in Sardis that did not defile their outer garments, and they shall walk with me in white ones, because they are

154

worthy. He that conquers will thus be arrayed in white outer garments; and I will by no means blot out his name from the book of life, but I will make acknowledgment of his name before my Father and before his angels. Let the one who has an ear hear what the spirit says to the congregations.' "—Revelation 3:1-6.

To the congregation in Sardis the glorified Jesus Christ identifies himself as the one who "has the seven spirits of God and the seven stars." As such, he held in the control of his right hand all the angel-like overseers who were symbolized by the "seven stars." So he had both the right and the obligation to direct himself to the "angel" of the Sardis congregation and to call to his attention what the condition of the congregation was in actuality and not just in name. The glorified Jesus Christ could discern the actual condition of it, for he has the "seven spirits of God." These seven spirits are first said to be before the throne of God, where they are pictured as being "seven lamps of fire burning before the throne." (Revelation 1:4; 4:5) They are illuminators, having power to enlighten and to throw light upon hidden things. For example, concerning the "things that God has prepared for those who love him," the apostle Paul wrote: "For it is to us God has revealed them through his spirit, for the spirit searches into all things, even the deep things of God." —1 Corinthians 2:9, 10.

However, the "seven spirits of God" are later pictured as eyes, "seven eyes" possessed by the symbolic Lamb, the Lord Jesus Christ, when he approaches God's throne and takes the scroll of mystery out of God's right hand. As to the meaning of those "seven eyes" the apostle John says: "which eyes mean the seven spirits of God that have been sent forth into the whole earth." (Revelation 5:1-7) The "seven spirits" would accordingly picture the full, complete power of observation, of discernment, or detection that the glorified Lamb of God now has, so that throughout the "whole earth" nothing escapes his notice. Nineteen centuries ago he was perfectly able to see the spiritual condition into which the "angel" had let the Christian congregation in Sardis come.

Yes, the Sardis congregation had a name for being something that it actually was not. In its membership it had a "few names" that were well known to the Lord Jesus Christ and that could be mentioned with credit. Each of the other members was in danger of having his name blotted out "from the book of life," and his name was becoming unworthy of being acknowledged by Christ in heaven before his Father and before his angels. This put the Sardis congregation and its angellike overseer in a serious situation, because a good name with God the Father is critically important.

Proverbs 10:7 says: "The remembrance of the righteous one is due for a blessing, but the very name of the wicked ones will rot," become an odious stench and not be worthy of a blessing. A favorable name with God is most precious: "A name is to be chosen rather than abundant riches; favor is better than even silver and gold." (Proverbs 22:1) While a Christian is alive, he can and should make a good name for himself with the Giver of life, Jehovah God. Correctly Ecclesiastes 7:1 advises: "A name is better than good oil [ointment], and the day of death than the day of one's being born."

Of course, the members of the Sardis congregation were alive as humans, but what were they as far as being real Christians is concerned? Their being alive as humans prospering in the things of this world and having a fine place in which to hold their congregational meetings was not the thing of central concern. What were they spiritually? Were they alive spiritually?

The deeds and works that they had been performing must have been "dead works," works not contributing to spiritual life, works that might appeal to the unchristian people in Sardis but that were not the special works that a Christian should perform as a follower of Christ who was born and came into the world, that he "should bear witness to the truth." (Hebrews 9:14; John 18:37) Jesus Christ had not found the deeds of the Sardis congregation "fully performed before my God." With the worldly people of Sardis the "angel" and the congregation that he represented may have had a name for being alive, but Jesus Christ, who has the seven spirits of God, saw and knew that they were dead in a spiritual way, as real Christians.

Except for a "few names" in the Sardis congregation it would really be dead spiritually, not shining like a lighted golden lampstand. Those "few names" may have been "the things remaining that were ready to die." They could be mortally affected by the dead spiritual condition of the majority of the congregation. From that standpoint, they were "ready to die." The overseer or "angel" who represented the congregation was asleep, as far as Christian responsibilities are concerned. He needed to wake up, to see the actual state of things, and to "become watchful" and to wake up the sleeping ones of the congregation and help them to "become watchful." The "angel" needed to "strengthen" those who were in danger of dying spiritually. Then he should use and cooperate with these in strengthening all others to live, act and serve as genuine Christians. To this end he needed to "repent."

WHY THE NEED FOR REPENTING

For the purpose of bringing himself around to sincere repentance, the angel must do something and must remind the others to do something. What was this? "Continue mindful of how you have received and how you heard." (Revelation 3:3) They had heard the message of God's kingdom that he will use for restoring his universal sovereignty to this earth and putting in perfect order all the affairs of mankind. They had heard the message of everlasting salvation that comes through the ransom sacrifice of God's Son, Jesus Christ. They had heard of how God was taking out from all nations of mankind a "people for his name" to be united with his Son Jesus Christ in the heavenly kingdom as his joint heirs.

Also, by now they had received almost the complete Bible, only the final writings by the inspired apostle John being yet to be produced and added. They had received water baptism in symbol of their full dedication of themselves to Jehovah God. They had been taken into the "new covenant" with him through the Mediator Jesus Christ and thus had become members of the "people for his name." This meant, too, that they had received the adoption as the spiritual sons of God and had been anointed with the spirit of God to be preachers of the Word of God to all the nations in order that other disciples of Christ might be made. They had received the wondrous hope of having a spiritual, heavenly resurrection from the dead and being made kings and priests with him for the blessing of all the world of mankind, living and dead.—Acts 15:14; Hebrews 8:6-13; 2 Corinthians 1:21, 22.

What precious things and O how many things they had received and had heard! But now because of verging on spiritual death they were in danger of losing these things forever. So they needed to become mindful again of these things and then "go on keeping" these most valuable things. They must have a change of mind. As Jesus Christ said to their "angel" overseer, they must repent! This would make them grieve over their having become so ungrateful and unappreciative to God from whom they had received so much favor and heard so much truth. Their repentance would lead to their reactivating themselves spiritually and then really living up to their name of being alive, truly alive as Christian personalities. They would awake from a spiritual deadness and would take part again in the right Christian works and would fully perform them before God.—Ephesians 5:14.

For the moment, Jesus Christ was warning the "angel" overseer of the Sardis congregation; but suddenly, at an unknown future hour, Jesus Christ as Chief Inspector would come upon the Sardis congregation for the final inspection and then take due action. At that time it would be too late for any unrepentant, spiritually dead Christians to repent and regain what they were in danger of losing. "Certainly," said the Inspector Jesus Christ, "unless you wake up, I shall come as a thief, and you will not know at all at what hour I shall come upon you." (Revelation 3:3) By coming at this unknown, unannounced time for final inspection he would find out whether they were living as true Christians, "not with acts of eyeservice, as men pleasers, but with sincerity of heart, with fear of Jehovah." (Colossians 3:22) "In the sincerity of your hearts, as to the Christ, not by way of eyeservice as men pleasers, but as Christ's slaves, doing the will of God wholesouled." (Ephesians 6:5, 6) They must not be hypocritical Christians, Christians in name only and for outward show. They need to be true Christians, because hypocritical ones will be rejected.

Today, in this twentieth century, Christendom or the so-called Christian world is filled with religious hypocrites. When World War I ended at eleven o'clock in the morning of the eleventh day of the eleventh month of the year 1918, Christendom had made a bad record for herself as a professed Christian institution. Christianity was then due to enter the most difficult period of its history. Would it survive? It was a most pressing time for a warning to come from Jesus Christ at God's spiritual temple to all those who professed to be Christians. Christendom, which claims to follow the Prince of Peace, Jesus Christ, had failed to prevent or stop World War I. It was really HER war, all twenty-eight nations taking part in that war being members of Christendom except four. As a force for the promoting of true Christianity she had proved to be dead. In fact, during World War I she showed herself to be a persecutor of true Christians who would not join her in bloodshed but who preached God's kingdom. Instead of God's kingdom, Christendom proposed a League of Nations for world peace and security and voted for it in the first postwar year, 1919.

What about the anointed remnant of dedicated Christians? During the critical war years of 1914-1918 they had undergone the persecution foretold by Christ in his prophecy found in Matthew 24:7-12. In the various lands at war much or all of their literature, as published by the Watch Tower Bible & Tract Society, had been banned. In the United States even the president and the secretary-treasurer of this Watch Tower Society and other members of its headquarters staff had been imprisoned at the height of the war hysteria. A fear toward the political authorities of the world acted as a restraint upon much of the public activity of this persecuted remnant of spirit-anointed Christians. Christendom hoped and trusted that she had silenced them forever as being a heretical, nonconformist religious group. Would her hope and trust prove true?

At the end of World War I on November 11, 1918, the warning message of Jesus Christ to the Sardis congregation was very appropriate. During the world conflict just ended the deeds of true Christianity had not been "fully performed before [Christ's] God" by the anointed remnant. Whatever features of the real Christianity were remaining with them "were ready to die," unless they would be strengthened. Would the remnant consider that their work on earth was ended? Would they form themselves into a restricted religious sect, thinking that the limit of Bible understanding had been reached? Would they stop all further preaching of God's kingdom, and stick strictly to themselves until their numbers died out? Would they finally have the name of being alive as a mere little, insignificant religious sect but really be spiritually dead to the worldwide Kingdom work that was then due to open up in the postwar era? There was actual danger of this. Therefore, the warning to the Sardis congregation was most suitable for the anointed remnant at that decisive time.—Revelation 3:1, 2.

There was dire need to be mindful of what they had received and what they had heard particularly since the first publishing of the religious magazine *Zion's Watch Tower and Herald of Christ's Presence* in July of the year 1879. The "times of the Gentiles"

as foretold by Christ in Luke 21:24 (*AV*) and as emphasized in the *Watch Tower* magazine had indeed ended in early autumn of the epoch-making year of 1914. At that time the invisible presence of Jesus Christ in his heavenly Messianic kingdom had begun. The anointed remnant had received the divine commission to preach, yes, to herald world wide, not Christendom's League of Nations as "the political expression of the Kingdom of God on earth," but the Messianic kingdom of God as now established in heaven at the end of the Gentile Times in 1914. (Matthew 24:14; Mark 13:10) It was indeed the urgent time for the anointed remnant to "repent" over its recent failures and any tendencies to deadness and to wake up and take the action now due. Otherwise the reigning King Jesus Christ would come upon the anointed remnant at a future unannounced hour and consign them to real death.—Revelation 3:3.

WALKING IN WHITE GARMENTS

In the case of the anointed remnant then, the situation was not one of spiritual death on the part of *all* members thereof. Neither was it so in the case of the Sardis congregation. Jesus Christ knew this, for he said to the "angel" of the Sardis congregation: "Nevertheless, you do have a few names in Sardis that did not defile their outer garments, and they shall walk with me in white ones, because they are worthy." (Revelation 3:4) These "few names" or persons had not made themselves unsightly as Christian personalities. They lived up to what they openly professed to be, imitators of Jesus Christ. Their "outer garments" would symbolize their outward profession, their religious claims. Despite all the defiling pagan influences of materialistic, idolatrous Sardis, they held onto a clean, irreproachable Christian appearance. They did not defile or pollute their "outer garments" of Christian profession. So doing, they brought no shame or reproach upon the Sardis congregation. They truly lived their Christianity.

For the comforting and strengthening of these undefiled living Christians, Jesus Christ said that they would at last "walk with me in white ones, because they are worthy." This meant that, after the establishment of his Messianic kingdom, he would resurrect them from their sleep in the graves to clean, spotless life with him in the heavens. They would then be clothed upon with shining righteousness, and with the office of underpriests to serve under him who, in the Revelation vision, is seen "clothed with a garment that reached down to the feet, and girded at the breasts with a golden girdle." (Revelation 1:13) In harmony with this, Revelation 6:9-11 states that 'white robes' were given as a reward to the martyred Christians whose souls were pictured as being under the altar. The worthy "few names" were an example to the rest of the Sardis congregation, who apparently had defiled their garments with the worldliness of pagan Sardis and who needed to repent and to clean up their "outer garments" of Christian profession. After World War I similar things applied to the surviving anointed remnant.

The closing words of encouragement to the "angel" of the Sardis congregation fittingly stress the importance of the "outer garments" of Christian profession. To this "angel" the glorious one "who has the seven spirits of God and the seven stars" says: "He that conquers will thus be arrayed in white outer garments; and I will by no means blot out his name from the book of life, but I will make acknowledgment of his name before my Father and before his angels. Let the one who has an ear hear what the spirit says to the congregations."—Revelation 3:5, 6.

For those members of the Sardis congregation of the first century and for the members of the anointed remnant of this twentieth century, "he that conquers" means an anointed Christian that has not defiled or polluted his symbolic outer garments that identify him as a follower of the Lord Jesus Christ. He may be in the midst of this world of mankind, of which the city of Sardis was once a part, but he does not let himself become a part of this world, any more than Jesus Christ himself when on earth as a man was a part of this same world. (John 15:19; 17:14-16) He practices the pure and undefiled Christian religion by keeping himself "without spot from the world," not loving the world nor the "things in the world." (James 1:27; 1 John 2:15-17) Because of his inborn sinfulness and weakness he may unknowingly or unwillingly sin; but when he realizes that he has sinned, he repents and asks God's forgiveness and gets cleansed of sin through the "blood of Jesus his Son." (1 John 1:7 to 2:2; Revelation 1:5) In this manner he keeps his outer garments undefiled.

The expression "he that conquers" also means the anointed Christian who without shame acknowledges Jesus Christ as his Ransomer and Lord and Master before all the world, even in the face of the danger of death by violence at enemy hands. In harmony with acknowledging Christ and in proof of it, the conqueror refuses to become the slave of political, religious and military men on earth. Paul says: "He that was called when a free man is a slave of Christ. You were bought with a price; stop becoming slaves of men." (1 Corinthians 7:22, 23) The conqueror also takes seriously Jesus' words: "Everyone, then, that confesses union with me before men, I will also confess union with him before my Father who is in the heavens; but whoever disowns me before men, I will also disown him before my Father who is in the heavens." (Matthew 10:32, 33; Mark 8:38; Luke 9:26) Since the conqueror is acknowledged by the glorified Christ before his heavenly Father and before his angels, it must be because he conquers by acknowledging Christ on earth.

All conquerors of such kind will be preserved for all eternity. Because of having followed Christ's steps and gone in through the narrow gate and got onto the cramped road that leads to life, they already have their names written tentatively in the "book of life." (Matthew 7:13, 14) By continuing on that cramped road and by conquering this world through Christian faith and faithfulness, the conqueror is assured of having his name kept in that "book of life." The Lord Jesus Christ assures him: "I will by no means blot out his name from the book of life." His heavenly inheritance of life will be immortality, and thus to endless eternity he will be able to walk "arrayed in white outer garments" as a worthy associate of the Lord Jesus Christ. This information is something worth being heard by the "one who has an ear" to hear what the spirit says to the congregations.

To the Angel

in Philadelphia

Fɴᴏᴍ the congregation in Sardis, the attention of the glorified Jesus Christ moves to the congregation in Philadelphia, a city lying thirty miles southeast of Sardis and about one hundred and thirty miles from the Isle of Patmos, where the apostle John received the special message for the Philadelphia congregation. Today the place is called Alaşehir (Reddish City, from the hills to its rear). Earthquakes occurred in that area, and the Philadelphia of John's day was the city rebuilt by the Roman emperor Tiberius Caesar after the earthquake of the year 17 C.E., and for a time it was called on Roman coins New Caesarea. As it lay in a wine-producing section, its chief false god was Bacchus or Dionysus, who corresponds with Nimrod "a mighty hunter in opposition to Jehovah," who was later bewailed by worshipers as Tammuz. (Genesis 10:8-10; Ezekiel 8: 13, 14) The ancient city of Philadelphia, the city of "Brotherly Affection," had a Jewish population besides a Christian congregation, but, according to the record, there was little brotherly affection for the Christian congregation on the part of the natural, circumcised Jews.

Near the end of the first century of our Common Era, what outlook was given to the Philadelphia congregation, not from man's standpoint, but from Christ's standpoint? This outlook was set forth in the message that the apostle John was told to send to the earthly overseer of the congregation, as follows:

"And to the angel of the congregation in Philadelphia write: These are the things he says who is holy, who is true, who has the key of David, who opens so that no one will shut, and shuts so that no one opens. 'I know your deeds—look! I have set before you an opened door, which no one can shut —that you have a little power, and you kept my word and did not prove false to my name. Look! I will give those from the synagogue of Satan who say they are Jews, and yet they are not but are lying —look! I will make them come and do obeisance before your feet and make them know I have loved you. Because you kept the word about my endurance, I will also keep you from the hour of test, which is to come upon the whole inhabited earth, to put a test upon those dwelling on the earth. I am coming quickly. Keep on holding fast what you have, that no one may take your crown.

" 'The one that conquers—I will make him a pillar in the temple of my God, and he will by no means go out from it any more, and I will write upon him the name of my God and the name of the city of my God, the new Jerusalem which descends out of heaven from my God, and that new name of mine. Let the one who has an ear hear what the spirit says to the congregations.' "—Revelation 3:7-13.

The glorious heavenly one sending this message to anointed Christians is deserving of confidence, for he is that one "who is holy, who is true." At a critical time when other Jews were going away from this "holy" one, Jesus Christ, because of a lack of faith, the Jewish apostle Peter said to him: "We have believed and come to know that you are the Holy One of God." (John 6:69) Later, after the heavenly glorification of Jesus Christ and during a time of persecution, the entire Christian congregation in Jerusalem spoke of him as holy when they prayed to Jehovah God, asking him to give them further privileges of preaching, "While you stretch out your hand for healing and while signs and portents occur through the name of your holy servant Jesus." (Acts 4:23-30) Because of his holiness he has been made God's high priest, one who "was suitable for us, loyal, guileless, undefiled, separated from the sinners, and become higher than the heavens."—Hebrews 7:26.

The glorified Jesus Christ could not be holy and at the same time be untrue, be a liar like the unholy Devil. So in identifying himself to the Philadelphia congregation he speaks the truth as to who and what he is. There is good Bible basis for him to say that he is the One "who has the key of David, who opens so that no one will shut, and shuts so that no one opens." (Revelation 3:7) The David, here mentioned for the first time in this Revelation to John, is the one concerning whom the glorified Jesus is said to be "the root of David" and also "the root and the offspring of David." (Revelation 5:5; 22:16) It is the ancient David, king of Jerusalem, with whom Jehovah God made a covenant for an everlasting kingdom. (2 Samuel 7:4-29) Of this David, Jesus became a royal descendant by being born as a human to the virgin Mary of David's royal family. (Matthew 1: 1-25; Luke 1:26-38; 2:1-21; 3:21-31; Romans 1:1-4) By being faithful to God to a martyr's death, Jesus Christ proved to be the Permanent Heir of David for the everlasting kingdom. So he has the "key" that King David had and that David would entrust to a faithful servant.

Not amiss, then, did the glorified Jesus Christ quote from the words of Isaiah 22:22, in which Jehovah God refers to a trusted servant of the king of Jerusalem, namely, to Eliakim, saying: "I will put the key of the house of David upon his shoulder, and he must open without anyone's shutting, and he must shut without anyone's opening." Thus this servant with the key had a great responsibility toward the household of King David, combined with large powers and authority. The king delegated to him the authority to open and to shut. It is here to be noted that at the time of this Revelation to John the glorified

Jesus Christ did not say that the "key of David" was in the hand of any bishop of the pagan city of Rome as an apostolic successor to the apostle Simon Peter, to whom the words of Matthew 16:18, 19 were said. No professed earthly representative of Christ, but the heavenly Jesus Christ himself holds onto the "key of David" with the powers symbolized by the "key" of opening and shutting firmly.

It was not the apostle Simon Peter nor any so-called apostolic successor of Peter in pagan Rome who set before the Philadelphia congregation "an opened door, which no one can shut." It was not even the apostle John, but was the glorified Jesus Christ, "the root and the offspring of David," who said to the overseer of the congregation in Philadelphia: "I know your deeds —look! I have set before you an opened door, which no one can shut—that you have a little power, and you kept my word and did not prove false to my name." (Revelation 3:8) Likewise, it was not any Pope Benedict XV (1914-1922 C.E.) of Rome who set before the faithful remnant of anointed Christians in the postwar year of 1919 an "opened door, which no one can shut." In fact, the popes of Rome and of Vatican City have been unable to shut that "opened door," because this symbolic "door" was actually opened, not by them or any other mere man, but by the Lord Jesus Christ himself.

To what privileges and opportunities that "opened door" permitted entrance by the Philadelphia congregation back there in the first century we do not exact-

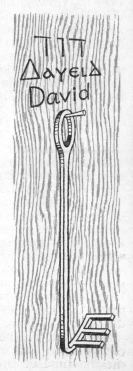

ly know today. But evidently it was to more Christian activity as a symbolic golden lampstand, because, just before speaking about the "door," the glorified Jesus Christ says to the congregation overseer: "I know your deeds." He knew that the congregation was able to go through the "opened door" and undertake the newly opened privileges and opportunities, because, as he said to the Philadelphia overseer, "you have a little power." Political power? No, but possibly power of influence with the Philadelphian people, and certainly the power of Christian devotion, courage and ability to keep moving forward after all that they had already endured as faithful Christians.

After the end of World War I in 1918 and at the beginning of the postwar year of 1919 the faithful remnant of anointed followers of Jesus Christ had no political power, no "pull" with the politicians, the judges, the militarists and the clergy of Christendom. Because of their sincere endeavors to preach God's kingdom by Christ instead of directly taking part in the international bloodshed, they were a persecuted religious minority. They were, as Jesus Christ foretold in his prophecy on the "conclusion of the system of things," nothing but "objects of hatred by all the nations on account of my name." (Matthew 24:3, 9) Their Bible literature, as published by the Watch Tower Bible & Tract Society, was under ban either in whole or in part in various lands. Many of them were held in military camps or in concentration camps and prisons. Even until March 25, 1919, the president and the secretary-treasurer and six other noted representatives of the Watch Tower Society were held in the Federal penitentiary of Atlanta, Georgia, U.S.A., on false wartime charges that were afterward thrown out of court. So no power of a worldly kind did they have.

The "little power" that the ancient Philadelphia congregation and its "angel" had when the "opened door" was given to them was the power to do as

Jesus Christ said: "You kept my word and did not prove false to my name." They observed and adhered to the word of Christ, the teaching and the commands that he had given to them. They did not deny that they were Christians either by word or by the way that they lived; they did not prove false to his name by acting contrary to how a Christian should speak, think, do and preach. They could therefore be expected to keep doing this after they had entered in through the now "opened door."

"AN OPENED DOOR"

No less can be said for the tried and tested remnant of anointed Christians that survived the persecution and hard conditions of World War I. Although from March of 1918 on there had been a suspension of the circulating of the bound book *The Finished Mystery* and its magazine edition (the special *Watch Tower* edition of March 1, 1918), and the series of tracts known as *Bible Students Monthly,* the anointed remnant continued to publish their official semimonthly magazine *The Watch Tower and Herald of Christ's Presence,* without a break. On Sunday night, April 13, 1919, they obeyed the command of the Lord Jesus Christ and celebrated the Lord's Supper in memorial of his death as the ransom sacrifice for all mankind. They tried to keep the word of Christ to the extent that they understood it. Whereas they denied the charges of the enemy that they were a religious sect following a human leader, they never did deny the name of Christ, disown him or willfully prove false to his name. They held fast to their hopes of being early united with him in his heavenly kingdom. As a result they had "a little power" as the postwar period opened.

Truly "an opened door" was set before the anointed remnant in 1919 by the glorified Jesus Christ, who has the "key of David." This opening came particularly with the significant event of Wednesday, March 26, 1919, in Brooklyn, New York, namely, the release on bail from Federal detention of the Watch Tower Society's president and secretary-treasurer and the six other prominent representatives.* The privileges and opportunities of the postwar period were opened up to all the anointed remnant, and these privileges and opportunities have continued and increased to them for already a half century (1969, at this printing). With what "little power" the anointed remnant had in 1919, they undertook an immediate reorganizing of Jehovah's dedicated people for the work ahead for as long as it should last.

Concerning the "door" opened to him the apostle Paul wrote to the Christians in Corinth, Greece (about 55 C.E.): "A large door that leads to activity has been opened to me, but there are many opposers." (1 Corinthians 16:9) Later he wrote them: "A door was opened to me in the Lord, I got no relief in my spirit . . . and departed for Macedonia." (2 Corinthians 2:12, 13) The Lord Jesus Christ, "who has the key of David," was the one that opened that door for the apostle Paul, and likewise he, and no man on earth, was the one that opened the door that leads to activity for the anointed remnant of spiritual Israelites in the spring of 1919 C.E. That "door" has proved to be one "which no one can shut," although there were many opposers to start with back in 1919. Russian communism, Italian Fascism, pope-directed Catholic Action, German Nazism, found it impossible to shut that door. Not even the militarism of World War II could shut that door. In 1939, the year of the outbreak of World War II, there were 71,509 witnesses of Jehovah reporting activity world wide. In 1945, after the war ended, there were 141,606 reporting witness work afield.

Today those who are actively associating with the anointed remnant have boosted the number of Jehovah's witnesses regularly preaching the Kingdom good news world wide to well over 1,225,000 early in

---

* See *The Watch Tower,* as of April 15, 1919, page 118, paragraph 2; also the book entitled "Light," Volume I, page 249, paragraph 2.

1969. This doubtless has something to do with fulfilling the promise that the Possessor of the "key of David" made to the ancient Philadelphia congregation: "Look! I will give those from the synagogue of Satan who say they are Jews, and yet they are not but are lying—look! I will make them come and do obeisance before your feet and make them know I have loved you."—Revelation 3:9.

"THE SYNAGOGUE OF SATAN"

Evidently the ancient Philadelphia congregation and its "angel" or overseer had encounters with natural circumcised Jews of that day. They may have tried to win back those of the Philadelphia congregation who were Jews by birth, like Christ's twelve apostles, but who had become Christian believers and hence spiritual Jews, spiritual Israelites. Or they may have tried to persuade these Jewish Christian believers to retain or take up again certain things of the ancient Mosaic law, such as fleshly circumcision, keeping the weekly sabbath day, and so forth. In any case such Jewish unbelievers opposed or tried to corrupt the Philadelphia congregation. Because of their efforts against the congregation of spiritual Israelites, they proved themselves to be the "synagogue of Satan" although they claimed to be the synagogue of the God of Abraham, Isaac and Jacob and of Moses. Jews they were in a natural, fleshly sense, but not in a spiritual sense. So they were not worthy of being called real Jews, such as Christ's apostles were. They said they were Jews, but, said the Lord Jesus Christ, "they are not but are lying." He ought to know.

Just how he made those falsely professing Jews to come and do obeisance before the feet of the Philadelphia congregation, there is no historic record to show. Today, according to *The World Almanac* for 1969 (page 224), there are 13,537,000 Jewish people throughout the earth. According to what the glorified Jesus Christ with the "key of David" said to the

Philadelphia congregation, it behooves such natural Jews to consider well how they deal with the anointed Christian remnant of spiritual Jews or Israelites. However, the main difficulty that the anointed remnant has is with those of Christendom who profess to be spiritual Jews, Jews "on the inside." (Romans 2:28, 29) Those opposing and persecuting the anointed remnant are principally such religionists who claim to be spiritual Jews, particularly their clergymen. Such opposers argue and proclaim that the anointed remnant are not spiritual Jews with circumcised hearts. No, say those religious opposers, but they themselves are the real spiritual Jews who are of the synagogue of the Most High God. Nevertheless, their conduct shows they are liars and of the "synagogue of Satan."

As far as being real Jews, spiritually, Jews "on the inside," the historical facts of this twentieth century are against the religionists of Christendom. They have seen and have had to admit that, as far as being real Christians, real spiritual Jews, is concerned, the anointed remnant of Jehovah's worshipers are the ones that have maintained true Christian integrity in the face of rabid opposition, persecution, dictatorships, militarism, nationalistic politics, materialism and criminal lawlessness. Rather than have the anointed remnant pay respects to them, they have had to bow down in acknowledgment to the anointed remnant of Jehovah's witnesses, unwillingly, of course, but necessarily because of the facts of the case. As concerns the anointed remnant who tremble at the written Word of Jehovah, it has been just as the prophecy of Isaiah 66:5 foretold:

"Hear the word of Jehovah, you men who are trembling at his word: 'Your brothers that are hating you, that are excluding you by reason of my name, said, "May Jehovah be glorified!" He must also appear with rejoicing on your part, and they are the ones that will be put to shame.'"—See also Isaiah 60:14.

To what are they led by this coming and doing obeisance before the feet of the Philadelphia congregation and knowing that Jesus Christ has loved this congregation? If some of such ones become Christians and members of the congregation, this would mean a growth in number of members of the Philadelphia congregation. Certainly such a development has been true of the anointed remnant of spiritual Israelites or Jews since 1919 C.E. The great majority of additional members have come from the various religious sects of Christendom.

Moreover, since the epochal year of 1935 C.E. more than a million persons have come out from Babylon the Great, the world empire of false Babylonish religion, and they have lined up with the anointed remnant in worshiping Jehovah as the only living and true God and in publishing abroad His name and his Messianic kingdom. This is uncontradictable proof that the glorified Jesus Christ loves the faithful anointed remnant; and the more than a million fellow worshipers who have been added since 1935 know that fact. They acknowledge the leadership taken by the anointed remnant in God's work and thus do obeisance to them, but do not depart from their worship of only Jehovah God.

"THE HOUR OF TEST"

For now more than half a century the anointed remnant have endured despite all the trialsome time that set in with the close of World War I on November 11, 1918. They have been kept from falling victim to the worsening world conditions and events that have tested Christian faith and integrity so much as to prove one either a hypocritical Christian or a true one. Very apparently they have endured, not in their own strength, but with help from above. This has been a fulfillment of what the Lord Jesus Christ said to the "angel" of the Philadelphia congregation: "Because you kept the word about my endurance, I will also keep you from the hour of test, which is to come upon the whole inhabited earth, to put a test upon those dwelling on the earth."—Revelation 3:10.

Since the close of the first world war in 1918, all persons dwelling on the earth, including the anointed remnant, have been put to this test. Pressures from human sources and from invisible demon sources have become terrific, in materialistic, faithless, rebellious, revolutionary, nationalistic directions. The test has been to determine before God whether one is a part of this system of things under Satan the Devil's invisible control or is in favor of God's Messianic kingdom and is seeking first its interests. The great temptation is for a person to yield to the worldly pressures and attractions and to become a part of this system of things. More than fifty years of twentieth-century history has proved that the anointed remnant have endured the test. In 1919, when Christendom went over to advocating and supporting the political League of Nations for world peace and security, the anointed remnant reaffirmed its own public stand for God's kingdom by Christ. They proceeded to preach God's kingdom as never before, as Jesus foretold in Matthew 24:14. Thus he has kept them from this "hour of test."

However, this worldwide test in this comparatively short time period like an "hour" is not over as yet. The faithful anointed remnant dare not become self-confident. Thus far they have been kept from falling victim to spiritual disaster under the continuing test, but the climax of the test is yet to come. Then the glorified Jesus Christ will come to make the final inspection and see whether the anointed remnant have endured to the end. This is why they need to pay heed to the warning given to the "angel" of the Philadelphia congregation: "I am coming quickly. Keep on holding fast what you have, that no one may take your crown."—Revelation 3:11.

The anointed remnant has had the "word about my [Christ's] endurance." They have kept this word by observing it and trying to measure up to the example of endurance about which it tells, namely, Christ's endurance when he was on earth as a man under test of his obedience to God. They have not proved false to his name, but have confessed him as their Leader and as God's anointed King in spite of nationalism and totalitarian dictators who have claimed to be the nation's only leader, the *Fuehrer*, the *Duce*. They have entered in through the "opened door" set before them by the Christ, who has the "key of David." The Christian activity in behalf of God's Messianic kingdom to which this "door" has admitted them they have refused to give up regardless of all the worldly opposition and persecution. Now they must still keep holding fast this Kingdom service till Christ comes, quickly now indeed. They have a good record with God for their Christian endurance and service. They have rightful hopes of ruling as kings with Christ in heaven. These things they need to keep holding fast. Then nobody else will take one's crown.

There are only a limited number of royal crowns in the heavenly kingdom with Christ, only 144,000 of such crowns. Every heavenly crown must at last be worn by a faithful worthy Christian. It would be a disappointing experience for an anointed, spirit-begotten Christian who received from God the hope of a heavenly crown to fail under the earthly test and thus prove unworthy of the promised crown, so that the crown would have to be reserved for someone else who becomes called to the Kingdom and who proves faithful to the end. In order to encourage the Kingdom heirs to hold fast to what they have and to make sure their title to the heavenly crown, Jesus Christ sends the following message by means of God's spirit to all the congregations:

"The one that conquers—I will make him a pillar in the temple of my God, and he will by no means go out from it any more, and I will write upon him the name of my God and the name of the city of my God, the new Jerusalem which descends out of heaven from my God, and that new name of mine. Let the one who has an ear hear what the spirit says to the congregations."—Revelation 3:12, 13.

Notice that in this message to the "one that conquers" the Lord Jesus Christ uses the expression "my God" four times. He did not claim to be the "second person" in a triune God in which each of the three "persons" was coequal and coeternal. No, but he recognized his heavenly Father as being his God whom he himself worshiped, served and obeyed. He recognized the spiritual "temple" as belonging to his God. He is the one whom his God lays as the "foundation cornerstone" in that spiritual temple in which God its owner dwells by his spirit. (Ephesians 2:20-22) But his God uses Jesus Christ as a fellow builder of this spiritual temple, and so Jesus Christ can speak of himself as setting up each "pillar in the temple of my God."

PERMANENT POSITION IN GOD'S TEMPLE

For a Christian conqueror to be made a pillar in that temple means for him to be given a fixed position in that spiritual structure. That is why the deputy builder Jesus Christ says very positively concerning such a spiritual pillar, "he will by no means go out from it any more." Nothing like an earthquake such as would shake the area of ancient Philadelphia could remove such a spiritual pillar from his position in God's temple. Forever, amid all events and circumstances, he would have the blessed privilege of serving as a pillar to uphold the divine truth and the universal worship of the only living and true God. (1 Timothy 3:15, 16; 1 Peter 2:4-6) What a highly dignified service and precious closeness to God this signifies for conquerors!

In this promise to conquerors Jesus Christ testifies that his God has a personal name. The Son of God has a personal name, Jesus, with the title "Christ" attached. So, too, his God has a name of his own. Jesus knows that name of his God and will write it upon each one of his followers "that conquers." Jesus Christ when on earth read the inspired Hebrew Scriptures, and he knew that in those Hebrew Scriptures God's name occurs thousands of times. There it is spelled with four Hebrew alphabetic characters, corresponding to JHVH or YHWH. Jesus Christ knew how to pronounce that name correctly. Today it is pronounced Jehovah, or more recently Yahweh. This name the Lord Jesus Christ promises to write upon each Christian conqueror, doubtless on what would correspond with the forehead where the name written could be plainly seen by all beholders. Just as in ancient Bible times a slave branded in the forehead with his master's name was thereby understood to belong to the master whose name he bore, so the "name of my God" written by Jesus Christ upon the conqueror stamps that conqueror as belonging to Jehovah, the God of Jesus.

The conqueror becomes marked also with another honorable name of which not to be ashamed, for the Lord Jesus adds: "I will write upon him . . . the name of the city of my God, the new Jerusalem which descends out of heaven from my God." Just as the old earthly Jerusalem was the seat of government, the capital city, of the united kingdom of Israel, so the "new Jerusalem which descends out of heaven from my God" will be the capital city, the capital organization, of all of God's creation in heaven and on earth. Later in the visions of the Revelation the apostle John saw this symbolic city, New Jerusalem, descending out of heaven from God in order to rule all mankind and to bless them with a perfect government. (Revelation 21:2-4) In itself, the name Jerusalem means "Possession of Peace." When a Christian conqueror is marked with the name of the new Jerusalem by the One with the "key of David," it means that he belongs to that symbolic city, he is a part of it, he is a citizen of it. According to Philippians 3:20, his "citizenship exists in the heavens."

He is a member of God's capital organization. What a high office!—Compare Psalm 87:5, 6.

The foremost one in God's capital organization is his Son Jesus Christ. Most properly, then, the Son adds to his promise to the "one that conquers" the closing words: "And I will write upon him . . . that new name of mine." (Revelation 3:12) Later Revelation 14:1-3 shows the 144,000 conquerors standing with the Lamb Jesus Christ on the heavenly Mount Zion and "having his name and the name of his Father written on their foreheads." There, though, it does not speak of his new name as being written on them. What his "new name" is, is not revealed, not even in Revelation 19:12, where it is said that "he has a name written that no one knows but he himself." It is kept secret from other creatures, like the name upon the "white pebble" that is to be given to the Christian conquerors: " . . . upon the pebble a new name written which no one knows except the one receiving it." (Revelation 2:17) Christ's "new name" in heaven would, of course, become known to his 144,000 disciples when he writes it upon them.

Christ's heavenly "new name" is, naturally, known to his God Jehovah, for God is the one that bestows it upon him. In due time Jesus Christ shares this "new name" with his 144,000 joint heirs by, as it were, writing it upon them. Their having his "new name" written upon them means that they are identified with him and belong to him in his new heavenly relationship with his God. No other creatures in heaven or on earth will be privileged to share in that very private, most intimate, new relationship of Jesus Christ with his God Jehovah. Thus written upon, the 144,000 Christian conquerors will bear the name of God the heavenly Father and the name of his Son Jesus Christ and the name of the heavenly city, the New Jerusalem. In this way they will be highly honored in a threefold manner as a reward for being conquerors, who heeded what the spirit said to the congregations.

To the Angel
in Laodicea

THE CITY of Laodicea got its name from the wife of the Seleucid ruler, Antíochus II, who was the grandson of General Seleucus Nicator and who came to be called *Theós*, "God." He founded and named Laodicea in the third century before our Common Era.*

Being well situated in the western part of Asia Minor, it became wealthy. It was a manufacturing city and also a banking center, whose bankers did business with the whole of the Roman Empire. It was noted for the worship of the god of medicine, Aesculapius, and appropriately had a medical school. It also produced a famous eye medicine known as Phrygian powder. However, because the city had no permanent water supply, water had to be piped to it from hot springs some distance away, the water likely being lukewarm by the time it reached the city limits. The city was linked by roads with Ephesus and Pergamum, where two of the "seven congregations that are in the district of Asia" were located. (Revelation 1:4, 11, 20; 2:1, 12) At the time that the apostle Paul wrote to Christians in Colossae, about 60-61 C.E., there was a congregation in Laodicea. —Colossians 2:1; 4:13-16.

During the several decades that elapsed since its founding, the congregation in that materially pros-

---

* He is connected with the fulfillment of Daniel 11:6. See pages 230, 231 of the book *"Your Will Be Done on Earth,"* published by the Watch Tower Bible & Tract Society of Pennsylvania in 1958.

perous city of Laodicea had suffered a severe spiritual decline. Doubtless very different from the letter that the "congregation of the Laodiceans" had received from the apostle Paul was the one that the apostle John was instructed to send to the "angel" or overseer of that congregation. (Colossians 4:16) In this letter, the seventh and last one of the letters dictated to the "seven congregations that are in the district of Asia" about the year 96 C.E., there is no word of praise to the Laodicean "angel." Here is what the apostle John was told:

"And to the angel of the congregation in Laodicea write: These are the things that the Amen says, the faithful and true witness, the beginning of the creation by God, 'I know your deeds, that you are neither cold nor hot. I wish you were cold or else hot. So, because you are lukewarm and neither hot nor cold, I am going to vomit you out of my mouth. Because you say: "I am rich and have acquired riches and do not need anything at all," but you do not know you are miserable and pitiable and poor and blind and naked, I advise you to buy from me gold refined by fire that you may become rich, and white outer garments that you may become dressed and that the shame of your nakedness may not become manifested, and eyesalve to rub in your eyes that you may see.

"'All those for whom I have affection I reprove and discipline. Therefore be zealous and repent. Look! I am standing at the door and knocking. If anyone hears my voice and opens the door, I will come into his house and take the evening meal with him and he with me. To the one that conquers I will grant to sit down with me on my throne, even as I conquered and sat down with my Father on his throne. Let the one who has an ear hear what the spirit says to the congregations.'"—Revelation 3:14-22.

In sharp contrast to the congregation at Smyrna (about 113 miles to the northwest), which was in poverty materially but in riches spiritually, the Laodicean congregation was materially rich but spiritually poor. Instead of the literal gold handled by the Laodicean bankers, instead of the garments of glossy black wool produced by the local clothiers, instead of the medicinal tablets or powder for the literal eyes as produced by the local medical profession, instead of the boiling hot medicinal waters from the hot springs at nearby Hierapolis, the Laodicean congregation needed things like these in a spiritual sense. It needed real Christian gold to enrich its personality, the white outer garments to give it an irreproachable Christian appearance with no unchristian features that were as shameful as bodily nakedness. It needed a spiritual eyesalve to be applied to take away its blindness to Bible truth and Christian responsibilities. It could buy these things from the One knocking at the door, if it let him in hospitably to entertain him. It needed to become stimulatingly hot or refreshingly cold, but not stay lukewarm.

Likewise, with the case of the anointed remnant of Christ's congregation in the postwar year of 1919 C.E. There was then a pressing need for the anointed remnant of dedicated, baptized Christians and for those who merely professed to be Christians in sectarian Christendom to place a proper value on things that had to do with true Christianity. Notwithstanding more than four years of World War I, Christendom remained rich in a material way and was due to increase her riches in money, lands and property and political power in the postwar epoch. But was she rich with real Christian spiritual riches? Would she now seek them? She had badly tarnished her religious appearance because of her responsibility for and support of gory World War I. Would she clean up her religious appearance to match the apostolic Bible teachings, standards and principles? Would she repent of her worldly ways? Would she allow spiritual "eyesalve" to be applied so that she could see the difference between man-made traditions and Bible truth and also see the now occurring fulfillments of Bible prophecies and what these mean and what God now wants Christians on earth to do?

The anointed remnant, although separate and distinct from Christendom, had to face the same issues of this "time of the end" as Christendom did. (Daniel 12:1-4) Any spiritual lukewarmness that may have resulted to them because of the persecutions and trials and dangers of World War I days they had to get rid of without delay. Let Christ vomit out of his mouth Christendom as something that he could not stomach, but the anointed remnant did not want to have that happen to them because of any lukewarmness toward God's will and work and his revelations of truth in this "time of the end." The remnant did not dare yield to the materialistic times that now set in as the world rebuilt the present system of things so frightfully damaged by World War I. Any material riches that members of the anointed remnant may still have had were not the things to rely upon as if they were all that was necessary for respectable Christians. Were they spiritually poor? Did they need to take Christ's advice and buy from him true riches, Christian "gold refined by fire," able to stand the fiery times ahead? This was the safe thing to do!

Furthermore, what about the remnant's outward garments of Christian professions and identity? These garments had been somewhat soiled by their compromises and failures during World War I. As with the ancient Laodicean congregation and its "angel," there was some "shame of your nakedness" that had become manifest and that called for them to repent before God. To do away with such nakedness the remnant needed to buy from the glorified Jesus Christ spiritual "white outer garments" that would mark and identify them as blameless Christians. How could they "buy" such white outer garments? Not with material gold, but by a reinvigorated devotion to Christ's example and by the decision to stick to true Christian neutrality in the midst of the world's political and military conflicts. This they did, as history proves. During World War II, which began twenty years later, they did not soil these "white outer garments." No, nor in later conflicts.

"EYESALVE" FROM "THE FAITHFUL AND TRUE WITNESS"

Did the anointed remnant need to buy any spiritual eyesalve? Yes, not from politically and religiously split Christendom, but from the now reigning Jesus Christ. He had now come to God's spiritual temple and was standing, as it were, at the remnant's door and knocking so as to be received hospitably inside to the midst of the remnant as his congregation. By forsaking the philosophies and man-made traditions of Christendom and heathendom, the anointed remnant had already had their eyes opened to see many truths of the Holy Bible and to discern God's purpose, God's organization and God's work for now. But their eyes were yet blind to many things about God's written Word and about his will and purpose and work for Christ's true followers in the "time of the end" that had begun in the year 1914 C.E. Many Bible truths were now about to be revealed. Bible prophecies were now due to be fulfilled and thereby correctly understood. The fact that God has a theocratic organization needed to be seen and acted upon. The progressive work that God has purposed for the remnant in this "time of the end" needed to be seen, undertaken.—Daniel 12:4-10.

Beyond all question there was need for the spiritual eyesalve to be bought from the invisibly present Jesus Christ and to be rubbed in the remnant's eyes of spiritual discernment. This called for them to make a direct study of the Holy Scriptures as never before, praying for God's holy spirit through Christ to direct them and open their eyes and to guide their decisions and course of conduct. The history of the past half century records that the remnant did so and gained a remarkable brightening up of their spiritual vision. In due time they saw the need to distinguish themselves from Christendom by embracing a name that had Bible foundations. Hence in the year 1931, by resolutions adopted world wide, they took the very responsible name, Jehovah's witnesses. (Isaiah 43:10-12; 44:8) In this way they were anxious to imitate their Leader Jesus Christ by themselves being what he called himself in his opening words to the "angel of the congregation in Laodicea." According to Revelation 3:14 he said:

"These are the things that the Amen says, the faithful and true witness, the beginning of the creation by God." Note those words, "the faithful and true witness." Of whom or of what was Jesus Christ

a witness? (Revelation 1:5) According to his own words, he was a witness of his heavenly Father, Jehovah God the Almighty, and also of God's kingdom and its being the divine means to sanctify God's name and cause his will to be done on our earth as it is also done in heaven. (John 18:36, 37; 1 Timothy 6: 13) He sent forth his disciples to be "witnesses." (Acts 1:6-8) He predicted to his disciples: "This good news of the kingdom will be preached in all the inhabited earth for a witness to all the nations; and then the end will come." (Matthew 24:14; Mark 13: 10) Above all other creatures, Jesus Christ deserves and applies to himself the title "the faithful and true witness."

"THE AMEN" AND THE FIRST "CREATION"

He also spoke of himself as "the Amen." How is he "the Amen" personified? It is well known that at the end of prayers addressed to Jehovah God in the name of Jesus Christ the word Amen! is properly adjoined. (1 Corinthians 14:16) It has the meaning of "Surely!" or, "So be it!" In Isaiah 65:16, in the Hebrew Masoretic text, Jehovah is called "the God of Amen," and some Bible translations render this "the God of truth," "the God of faithfulness," or "the true God." (RS; JPS; Ro; Le; NW) This indicates that the word Amen! is an affirmation or guarantee that something is true or is bound to come true and be realized. God has sent forth his faithful Son as an "Amen" to all the divine promises made in his Word. "For," says 2 Corinthians 1:20, "no matter how many the promises of God are, they have become Yes by means of him. Therefore also through him is the Amen said to God for glory through us." Hence prayer that is not offered to God through Jesus Christ will not be answered, for Jesus said to his apostles:

"No matter what you ask the Father in my name he [will] give it to you." "If you ask the Father for anything he will give it to you in my name. Until this present time you have not asked a single thing in my name. Ask and you will receive, that your joy may be made full." "Also, whatever it is that you ask in my name, I will do this, in order that the Father may be glorified in connection with the Son. If you ask anything in my name, I will do it." —John 15:16; 16:23, 24; 14:13, 14.

Appropriately, then, the apostle John closed the writing of the book of Revelation with the words: " 'Amen! Come, Lord Jesus.' May the undeserved kindness of the Lord Jesus Christ be with the holy ones." (Revelation 22:20, 21) Correspondingly, at its opening this book notes the fact that it is "a revelation by Jesus Christ, which God gave him, to show his slaves the things that must shortly take place." (Revelation 1:1) Since Jesus Christ is "the Amen," this assures that all the things shown to his Christian slaves in the Revelation will without fail take place, and that "shortly." What yet remains of this Revelation to take place will do so "shortly."

But in the message to the "angel" of the congregation in Laodicea, did the glorified Jesus Christ really say that he is "the beginning of the creation of God"? (Revelation 3:14, AV; AS; ER; Dy; Ro) In the language in which he spoke to the apostle John, did he really say that he was "the beginning" rather than 'the beginner' of the creation of God? In the language in which John wrote down the Revelation the Greek word is arkhé. This word occurs fifty-eight (58) times in the Greek text of the Authorized or King James Version and yet never is it translated as 'beginner' or 'originator.' In all of the apostle John's Bible writings (one Gospel, three letters and the Revelation) he used the Greek word arkhé twenty-three (23) times, and always in the sense of "beginning." In the Revelation alone he used this Greek word four (4) times and in three cases (Revelation 1:8; 21:6; 22:13, AV) John sets it in opposition to the "end" or "ending." So it is not consistent to think that in Revelation 3:14 the apostle John switches the meaning of *arkhé* from "beginning" to 'beginner' or 'originator.'

Other Scriptures, both in John's writings* and in other books of the Holy Bible, prove that Jesus Christ is the "beginning" or 'original one' of all creation by God. Jesus always spoke of himself as the Son of God, which proves that he received life from God as his heavenly Father and thus had a beginning of life as the "only-begotten Son" of God. (John 10:36; 3:16; 5:26) Also, in Colossians 1:15, 18 (*AV*) it is written that he "is the image of the invisible God, the firstborn of every creature: And he is the head of the body, the church: who is the beginning [*arkhé*], the firstborn from the dead; that in all things he might have the preeminence." His being the "first-born from the dead" means that he himself was once dead, and his being the "firstborn of every creature" means that he himself was created by his heavenly Father.—Revelation 1:5, 17, 18; Acts 2:22-32.

It is not to Jesus Christ but to God that the apostle Peter applies the title "Creator" in 1 Peter 4:19. It is to this Almighty God on his heavenly throne that the creatures in heaven say: "Holy, holy, holy, is the Lord God Almighty, who was and is and is to come!" "Worthy art thou, our Lord and God, to receive glory and honor and power, for thou didst create all things, and by thy will they existed and were created." (Revelation 4:8-11, *RS*) It is to this Almighty God the Creator that Jesus Christ, the Lamb of God, comes to receive the mysterious scroll out of the right hand of that One on the heavenly throne. (Revelation 5: 1-10) It is by this Almighty God the Creator that the angel swears, according to Revelation 10:5, 6. All these things being taken into account, it is plain from the Bible itself that Jesus Christ the Son of God is not the Creator but that Almighty God the Creator used his only-begotten Son as his instrument

* See the 64-page booklet entitled " 'The Word'—Who Is He? According to John," published in 1962 by the Watch Tower Bible & Tract Society of Pennsylvania.

in creating all other creatures or creations. (John 1:1-3; Ephesians 2:10, 15; 3:9; Colossians 1:16, 17; Revelation 19:13) Jesus Christ is the oldest of God's creatures, for he is the *beginning* of God's creation. He is not ashamed to call his spirit-begotten, anointed followers his "brothers." (Hebrews 2:11) As the oldest fellow creature and oldest spiritual brother he said to the "angel" of the Laodicean congregation: "All those for whom I have affection I reprove and discipline. Therefore be zealous and repent." (Revelation 3:19) In the year 1919 C.E. the anointed remnant that had survived World War I needed to repent with respect to a number of things that were revealed to them as shortcomings. But they showed themselves zealous to do so and they were forgiven through Jesus Christ. They needed to be reproved, to be set straight as respects a number of things, and also to be disciplined especially with regard to theocratic organization. But they were glad to accept this reproof and discipline through Jesus Christ their oldest Brother, because they knew that all this was a display of his fondness or affection for them. They remembered what is written down in Hebrews 12: 2-11 concerning divine discipline. Just as Jesus had accepted discipline, so too the remnant did.

WHAT THE KNOCKER AT THE DOOR PROMISES

Their repenting and accepting discipline was to open the way to many spiritual privileges. This fact is made evident from the very next words of their oldest Brother: "Look! I am standing at the door and knocking. If anyone hears my voice and opens the door, I will come into his house and take the evening meal with him and he with me." (Revelation 3:20) Who was more worthy of their hospitality than their oldest spiritual Brother? Having accompanied his heavenly Father to the spiritual temple in the spring of 1918 for the work of inspection and purification, he was indeed invisibly standing at the door of receptiveness of the anointed remnant who needed so much spiritual help at the close of World War I on November 11, 1918.—Malachi 3:1-5.

The anointed remnant did show hospitality toward the Christ in his second but unseen presence and received him into their organizational "house." This meant the putting of themselves into position to receive many blessings, for now they received him as the reigning King, enthroned on the heavenly throne in 1914 C.E. He knocked at the door at the time of the "evening meal," or at supper. Back there in the days of the apostle John the main meal was the supper. It meant that the day's labor was over and that the family could come together. (Luke 17:7-9) At sunset the old day in which labor had been performed was ending, and a new day was beginning. Correspondingly, for the anointed remnant one feature of their work had ended, and with the start of the postwar period a new feature of their earthly work was opening up that had to do with God's established Messianic kingdom. For this they needed instruction and encouragement. Their guest at the evening meal or supper was the one to give this to them.

When Jesus was on earth as a man, those who invited him in to sup with them would always receive something greater in return, by the spiritual instruction and upbuilding that he would give in connection with the supper. (John 12:1-11) On one occasion when a ruler of the Pharisees had Jesus in for a meal at his house, a certain fellow guest was so moved by what he heard Jesus say that he exclaimed: "Happy is he who eats bread in the kingdom of God." Jesus immediately proceeded to give the parable of the "grand evening meal" to which many were invited. (Luke 14:1-24) It was like this when the invisibly present Jesus Christ knocked at the door of the anointed remnant by unfolding to their understanding the Bible prophecies then due to be understood regarding the world situation and their work. Then the responsive remnant opened up to receive him. This resulted in a great blessing for their hospitality. This spiritual supper that ensued meant a tremendous period of instruction and upbuilding for them from their heavenly Guest. More than *his* having the supper with them, they were rather having supper with *him*.

When he said: "I will come into his house and take the evening meal with him and he with me" (Revelation 3:20), the glorified Jesus Christ may have meant more than just the spiritual feast on earth that the hospitable remnant began to enjoy in the year 1919. He may have also had in mind their going into the heavenly "wedding celebration" into which the five wise virgins with lighted lamps were pictured as being admitted in his parable of the wise and foolish virgins, in Matthew 25:1-12. He may have been referring to the heavenly happiness spoken of in Revelation 19:9: "Happy are those invited to the evening meal of the Lamb's marriage." He may have meant the eating of "bread in the kingdom of God" through a resurrection from the dead to immortal life in the spirit heavens, there to eat bread, as it were, with the enthroned reigning King Jesus Christ. At least, the responsive remnant's opening the door after hearing his knock and voice in the year 1919 leads to such a blessed heavenly "supper."

Because of the timing and the circumstances, the "evening meal" begun in 1919 had to do with Kingdom matters. Not inappropriately, then, the glorified Jesus Christ went on from mentioning the "evening meal" to make the following promise: "To the one that conquers I will grant to sit down with me on my throne, even as I conquered and sat down with my Father on his throne." (Revelation 3:21) At the time of his message to the Laodicean congregation, about the year 96 C.E., Jesus Christ had already sat down with his heavenly Father on his throne and at his right hand. (Acts 2:32-36; 7:55, 56; 1 Peter 3:22) But since the end of the Gentile Times in the year 1914 C.E. and since his installation as king to reign in the midst of his enemies in fulfillment of Psalm 110:1-6, he grants to his conquering followers to sit on the heavenly throne with him as reigning King. This he grants by raising them from the dead to be with him as his joint heirs. Inasmuch as he came to God's spiritual temple in the spring of 1918 C.E., those of the anointed remnant dying physically since then did not need to sleep on in death awaiting his return; they were given an instantaneous resurrection as spirit creatures into his heavenly presence.—Revelation 14:13; 1 Corinthians 15:50-54.

The promise of such a glorious thing is worth listening to and striving to make one's very own. Hence the closing words of the message to the "angel" or overseer of the congregation in Laodicea: "Let the one who has an ear hear what the spirit says to the congregations."—Revelation 3:22.

Now that the special messages to all "the seven congregations that are in the district of Asia" have been delivered to their "angels," it is overwhelming, especially for the anointed remnant on earth, to consider all the things that the spirit of God has said to the congregations by way of promising rewards to the conquerors. To everyone that conquers within these congregations of spirit-begotten, anointed Christians is to be granted "to eat of the tree of life, which is in the paradise of God." (Revelation 2:7) He is to be given the "crown of life" and "will by no means be harmed by the second death." (Revelation 2:10, 11) He will be given "some of the hidden manna" and also a "white pebble, and upon the pebble a new name written which no one knows except the one receiving it." (Revelation 2:17) He will be given "authority over the nations, and he shall shepherd the people with an iron rod so that they will be broken to pieces like clay vessels." He will also be given "the morning star."—Revelation 2:26-28.

Each worthy conqueror will walk with the glorified Christ "in white," yes, "arrayed in white outer garments," and there will be no move to "blot out his name from the book of life," but, says Christ, "I will make acknowledgment of his name before my Father and before his angels." (Revelation 3:4, 5) Each conqueror will, as Christ says, be made a "pillar in the temple of my God, . . . and I will write upon him the name of my God and the name of the city of my God, the new Jerusalem which descends out of heaven from my God, and that new name of mine." (Revelation 3:12) To each conqueror the glorified Christ also promises: "I will grant to sit down with me on my throne, even as I conquered and sat down with my Father on his throne."—Revelation 3:21.

Only 144,000 spirit-begotten anointed Christians will prove worthy conquerors and share in all those magnificent rewards according to the will and power of God through Christ. They will form the heavenly spiritual Israel, in twelve equal tribes, as it were. During the past nineteen centuries, since the festival day of Pentecost of 33 C.E. the work of sealing them in their spiritual foreheads with the spirit of God has been taking place, openly marking them as the special property of the God of spiritual Israel. Before the stormy "four winds of the earth" are permitted to blow in the approaching "great day of God the Almighty," all the remnant that are yet needed to complete the full final number of 144,000 spiritual Israelites must be sealed with God's spirit as a token of their future heavenly inheritance with Christ. —Revelation 7:1-8; 16:14.

This sealing work is nearing its end. Then there will come upon all the world of mankind tribulation surpassing any trouble yet experienced on earth by men. After that comes the imprisoning of Satan the Devil and his demons, and then, O joy! the thousand-year reign of Jesus Christ and his Kingdom joint heirs, for the glory of God and the blessing of mankind with life in a paradise earth.—Matthew 24:21, 22, 31; Revelation 19:11 to 20:6; Luke 23:43.

CHAPTER 15

Earthly Survivors of "The Great Tribulation"

WITH inspired vision the Christian apostle John looked far beyond his own imprisonment on the penal isle of Patmos and saw the worst of troubles ever to hit mankind brewing. Why has it not hit the earth before now? Because Almighty God is holding it back by his angels until 144,000 spiritual Israelites will have received the stamp of His ownership, the identifying seal in their forehead, figuratively speaking. This reason for holding back the earth-wide storm of destructive trouble was foretold and illustrated to the inspired apostle John. (Revelation 7:1-8) This holding back of the storm has benefited more than the remnant of those sealed as spiritual Israelites who are in the new covenant with Jehovah God. It has benefited and will yet benefit a crowd of unsealed humans, the number of whom has not been fixed or declared like the number of the spiritual Israelites. Why, then, this benefit to them, since they are not sealed? Who are they anyhow? Will they be fatally hurt by the storm soon to be let loose? What can we learn on this from what John saw and heard?

After hearing the number of those who were to be sealed as spiritual Israelites but before seeing the terrific storm let loose from the four corners of the earth, the apostle John says: "After these things I saw, and, look! a great crowd, which no man was able to number, out of all nations and tribes and peoples and tongues, standing before the throne and before the Lamb, dressed in white robes; and there were palm branches in their hands. And they keep on crying with a loud voice, saying: 'Salvation we owe to our God, who is seated on the throne, and to the Lamb.'" (Revelation 7:9, 10) John sees here, not the gathering of the "great crowd" in progress, but the completed picture, the fully gathered though unnumbered "great crowd." An older person speaks of them as the comers out of the great tribulation, as those who "have come out of the great tribulation." (Revelation 7:14, *RS; Mo; NEB*)* Since they are standing before the throne of God and before the Lamb Jesus Christ, are they up in heaven?

No! They are on earth and they will stay on earth. They do not need to be up in heaven as spirit creatures in order to stand before the throne of Almighty God and before his Lamb any more than "all the nations" have to be up in heaven when they are gathered before the Son of man when he comes and sits down on his glorious throne to separate the "sheep" and the "goats."—Matthew 25:31, 32.

In this age of radar and television we can appreciate how the Almighty God and his Lamb Jesus Christ can have before them this "great crowd" even though here on earth. (Psalm 11:4, 5; Proverbs 15:3; Revelation 5:6) Also, by eyes of faith this "great crowd" has had God on his throne of the universe and also his heavenly Lamb in view. It is with them as Psalm 16:8 says: "I have placed Jehovah in front of me constantly." (Acts 2:25) They recognize that there is only one living and true God and that he is King over all, the divine Ruler of heaven and earth, and they acknowledge themselves as being His earthly subjects. Besides this they acknowledge the Lamb, that is, Jesus Christ, the one who was slaughtered like an inoffensive, unresisting lamb in sacrifice to God.

It is not to any earthly throne and its occupant

---

* See the interlinear reading under the Greek text of Revelation 7:14 in *The Kingdom Interlinear Translation of the Greek Scriptures*, published in 1969.

that they address themselves. Rather, to the heavenly throne and its divine Occupant and to his once sacrificed Lamb they address themselves, saying: "Salvation we owe to our God, who is seated on the throne, and to the Lamb." For thus openly confessing that their salvation comes from the Ruler of the universe and through his lamblike Son, they are indeed standing before God's throne even though they are in the flesh on earth. No occupant of a throne on earth hears such an ascription of salvation from this "great crowd"; only the heavenly enthroned God does, and so does His Lamb. This works for their having a spotless appearance in God's eyes. To picture this, they are said to be "dressed in white robes," with nothing unseemly showing to make them offensive in appearance before the enthroned God and his Lamb. This obliges them to put the law of God above the law of man; and, when there is any conflict between the law of God and the law of earthly man, they take the stand of the apostles of the Lamb Jesus Christ, saying: "We must obey God as ruler rather than men."—Acts 5:29.

Although this "great crowd, which no man was able to number," keeps coming "out of all nations and tribes and peoples and tongues," yet they do not let their tribal, national, racial or language differences set them at odds with themselves. They surmount all these divisive things of this world and stand united in openly confessing the reigning God Jehovah and his Lamb Jesus Christ as the source and the channel of their salvation. They salute no humans or emblems in an attributing to these their salvation. With the inspired psalmist they say: "Salvation belongs to Jehovah." (Psalm 3:8, NW; AS; Yg) They are jubilant about their God of salvation and about his Lamb, and this fact is pictured by this feature of the "great crowd": "There were palm branches in their hands," and "they keep on crying with a loud voice, saying: 'Salvation we owe to our God, who is seated on the throne, and to the Lamb.'"

(Revelation 7:9, 10) Such palm branches in their hands do not mean that they suffered a martyr's death or gained victory, but they ascribe the victory to their God and to his Lamb who died as a perfect human sacrifice. They hail these ones as Saviors.

At the vision of this the apostle John quite likely thought of what he witnessed at the time of the triumph-like ride of the Lamb Jesus Christ into Jerusalem on Nisan 9 of 33 C.E. About this John himself wrote, saying: "The next day the great crowd that had come to the festival, on hearing that Jesus was coming to Jerusalem, took the branches of palm trees and went out to meet him. And they began to shout: 'Save, we pray you! Blessed is he that comes in Jehovah's name, even the king of Israel!'" (John 12:12, 13) John could remember also that at the celebration of the joyous festival of booths in the seventh lunar month (Tishri) his people were told to use the fronds of palm trees. (Nehemiah 8:14, 15) Palm branches were very suitable to be waved before Jehovah God on his throne because, on the walls of the temple built by wise King Solomon at Jerusalem, there were carved palm-tree figures as well as cherubs.—1 Kings 6:29-35.

In the Revelation vision to John it appeared very appropriate that the unnumbered "great crowd" should be standing before the enthroned God and his Lamb holding up palm branches in symbol of their great joy and their grateful appreciation to these Saviors.

Those making up the "great crowd" in this twentieth century can be much encouraged by the fact that the holy creatures of the invisible heavens back them up in what they are crying out by exclaiming Amen! Right after describing the vision of the "great crowd," the apostle John proceeds to add: "And all the angels were standing around the throne and the older persons and the four living creatures, and they fell upon their faces before the throne and worshiped God, saying: 'Amen! The blessing and the glory and the wisdom and the thanksgiving and the honor and the power and the strength be to our God forever and ever.' " (Revelation 7:11, 12) Thus all those other creatures worship the same God as the "great crowd" on earth does. They render to Him glory, thanksgiving and honor, and they confess that He is the divine Source of all blessing, wisdom, power and strength. If it were not for God's blessing, wisdom, power and strength, the salvation of the "great crowd" could not be brought about through the Lamb Jesus Christ.

WHO ARE THEY AND FROM WHERE?

The apostle John knew that this "great crowd," for whom no man can fix a definite number, was not the same as the 144,000 spiritual Israelites with the seal of the living God in their foreheads, and was not a part of those 144,000 spiritual Israelites. Well, then, was the "great crowd" a picture of all the saved ones of mankind? Or whom does the "great crowd" picture? John had to admit that he did not know, when the question was put to him by one of the twenty-four older persons who had earlier been seen seated on thrones about God's central throne. (Revelation 4:4-6) The information that John got he shares with us, writing:

"And in response one of the older persons said to me: 'These who are dressed in the white robes, who are they and where did they come from?' So right away I said to him: 'My lord, you are the one that knows.' And he said to me: 'These are the ones that come out of the great tribulation, and they have washed their robes and made them white in the blood of the Lamb. That is why they are before the throne of God; and they are rendering him sacred service day and night in his temple; and the one seated on the throne will spread his tent over them. They will hunger no more nor thirst any more, neither will the sun beat down upon them nor any scorching heat, because the Lamb, who is in the midst of the throne, will shepherd them, and will guide them to fountains of waters of life. And God will wipe out every tear from their eyes.' "—Revelation 7:13-17.

The group of twenty-four older persons is one of the several Revelation symbols of the 144,000 spiritual Israelites who are to reign with the Lamb Jesus Christ during the coming millennium. So the one older person who gave the apostle John this information would stand for a part of that congregation of Kingdom heirs. Ever since the end of the first world war on November 11, 1918, there has been a remnant of these Kingdom heirs on earth. In recent years their number has been dwindling, whereas the number of the "great crowd" has been increasing steadily. Quite nicely, then, John's getting the explanation from the informative older person prefigured that in this time of the fulfillment of the Revelation the enlightening information about who and from where are the "great crowd" would be given through this anointed remnant as God's visible channel.

Indeed, the long-looked-for, satisfying information did come to us just that way, in the year 1935. In that year the Watch Tower Bible & Tract Society, the board of directors of which must all be members of the anointed remnant, published in its official magazine (*The Watchtower and Herald of Christ's Presence*) its latest explanation of Revelation 7:9-17 concerning the "great crowd," or, "great multitude." (*AV; AS; RS*) This appeared in the August 1 and 15, 1935, issues of *The Watchtower*, in the two-part article entitled "The Great Multitude." However, eight weeks earlier that same year, on Friday evening, May 31, at 5:00-6:30 p.m., at the Washington, D.C., convention of Jehovah's witnesses, this same information was presented to the visible audience and to the invisible radio audience by the then president of the Watch Tower Bible & Tract Society, Pennsylvania corporation, namely, Joseph F. Rutherford, who spoke on the subject "The Great Multitude." Both this convention talk and the later *Watchtower* article set forth that the "great multitude" was not to go to heaven but was to live forever on a paradise earth.

Since the older person told John that "these are the ones that come out of the great tribulation," does this mean that they must go through great persecution? It would not altogether exclude that, inasmuch as in the Revelation the word "tribulation" is used at times to mean persecution or suffering as a Christian, specifically of the congregation of spirit-begotten, anointed ones. (Revelation 1:9; 2:9, 10) However, the "great crowd" are foretold to "come out of the great tribulation," and this could hardly mean that the "great crowd" suffer more persecution and hardship than the anointed remnant does so that theirs is "the great tribulation." The "great crowd" may suffer persecution along with the anointed remnant, but the persecution upon the "great crowd" is not to be put separate and magnified by the expression "the great tribulation." What, then, appears more reasonable as the meaning of that expression? This, namely, the exceptional "tribulation" that comes when the "four angels" at the four corners of the earth let loose the "four winds of the earth" to blow upon the earth, sea and trees.—Revelation 7:1-3.

When the Lord Jesus Christ gave to his disciples the prophecy on the "sign" of his invisible second presence and the "conclusion of the system of things," he foretold "great tribulation" that would come in connection with the destruction of antitypical Jerusalem (or, Christendom). He said: "Then there will be great tribulation such as has not occurred since the world's beginning until now, no, nor will occur again. In fact, unless those days were cut short, no flesh would be saved; but on account of the chosen ones those days will be cut short." (Matthew 24:3, 21, 22; also Mark 13:19, 20) There the expression "great tribulation" hardly means persecution of Christians or suffering as Christians, but means the execution of God's righteous judgment, outstandingly against Christendom, inasmuch as Christendom was foreshadowed by the unfaithful Jerusalem that was destroyed in a horrible time of trouble in the year 70 C.E. Of course, thus far a large part of the "great crowd" has come out from Christendom, the antitypical Jerusalem. However, the "great tribulation" spoken of in Revelation 7:14 is not there mentioned in connection with any city. Hence this "great tribulation" means the execution of God's judgment against the whole world of mankind, the "four corners of the earth."—Revelation 7:1.

Out of this, "the great tribulation," the white-robed "great crowd" will come as earthly survivors, whereas this wicked system of things and all those who support it will be destroyed. This distinguishing feature about the "great crowd" makes it certain that the "great crowd" does not picture all of mankind who will eventually be saved to live in an earthly paradise, for it cannot be said of all these that they have "come out of the great tribulation." The patriarch Noah and his family, eight human souls all together, came out of the tribulation of the year 2370-2369 B.C.E., the earth-wide deluge. But at this "time of the end," the as yet unknown number of the "great crowd" of earthly survivors will come "out of the great tribulation" that destroys this system of things and its supporters. (Matthew 24:36-39) Since those of the "great crowd" "come out of the great tribulation," that is, survive it, the gathering of them must have begun during the time that the four angels at the "four corners of the earth" were holding back the "four winds" from harmfully blowing upon the earth.—Revelation 7:1-3.

WASHING THEIR ROBES WHITE

Since the year 1935 C.E. and its identification of the mysterious "great crowd" the faith that Christendom claims to have in the perfect human sacrifice of the Lamb Jesus Christ as a ransomer has been shown to be dead. How so? Because Christendom's profession of faith therein is not proved by her works.

(James 2:20-26) For this reason she will not be preserved through the "great tribulation." Not so, however, with the white-robed members of the "great crowd." Their faith is alive and is portrayed in the fact that the older person said of them: "And they have washed their robes and made them white in the blood of the Lamb." (Revelation 7:14) Prior to this, when they were people of the sinful world, their robes of identification were soiled and spotted with the world, not presentable in God's sight. (James 1:27) They could not wash these robes and make them white in their own blood through its being shed in violent martyrdom. Neither are they forced into washing and whitening them by being put through any future disciplinary "great tribulation." They could wash them spotlessly white only in the "blood of the Lamb." How?

They did their washing by acting out their belief that "unless blood is poured out no forgiveness takes place" and that Jesus Christ is "the Lamb of God that takes away the sin of the world." (Hebrews 9:22; John 1:29, 36) How? By dedication to God. In the issue of August 15, 1934, pages 249, 250, of *The Watchtower* it was published that, even for a person to put himself in line for gaining everlasting life on the paradise earth in God's new order, he must make an irrevocable dedication of himself to Jehovah God and then symbolize this dedication by complete baptism in water. He could not be a disciple of Jesus Christ unless he did so, in obedience to Jesus' words in Matthew 28:19, 20.

It is Jehovah God who determines whether the dedicated, baptized person shall be called with the heavenly calling to the Kingdom or shall be assigned to life and service on earth in His new order of things. Such a dedication can be made to God and accepted only if one makes this dedication through the Lamb Jesus Christ, believing that his shed blood provides for God to forgive one's sins and thus make one acceptable in God's sight.

So, by making this unconditional dedication of themselves to God through the Lamb whose blood was shed, those who came to be of the present-day "great crowd" figuratively "have washed their robes and made them white in the blood of the Lamb." That is how they can stand before God on his throne, in white robes and with palm branches in their hands. They keep these robes white by openly confessing before men their faith in the Lamb's blood and by continually asking God to forgive them their sins through the shed blood of his Lamb. Particularly since the year 1938 they have been attending the annual celebration of the Lord's Supper (or evening meal) as celebrated by Jehovah's witnesses on the anniversary of Christ's introduction of the Lord's Supper on the Passover night of the year 33 C.E. Although at such annual celebrations of the memorial of Christ's death they do not partake of the emblems as the anointed remnant does, they do believe that the unleavened bread means Christ's body and the red wine means Christ's shed blood. In 1969 the "great crowd" attended such a memorial of Christ's death on Tuesday, April 1, after 6 p.m.*

At the opening of the sixth seal of the mysterious scroll by the Lamb of God, the guilt-stricken, frightened worldlings of this system of things were shown calling upon the mountains and the rock-masses to hide them. Hide them from what? "From the face of the one seated on the throne and from the wrath of the Lamb, because the great day of their wrath has come, and who is able to stand?" (Revelation 6:15-17) The "great crowd" does not join those worldlings in calling upon earthly strongholds to hide them. They seek the face of the divine One seated on the heavenly throne, and they do not fear the "wrath of the Lamb." In answer to the question raised

---

* World wide this celebration of the Lord's Supper in 1968 was attended by a total of 2,493,519, of whom only 10,619 took of the bread and the wine as evidence of their being of the anointed remnant. Among the remaining 2,482,900 were included members of the faithful "great crowd."

by the self-condemned worldlings, "Who is able to stand?" the faithful ones of the "great crowd" show who is able. They stand, yes, before the throne of God and before the Lamb, "dressed in white robes" and having "palm branches in their hands." They ascribe their salvation, not to the mountains and the rock-masses, but to their God Jehovah and to his Lamb Jesus Christ.

Because of their clean appearance in washed, whitened robes, this "great crowd," although not being spiritual Israelites, are in a proper spiritual condition to have a standing before God, who is seated on the throne of the universe, as pictured in Revelation 7:9. "That is why," explains Revelation 7:15, "they are before the throne of God; and they are rendering him sacred service day and night in his temple." They clearly recognize that Jehovah God reigns by means of his Messianic kingdom that he brought to

birth at the end of the Gentile Times in 1914 C.E. In turn, the reigning God is pleased to give them recognition from his heavenly throne by assigning to them a part in the fulfillment of Jesus' prophecy: "This good news of the kingdom will be preached in all the inhabited earth for a witness to all the nations; and then the end will come." (Matthew 24: 14) The "great crowd" carries on an expanding part in this Kingdom preaching along with the anointed remnant of spiritual Israelites, who act as "ambassadors substituting for Christ." (2 Corinthians 5:20) The "great crowd" act as envoys under supervision of these Kingdom heirs.

RENDERING SACRED SERVICE IN GOD'S TEMPLE

The work that the members of the "great crowd" are doing is a sacred work. It is said that "they are rendering [God] sacred service day and night in his temple." This does not make them priests of God such as the anointed remnant are. (1 Peter 2: 5, 9) It is not said that, as Jesus Christ said to the congregation in ancient Philadelphia, those of the "great crowd" are made pillars in the temple of his God. (Revelation 3:12) Neither is it said of those of the "great crowd" that "they will be priests of God and of the Christ, and will rule as kings with him for the thousand years." (Revelation 20:6) Hence those of the "great crowd" are not a priestly class. Why or how is it, then, that they are seen rendering sacred service "day and night in his temple"?

It is because there are still an anointed remnant of members of the spiritual temple class yet on earth. So, since 1934-1935 C.E., the white-robed "great crowd" has been rendering their continual service to Jehovah God in immediate contact with this remnant of the temple class, those spiritual 'pillars' in the temple of God. Thus they are in, but not a part of God's temple. Besides that, they put God's worship foremost in their lives, but they cannot worship God except through his spiritual temple of which Jesus

Christ is the "foundation cornerstone." (Ephesians 2:20-22) Through it they will forever serve God.

Because they refrain from the profane, death-dealing works of this unholy world but constantly render service of a sacred kind to Jehovah God, he protects and shelters them. It is as Revelation 7:15 says: "The one seated on the throne will spread his tent over them." Furthermore, after the "great crowd" survives "the great tribulation," it will be true of them as well as of mankind who are thereafter to be resurrected, as foretold in Revelation 21:3: "Look! The tent of God is with mankind, and he will reside [tent; tabernacle, *Greek*] with them, and they will be his peoples. And God himself will be with them." So since God now spreads his tent over the "great crowd," it means that he protectively takes care of them and that they have close fellowship with him.

"OTHER SHEEP"

The God to whom the members of the "great crowd" are now 'rendering sacred service day and night in his temple' also sets a Shepherd over them. The benefits of having this shepherd are told in Revelation 7:16, 17: "They will hunger no more nor thirst any more, neither will the sun beat down upon them nor any scorching heat, because the Lamb, who is in the midst of the throne, will shepherd them, and will guide them to fountains of waters of life. And God will wipe out every tear from their eyes."

In this way persons belonging to the "great crowd" are likened to sheep and the Lamb of God is likened to their Shepherd. Evidently this is the beginning of the gathering work that Jesus Christ foretold after speaking of himself as "the fine shepherd," over the fold of 144,000 sheep who have the heavenly calling. He said: "And I have other sheep, which are not of this fold; those also I must bring, and they will listen to my voice, and they will become one flock, one shepherd." (John 10:1-16) Since those of the "great crowd" are brought by the "fine shepherd" before the great tribulation, they are the first ones of the "other sheep" of ransomed mankind whom the "fine shepherd" brings. Because this bringing of these "other sheep" occurs while the anointed remnant of Kingdom heirs are yet on earth, the "great crowd" of "other sheep" now become "one flock" with the remnant under the "one shepherd." Due to such unification this "one flock" of symbolic sheep on earth has already grown to far more than 144,000 clear around the inhabited earth, but all are under the "one shepherd," the glorified Jesus Christ, "the Lamb of God."

A faithful shepherd sees to it that his sheep are fed and watered well. Just so, too, the "great crowd" of "other sheep" do not hunger or thirst anymore in a spiritual sense. They are regularly taught and given an understanding of the nutritious Word of God, the Holy Bible, and they are given a generous share in Kingdom service, "sacred service," which is like food and drink to them, as in Jesus' own case.—John 4:32.

Besides such food and drink, the "fine shepherd" finds ample shade for his "other sheep." It is not the hot wrath of man that they have to fear because of their doing what is right; it is, rather, the burning wrath of God that they need to fear because of doing anything to merit his displeasure. So their "fine shepherd" guides and instructs them in doing God's will in order that they may have the divine approval, blessing and refreshment. Through their "fine shepherd" they can gain God's forgiveness of their sins, and keep their symbolic white robes clean. Their "fine shepherd" will shield these "other sheep" from the "scorching heat" that will blast down during the great tribulation.

Instead of burning rays from the sun and scorching heat from God's displeasure, there will be refreshment for the "great crowd" of these "other sheep" by means of his Shepherd Guide. They will not suffer death-dealing dehydration and desiccation and fatal lack of mineral salts. The "fine shepherd" "will guide them to fountains of waters of life." No piped, chemically tainted water this, but clear, cool, wholesome water right from the fountains. These symbolic waters mean not just waters in the sense of Bible truths but, rather, all of God's provisions for the "great crowd" to attain to everlasting perfect human life in happiness amid the earthly paradise of God's new order.

Thus through associating with the anointed remnant of the "little flock" before the "great tribulation," this "great crowd" of "other sheep" now enjoy things similar to those that were foretold for the remnant after they got out of Babylon the Great and were restored to Jehovah God's organization: "They will not go hungry, neither will they go thirsty, nor will parching heat or sun strike them. For the One who is having pity upon them will lead them, and by the springs of water he will conduct them." —Isaiah 49:10.

God loves this growing "great crowd" of these "other sheep" who are rendering sacred service to him day and night at his spiritual temple. Whereas in the past they may have wept because of their religious ignorance and because of their bad relationship with the one living and true God, now in their cleansed standing before God's throne and in their precious sacred service to him at his temple they weep no more. His promise regarding them is being fulfilled: "And God will wipe out every tear from their eyes." (Revelation 7:17) They rejoice in the salvation they owe to him through his Lamb Jesus Christ. But they look higher than their own personal salvation through the Lamb. They joyfully look forward to seeing the universal sovereignty of Jehovah God vindicated and his glorious name sanctified by his bringing the "great tribulation" that will cleanse the whole earth of the present wicked system of things of which Satan the Devil has been the god. What a joy it will be for them to survive that great tribulation!

CHAPTER 16

The Blowing
of the First
Four Trumpets

WITH the revelation concerning the earthly "great crowd" that stood before God's throne and before the Lamb Jesus Christ, the things to be disclosed by the opening of the sixth seal of the mysterious scroll were finished. One more seal, the seventh one, remained to be opened on this scroll that the Lamb had accepted from the right hand of God, who was seated on his glorious heavenly throne.

The opening of the sixth seal had revealed the "four angels" at the four corners of the earth holding back the "four winds of the earth" till God's preliminary work is finished and he gives the signal for the angels to let go and thus let the storm of worldwide destruction from him break upon the wicked earthly system of things. The time to hold back the Biblically predicted storm was evidently at the close of World War I on November 11, 1918, or, Kislev 6/7, 1918, Jewish calendar. As the historic facts show, God's tremendous pre-Armageddon work was by no means finished at that date and time as regards the sealing of the remainder of the 144,000 spiritual Israelites and the later gathering of the numberless "great crowd" of his earthly subjects and worshipers. —Revelation 7:1-17.

Reasonably, then, the time for the opening of the seventh seal of God's mysterious scroll would be at the start of this period of holding back the outbreak of the earth-wide storm upon all humankind. Let us accordingly locate ourselves at the start of the postwar period at the transition of the year 1918 to 1919. From this standpoint we watch to see what the apostle John saw start occurring when the Lamb Jesus Christ broke the seventh and last seal of the revelatory scroll: "And when he opened the seventh seal, a silence occurred in heaven for about a half hour. And I saw the seven angels that stand before God, and seven trumpets were given them."—Revelation 8:1, 2.

Silence in heaven for about half an hour! But why? It was evidently a time for prayer to be heard from the earth. Whose prayers? The seven angels were not permitted to sound their trumpets until those prayers were heard by God on his throne. At the temple in earthly Jerusalem the offering of incense by the priest upon the altar of incense in the Holy of the temple took about half an hour. During this time the people worshiping outside in the court of the temple kept silence while they engaged in mental prayer to God to whom the incense was ascending. (Exodus 30:1-8; Luke 1:8-10, 21) Agreeable to this, Psalm 141:1, 2 reads: "O Jehovah, I have called upon you. Do make haste to me. Do give ear to my voice when I call to you. May my prayer be prepared as incense before you." In the transition period of 1918-1919 it was indeed a time calling for earnest prayer to God on the part of the anointed remnant on earth. Would heaven be silent to hear?

By God's mercy and forbearance the anointed remnant had survived the hardships and persecutions of World War I. Why had he preserved them and kept them on earth instead of taking them to heaven at the close of the Gentile Times, as they had expected? What was his will and his work for them in the now opening postwar period? The remnant wanted to know.* They wanted to be freed from the fear and

---

* See the article entitled "The Harvest Ended—What Shall Follow?" in the issue of *The Watch Tower and Herald of Christ's Presence,* dated May 1, 1919, pages 133-139.

restraints imposed upon them by the militarized political powers and their religious concubine, Babylon the Great, the world empire of false Babylonish religion. For divine help, enlightenment, guidance and reactivation they needed to pray to the God of heaven. This is what they promptly did, along with deeper searching of the Holy Scriptures. As never before, they needed to live up to the name by which they were generally known throughout the earth, International Bible Students Association. Their prayers through Christ needed to be acceptable just like sweet incense to God in his heavenly temple. They needed to learn that God's angels were preparing to sound seven symbolic trumpets.

This historic season of prayer and the stirring things that followed upon it were forevisioned by the apostle John, according to Revelation 8:3-6, where John writes: "And another angel arrived and stood at the altar, having a golden incense vessel; and a large quantity of incense was given him to offer it with the prayers of all the holy ones upon the golden altar that was before the throne. And the smoke of the incense ascended from the hand of the angel with the prayers of the holy ones before God. But right away the angel took the incense vessel, and he filled it with some of the fire of the altar and hurled it to the earth. And thunders occurred and voices and lightnings and an earthquake. And the seven angels with the seven trumpets prepared to blow them."

The eighth angel acted like an Aaronic priest in the temple at Jerusalem in offering incense accompanied by the prayers of God's holy ones. (In Revelation 5:8 the incense offered by the twenty-four older men is itself said to mean the "prayers of the holy ones," the twenty-four older ones themselves picturing such "holy ones.") The eighth angel thus served in behalf of the "holy ones" in order to make their prayers acceptable to God, during the heavenly silence of "about a half hour." All the evidence of that critical year of 1919 goes to show that the contrite prayers of the anointed remnant of "holy ones" were favorably heard by Jehovah God through his "messenger [angel] of the covenant," Jesus Christ. (Malachi 3:1) The symbolic "smoke of the incense" ascended from his hand along with the prayers of the repentant anointed remnant, who sought renewed right relations with God and His guidance in doing their further work on earth. (Revelation 2:5, 16, 21, 22; 3:3, 19) However, action must now follow prayer, and promptly the eighth angel proceeded to act and stir up action.

FIRE HURLED ONTO THE EARTH

Back in the year 32 C.E. Jesus Christ on earth said: "I came to start a fire on the earth, and what more is there for me to wish if it has already been lighted?" (Luke 12:49, NW; Ro) He certainly "set fire to the earth" (NEB), raising an issue that caused great heat of controversy and resulted in the consuming of many false teachings, claims and pretensions by men and institutions.

No less so the eighth angel threw fire onto the earth when he filled the incense vessel with fire from the altar and hurled it to the earth. From being a prayer vessel the censer was converted into a starter of fire on the earth. The fire of the heated controversy over God's Messianic kingdom was to be started, for the fire was taken from God's holy altar. Indeed, the fire of the heated issue of God's kingdom was thrust upon the earthly stage by the anointed remnant in 1919, undoubtedly under angelic guidance, yes, under Christ's guidance. Testifying to that fact are the articles in issues of The Watch Tower that year, such as "Heralds of the Kingdom 'Killed'" (issue of May 1, 1919), "Kingdom of Heaven at Hand" (May 15, 1919), "The Kingdom of God" (August 1, 1919), and "Announcing the Kingdom" (September 15, 1919).

Expressions of God's supernatural power followed, as pictured in Revelation 8:5 as "thunders," "voices," "lightnings," and "an earthquake." There were thunderous storm warnings; there were stormy voices or sounds; lightnings of divine enlightenment and revelation flashed forth and struck at targets; and there was earthly unsettlement and upheaval. Notable that year was the week-long general convention held by the International Bible Students Association at Cedar Point, Ohio, September 1-8, which was attended by about 6,000 of these Bible students. The public talk "The Hope for Distressed Humanity" was given Sunday afternoon, September 7, by the then president of the Watch Tower Bible & Tract Society, J. F. Rutherford, who had been released from unjust imprisonment five and a half months earlier. Reporting the next day on this speech, the Sandusky (Ohio) *Star-Journal* said:

President Rutherford spoke to nearly 7,000 persons under the trees Sunday afternoon. He declared a League of Nations formed by the political and economic forces, moved by a desire to better mankind by establishment of peace and plenty would accomplish great good, and then asserted that the Lord's displeasure is certain to be visited upon the League, however, because the clergy —Catholic and Protestant—claiming to be God's representatives, have abandoned his plan and endorsed the League of Nations, hailing it as a political expression of Christ's kingdom on earth.—*The Watch Tower*, under date of October 1, 1919, page 298.

Did such a declaration by voice and in print kindle a fire? A half century later the fire still burns hotly over the issue of God's Messianic kingdom and a man-made international organization for world peace and security, now the United Nations. Thunderous storm warnings from God's Word through his anointed remnant of Kingdom heirs still peal forth. There are stormy voices or sounds; divine lightnings of enlightenment flash to illuminate Bible prophecies and truths. The peoples of the earth feel themselves disturbed and shaken by the continuous preaching of God's Messianic kingdom and of the fast-approaching day of his vengeance against mankind's earthly system of things. Now that the prayerful silence "for about a half hour" had ended by the year 1919, it became the due time for the heavenly "seven angels with the seven trumpets" to prepare to blow them.

Among Jehovah God's ancient people trumpets were used to call the congregation and to give signals, to celebrate the beginning of the new lunar months, to blow over burnt offerings and communion offerings at the temple, to sound a war call to gain victory with Jehovah's help, and to mark their festival occasions.* Inasmuch as the trumpet sound was heard over a wide area, the trumpet sounding was a public calling to notice that something of public interest was being enacted or was to be enacted or was to be proclaimed. When "the seven angels" of heaven prepared to blow the "seven trumpets" after the eighth angel had taken action, as described in Revelation 8:1-6, the anointed remnant of Kingdom heirs on earth for whom the angels are "spirits for public service" became involved. (Hebrews 1:14) The remnant had prayed; now they must take action to harmonize with the seven heavenly trumpeters. They must proclaim the meaning of what the apostle John saw happen in symbols after each trumpet blast.

Meantime, the special issue, No. 27, of the new thirty-two-page magazine *The Golden Age* (now *Awake!*), as of September 29, 1920, began to be distributed to the number of 4,000,000 copies. Its feature article was " 'Distress of Nations': Cause, Warning, Remedy." (Luke 21:25, *AV*) It laid bare much of the ungodly persecution heaped upon the International Bible Students during World War I by the religious clergymen of Christendom and their allies, political and military. Just prior to this, in June of 1920, the book entitled "The Finished Mystery," now released from under government limitations or ban, began to be advertised and circulated again, both in magazine form and in bound-book form, to Christendom's displeasure. Late in the following year (1921) the 384-

---

* Leviticus 25:8-11; 23:24; Numbers 10:1-10; Psalm 81:2-4; 2 Chronicles 5:11-14; Joshua 6:4-20; 2 Kings 9:13; 11:14; 2 Chronicles 13:12-16.

page bound book entitled "The Harp of God," dealing with prominent fundamental doctrines of the Bible, was published and began what was to be a phenomenal circulation of 5,819,037, in 22 languages. A short interval followed, and then came an event that the first angelic trumpeter could well use—an international convention of the anointed remnant in Cedar Point, Ohio, September 5-13, 1922!

THE FIRST ANGEL BLOWS HIS TRUMPET

Prophetically the apostle John wrote: "And the first one blew his trumpet. And there occurred a hail and fire mingled with blood, and it was hurled to the earth; and a third of the earth was burned up, and a third of the trees was burned up, and all the green vegetation was burned up."—Revelation 8:7.

A "third of the earth" was pounded with hail, causing great damage, fragile things being beaten down. Likely the fire that was thrown down was lightning; it was not for the purpose of enlightening, but for consuming combustible things. The blood accompanying the fire was nothing drinkable from heaven, drinking blood being contrary to God's law to the patriarch of all mankind, Noah. Like shed blood, it spelled death and stained up all upon which it was thrown down. It resembled the plagues of blood and of hailstones and fire upon ancient Egypt in Moses' day. (Exodus 7:15-25; 9:22-33) But upon what "third of the earth" was this destructive downpour hurled after the first trumpet peal?

In the Bible the number three is used to signify emphasis, a thing being said or done three times being thus made very emphatic. Likewise a third of anything would signify a sizable or considerable part. (Ezekiel 21:27; Revelation 4:8; Ecclesiastes 4:12) Although it was a significant, important part of the earth, that fact would not itself identify which "third of the earth" it was. However, in Isaiah 19:23-25 Jehovah God mentions a vital "third," namely, ancient Israel as taken along with Assyria, the northern

Second World Power of Bible history, and Egypt, the southern First World Power. This helps us to identify the "third," for, in Bible prophecy, unfaithful Israel, which was in the old Law covenant with Jehovah God, typifies modern-day Christendom, which claims to be spiritual Israel and to be in the new covenant with God through Christ the Mediator. Well, then, was Christendom the "third [part] of the earth" upon which the things that followed the blowing of the first of the seven trumpets were hurled? Yes, indeed.

On "The Day," Friday, September 8, 1922, at the second Cedar Point, Ohio, convention, the president of the Watch Tower Bible & Tract Society gave the speech on the Bible text, "The kingdom of heaven is at hand." (Matthew 4:17, *AV*) This stirring speech declared that Christendom is fatally smitten by God and doomed to eternal death because it had renounced God's kingdom by Christ and had recommended, approved and supported the human makeshift, the League of Nations, as "the political expression of the Kingdom of God on earth." Sunday afternoon, September 10, after his public address to an audience of 18,000, the president, J. F. Rutherford, read and moved the adoption of a resolution entitled "A Challenge." The vast audience rose to its feet, with mighty applause, in endorsement of this resolution that pointed out the disloyalty of Christendom's clergy to God in supporting the bloody World War I and thereafter repudiating God's Messianic kingdom by espousing the political League of Nations and trusting in it for world peace and security. The following month upward of forty-five million copies of this resolution and supporting material began to be distributed world wide.

From then on till now Christendom has, figuratively speaking, suffered what followed the first angel's blowing his trumpet in heaven. She, and especially her clergy, Catholic and Protestant, has been pelted, not with drops of refreshing rain of God's blessing, but with hardened water of a pounding hail in the form of strong, heavy charges and exposés based on Bible truth and prophecy, betokening God's curse. The fiery expressions of his wrath, couched in Biblical language, have been cast at her, consuming the false Christian cloak under which she carries on her religious hypocrisy. For all the human blood that she has shed and caused to be shed so wantonly God has doused her with blood, showing her to be blood-stained and deserving of death at God's hands. He will make her drink blood in her own destruction.

Christendom, the population of which is today reported to be 977,383,000 members, almost a third of the total population of the earth, is the "third of the earth" that has been spiritually "burned up" by that symbolic fire from heaven. Her religious organization, long thought to be so stable and reliable, is blackened from the scorching heat and proved to be pagan, not Christian. She is under God's fiery wrath and not his reviving blessing. Her prominent ones, the clergy, Catholic, Orthodox and Protestant, are the "third of the trees" that are "burned up" as being no ordained Christian ministers of His. Her hundreds of millions of church members, multitudinous like the blades of green grass, are the vegetation, "all the green vegetation," that was "burned up" as not being real followers or imitators of Jesus Christ, practicers of true Christianity.

The result of the downpour of symbolic hail, fire and blood upon Christendom shows her to be barren of Christian fruitage to God. Her appearance reminds us of the soil that is described in Hebrews 6:8, that is "rejected and is near to being cursed; and it ends up with being burned." This religiously burned-up condition is becoming more and more manifest in Christendom all the time.

THE SECOND ANGEL BLOWS HIS TRUMPET

Was that shocking—calculated to hurt religious feelings? But brace yourself to look at what is next portrayed. The apostle John writes: "And the second angel blew his trumpet. And something like a great mountain burning with fire was hurled into the sea. And a third of the sea became blood; and a third of the creatures that are in the sea which have souls died, and a third of the boats were wrecked."—Revelation 8:8, 9.

Catching up, as it were, the loud peal of the trumpet blown by the second angel, the members of the anointed remnant on earth echoed forth ear-tingling pronouncements as "faithful witnesses" during the year 1923 and into the early part of 1924. These Biblically supported proclamations did have an important impact upon the symbolic "sea." Not stable like the earth, the sea symbolizes the fluid-like, heaving, radical, revolutionary and aggressively militaristic elements of humankind. Although dissatisfied and in revolt against the long-established system of things, this element does not look to God for his promised Messianic kingdom as the cure-all for humanity's ills but is against that theocratic government. Lacking Bible faith, it is ungodly and is foaming forth its own worldly propaganda and schemes, with threats of force and violent measures. (Isaiah 57:20; 17:12, 13) But what was the fiery thing that was hurled into this symbolic sea?

It was not a mountain, but was "something like a great mountain burning with fire." It was a large earth-mass of the size of a "great mountain." It was hurled, not from heaven, but from the symbolic earth, it being wrenched from this "earth" and moved with a swift pitch into the "sea." Since in the Bible a mountain is used to symbolize a political government of the stable earth, this burning earth-mass of mountainous proportions pictures the issue of radical, socialistic, revolutionary government that was hurled into the sea of restless, revolt-minded people, a considerable part of mankind, forasmuch as a "third of the sea" became affected.

At this particular time this political issue was

being thrust upon the people. On November 7, 1917, the radical Bolsheviki overthrew the Russian government and set up an ungodly communist government. On October 30, 1922, Benito Mussolini and his radical party (founded in Milan, Italy, March 23, 1919) made their "march on Rome" and established a Fascist corporative state. On November 8, 1923, in Munich, Germany, Adolf Hitler, assisted by General Erich Von Ludendorff, organized the revolt known as the Hitler putsch, in favor of Nazism. How was all this going to affect the unstable, restless elements of humankind—for good or for ill?

A THIRD OF THE "SEA" BECOMES BLOOD

What did God foresee and foreshow? To him this great mass of mountainous proportions, wrested from the stable earth, was not to be a blessing. True, it was a fiery issue and still is, but to God it was like a self-consuming mountain; it was, like ancient Babylon, a "ruinous mountain," a "burnt-out mountain." (Jeremiah 51:25) So, in Revelation 8:8, God pictured this issue and political movement for radical, revolutionary government as "something like a great mountain burning with fire." It was very different from the symbolic mountain of his Messianic kingdom described in Isaiah 11:9; 25:6-8. That this violent thrusting of this revolutionary, socialistic, communistic type of government would bring no blessing is portrayed by the effect that the 'burning mountain' mass had upon the symbolic sea into which it was hurled: "A third of the sea became blood."

Despite the claims made for human blood transfusions in this twentieth century, no creatures could live in that large sea area that had been turned to blood. During the plague of blood upon ancient Egypt in Moses' day, the fish in the bloodied waters died, the Nile River began to stink, and the Egyptians were unable to drink from their deified Nile River. (Exodus 7:20, 21) Likewise, with the symbolic "third of the sea" that was turned to blood by the plunging in of the mountainlike fiery mass: "A third of the creatures that are in the sea which have souls died." (Revelation 8:8, 9) Thus God portrayed that life in a materialistic paradise on earth was not possible through any of these radical, revolutionary political movements. By Communist aggressions since 1917 across many countries, and with the establishing of Communist China on the Asian mainland in 1949, a third of the world's population have now been brought under atheistic Communist rule. Now, after all these years of Communist rule, what is the condition, what is the future outlook, of this "third of the sea" of humanity? Just like God's prophetic portrayal after the second angel trumpeted. Like dead men's blood!

Fulfillment of Bible prophecy indicates that, since the year 1918 C.E., Jesus Christ has been present in the spiritual temple of God and dividing the peoples of all the nations the same as a shepherd of the Mideast divides the sheep of his flock from the goats. (Matthew 25:31-46) Certainly the violent, aggressive, radical, revolutionary movements and governments have so functioned as to shove their subjects over onto the side of symbolic goats, namely, those who are to be destroyed in the coming war of Arma-

geddon for their faulty treatment of the anointed remnant of Christ's spiritual brothers. Quite appropriately, then, and manifestly under the guidance of the second angelic trumpeter, the International Bible Students Association held a regional convention in Los Angeles, California, U.S.A., August 18-26, 1923. On Saturday, August 25, the president of the Watch Tower Bible & Tract Society, J. F. Rutherford, spoke on the closing parable in Jesus' prophecy on the "conclusion of the system of things." It was the parable of the sheep and the goats.—Matthew 24:3 to 25:46.

Then the speaker presented to his audience of 2,500 a historic resolution entitled "A Warning." By an overwhelming response the audience expressed their approval of the resolution, which exposed the failure of the clergy of Christendom to aid Christ's spiritual brothers in proclaiming world wide the good news of God's kingdom, the religious clergy thereby showing goatish qualities. In conclusion the resolution appealed to the sheeplike people to turn, not to the clergy-supported League of Nations, but to God's kingdom as the "only remedy for national and individual ills." On Sunday, August 26, this same resolution was adopted at the convention's public meeting attended by 30,000. In the October 15, 1923, issue of *The Watch Tower* appeared the eight-page article entitled "The Parable of the Sheep and the Goats." Later, in December of the same year the manufacture began on the tract entitled "Proclamation—A Warning to All Christians" and containing the convention resolution. In the United States alone 13,478,400 copies were printed for circulation. Other millions were published abroad.

It has been publicly admitted by religious clergymen that the failure of the clergy of Christendom was largely responsible for the growth and spread of communism in eastern Europe, in Russia and neighboring lands that had been for centuries a powerful part of Christendom. It is well known that till now the Russian Orthodox Church has been acting as the handmaid of the Communist regime, but the dedicated Christian witnesses of Jehovah have been driven underground. By the banning and persecuting of these Christian witnesses the radical, revolutionary ruling elements of this world are acting anything but like the "sheep" of Jesus' parable. The parable sets out that the symbolic "goats" are cursed by the God of heaven. (Matthew 25:41-46) In agreement with this divine curse the radical, revolutionary, socialistic, communistic movement is death-dealing; it is lifeless, like the shed blood of a dead man. Being cast into the vast sea of mankind, it has caused a considerable part, "a third of the sea," to be turned to blood. Proportionately, a "third of the creatures that are in the sea which have souls" face death at Armageddon's war.

The inability of the "red" socialistic and communistic movement to give life, happiness and peace to the people was further emphasized even while the tract "Proclamation—A Warning to All Christians" was being circulated. On February 15, 1924, the sixty-four-page booklet bearing the name "A Desirable Government" was published by the Watch Tower Bible & Tract Society, and before the year was ended the Society had sent out 741,449 copies of this revealing booklet. It pointed forward to the approaching death of all worldly man-made governments, especially following the subheading "Government Failure—A Malady."

Though Russia was then in only the seventh year of Bolshevik, Communist, Red rule, page 5, paragraph 2, of *A Desirable Government* said: "Leading men of the world have advanced various schemes or methods for governmental reform. But these all have proven abortive." This included the attempted political reform in Russia, for page 23 took note of the "great revolution in Russia, Germany, Austria, and other European countries." Page 54 was quite correct in speaking of more trouble "similar to what Russia has already undergone."

The radical, revolutionary organizations that ride

the waves of this bloodied "sea" and that exploit the creatures in such symbolic sea are likewise doomed to be destroyed in the storm of Armageddon. This is what was prophetically pictured after the second angel trumpeted: "And a third of the boats were wrecked." (Revelation 8:9) The radical, revolutionary, socialistic, communistic rulerships will not succeed, for they hate and are working against the long-prayed-for kingdom of God by his Christ. Today there is no reason to think differently from what the Watch Tower Society's book, entitled "Government" and published in 1928, said:

The soviet government has not been a success and never can be, and is far from being satisfactory to the people who have tried it. As in all other forms of government where the people are supposed to have a voice, the demagogues and party men dominate the various councils; and therefore the government has presented no advantages over any other government. In fact, bolshevism has resulted in great suffering of the people, and it is feared by many of the other nations and governments of the earth.

Every form of government man has tried, whether that be monarchy, aristocracy, democracy, republic or social, has been unsatisfactory.—Pages 244, 245.

To this day Jehovah's Christian witnesses, the worldwide advocates and proclaimers of God's kingdom, continue to sound out everywhere the information that was pictorially disclosed after the second heavenly "angel" blew his trumpet back in 1923.

THE THIRD ANGEL BLOWS HIS TRUMPET

The time for the sounding of the third trumpet arrives, and what the apostle John sees in vision is a "star," but not one of the "seven stars" in the right hand of the glorified Jesus Christ and which stars symbolize the seven "angels of the seven congregations." (Revelation 1:16-20) Writes John: "And the third angel blew his trumpet. And a great star burning as a lamp fell from heaven, and it fell upon a third of the rivers and upon the fountains of waters. And the name of the star is called Wormwood [*Greek*,

The Absinthe]. And a third of the waters turned into wormwood, and many of the men died from the waters, because these had been made bitter."—Revelation 8:10, 11.

Here not the salty sea, but the fresh waters, the rivers and the fountains of waters, were affected. The "great star" that plunged from heaven into these fresh waters evidently pictures a class of persons who enjoyed religious privileges like those of the symbolic "seven stars" but who fall from the high level of privilege and opportunity that the Bible assigns to religious "stars." True dedicated, baptized, spirit-begotten Christians are said to be raised up and seated together "in the heavenly places in union with Christ Jesus." (Ephesians 2:1-6) But this symbolic "great star" does not live up to its profession of being up there. Instead, by its course of action it falls and comes short of being on such a high spiritual elevation. It could have been a spiritual illuminator, but, as it drops from heaven, it is "burning as a lamp" or like a torch, ablaze, on fire to its own destruction. So its name is Wormwood, literally, Absinthe, that name of a bitter plant of which there are several varieties in the Middle East. Its effect upon the fresh waters into which it falls is not sweetening, but is embittering, turning them into wormwood.

In view of these features about it, what religious class of people could this blazing, falling "great star" picture but the apostate Christian clergy of Christendom, Catholic, Orthodox and Protestant and otherwise sectarian? Especially since the days of Roman Emperor Constantine the Great of the fourth century C.E., the religious clergy of Christendom have pretended to offer to the people in their churches the fresh water of the truth that is life-giving, life-sustaining. But what has been the effect of the clergy's fall from true Christianity into apostasy upon the symbolic rivers and water springs of Christendom, the area of which has embraced a large section of the world's population? The people need fresh water from rivers and fountains in order to live. But what should have been spiritual "water" to sustain the spiritual life of the peoples, the apostate Christian clergy have turned into undrinkable, deadly, bitter wormwood waters. How? By teaching their church members false, pagan, unchristian, unbiblical doctrines, such as eternal torment in hellfire, and by leading the peoples into unchristian practices such as bloody, carnal warfare.

How embittering, how death-dealing the doctrines and religious course of the apostate Christian clergy have been to the peoples of Christendom was specifically emphasized in the year 1924 C.E. As though it was designed to proclaim publicly the facts about this by an ear-splitting trumpet blast, the International Bible Students Association held a general convention in Columbus, Ohio, U.S.A., July 20-27, 1924. On Friday, July 25, the president of the Association delivered the address on "The Temptation—Fall and Victory." At its close he introduced a resolution designated "The Indictment," which was overwhelmingly adopted by the conventioners. The following Sunday, July 27, the president delivered the public address entitled "Civilization Doomed," this doomed civilization including outstandingly Christendom.

That resolution, which featured the Columbus convention—what an "indictment" indeed it was against the apostate religious clergy of all Christendom! How the section thereof under the subheading "Doctrines" exposed the false, God-defaming doctrines of the clergy. It showed the deadliness of the religious course in which the clergy, along with their comrades in politics, were leading the people of Christendom! The clergy were making the people drink what was religiously bitter to them, like wormwood, yes, drink what meant spiritual death to them now and, at Armageddon, eternal physical destruction.

The extent of the damage done by the starlike clergy was well portrayed by what the apostle John saw in the vision, namely, that "many of the men died from the waters, because these had been made bitter." (Revelation 8:11) What misleading "stars" these clergy have been to Christendom, which claims to be most civilized! Instead of guiding people to God's kingdom, they have steered the people into the League of Nations and the United Nations. In contrast with Bible-student Christians who are true "ambassadors substituting for Christ," what a fall the clergy have had!—2 Corinthians 5:20.

As if by a trumpet this indictment of the clergy of Christendom was pealed throughout the earth, including Australia. In the United States alone 13,545,000 copies of the resolution "The Indictment" were printed for circulation. Other millions of copies, in foreign languages, were printed abroad. Worldwide distribution began in the following October, over 50,000,000 copies being distributed finally. The Indictment also went out through the columns of *The Watch Tower* in its issue of September 1, 1924. That was only a beginning of the proclamation of the things that were disclosed after the trumpet blast by the third heavenly angel. Again and again thereafter, by radio stations, singly and in chains, by public lectures, by books, booklets, magazines and tracts, the proclamation of the apostasy of Christendom's clergy and its effects upon the people has been unsparingly made. In 1963 was published the 704-page book *"Babylon the Great Has Fallen!" God's Kingdom Rules!*, and by 1968 2,803,296 copies had been printed. In 1969 appears the book *Is the Bible Really the Word of God?* in eleven principal languages, its first edition being three million copies. This book further exposes the falling away of the clergy from true Christian faith.

However, the overall panoramic picture of things in this present system of things is not yet complete. There are four more heavenly angels yet to be heard from. Let us not be afraid to see the whole picture presented, and so let us continue to look with the apostle John at the continuing vision as it is unveiled.

THE FOURTH ANGEL BLOWS HIS TRUMPET

"And the fourth angel blew his trumpet. And a third of the sun was smitten and a third of the moon and a third of the stars, in order that a third of them might be darkened and the day might not have illumination for a third of it, and the night likewise." —Revelation 8:12.

From such an unusual happening as this in outer space, a third of the earth or its inhabitants would not have any light from heaven either by day or by night. This would cover an area of the earth greater than ancient Egypt, which, in the days of the prophet Moses, was smitten with three days of complete darkness day and night, so intense that it could be felt. That ancient affliction on Egypt was considered to be a blow, a plague, its ninth in a series of ten plagues from the hand of Jehovah God. (Exodus 10:21-23) However, Jehovah's oppressed people in Egypt were made an exception; they did have "light in their dwellings." Today the faithful remnant of anointed Christians, together with the "great crowd" of companion worshipers of Jehovah God, do have spiritual light from heaven in their dwellings. They point to the darkness upon the "third" of the earth.

The Holy Scriptures have been outspoken in declaring that all the Gentile peoples of the earth, those not belonging to Jehovah's chosen people, were in religious darkness, these being alienated from the true God. (Ephesians 5:8; 6:12; Colossians 1:13; 1 Thessalonians 5:4, 5; 1 Peter 2:9; Isaiah 60:1, 2) So it would be nothing strange to portray the so-called pagan peoples as being in spiritual darkness. But what about Christendom, which distinguishes herself from the "pagans"?

Christendom, which now comprehends about one-third of the world's population, claims to be basking in spiritual light from heaven day and night. She has the Holy Scriptures circulated throughout her realm to the number of two billions of copies, in 1,337 tongues. She boasts of having the clergy, Catholic,

Orthodox and Protestant, as being the only duly ordained ministers of Christian religion and as being the only ones authorized to explain the Holy Bible. She assumes to have the light of divine favor because she can brag of having the prominent politicians, the top-ranking military men and the wealthy businessmen as the leading men of her churches. She has the protection of the political state. From Christendom's viewpoint, she enjoys alone the spiritual light from the heavens, as represented by the sun, the moon and the stars. But what does the "fourth angel" reveal to be the facts?

As can be appreciated today, under the guidance of the fourth heavenly angel a regional convention of the International Bible Students Association was held in Indianapolis, Indiana, U.S.A., August 24-31, 1925. Friday afternoon, August 29, the then president of the Association delivered to the thousands of conventioners the speech on the theme "A Call to Action," based on the prophecy of Isaiah 62:10. At the close he introduced the resolution that came to be called "Message of Hope." This resolution dealt principally with Christendom, which claims to be the spiritual light of the world. But note what paragraphs 6, 7 say:

> Catholicism claims and assumes that which justly belongs exclusively to God. Modernists deny God, deny His Word and His plan of redemption, and offer blind force as a remedy for man's undone condition. Fundamentalists, while professing to believe the Bible, by their course of action deny the same. They teach false and God-dishonoring doctrines, and together with Catholics and Modernists are allied with the political and commercial powers of the world in blasphemously claiming the ability to establish God's kingdom on earth. All of these have combined under Satan their superlord to push God into a corner and to dishonor his name.

> The results are that the people are smarting under the oppressive weight of commercial profiteers and their allies, have lost faith in the political leaders, and no longer have respect for the religionists who have misled them. Being guided by the false light of such an ungodly and unholy alliance, the peoples have fallen into darkness. . . .

By a rising vote the conventioners adopted the resolution that proclaimed such revealing facts as these. Sunday afternoon, August 31, the president delivered the public address on the subject "Lifting Up a Standard for the People," which was attended by around 10,000 persons. Before this address was delivered, the resolution "Message of Hope," previously adopted by the convention, was read to the public. At the close of the public talk the great audience rose in approval of the Resolution and the supporting argument. The resolution was also published in the magazines *The Watch Tower* and *The Golden Age,* but on Saturday, October 31, 1925, the distribution of this "Message of Hope" in tract form began in a number of English-speaking countries of Christendom. Finally around 50,000,000 copies in various languages were circulated. Thus, far and wide it was disclosed to the people that in the case of Christendom as a religious third of the population, "the day might not have illumination for a third of it, and the night likewise." (Revelation 8:12) She was not enjoying the light of heaven's truth and favor.

Christendom's floundering around helplessly in the chaos of world affairs painfully plays up the utter religious darkness in which she finds herself. The anointed remnant of Christian witnesses of Jehovah has fearlessly kept on pointing out the bedarkened situation that was symbolically disclosed after the blowing of the fourth trumpet. Attention was specially focused on the deepening darkness of Christendom by the publishing, in 1955, of the thirty-two-page booklet entitled "Christendom or Christianity—Which One Is 'the Light of the World'?" This was given wide circulation in a number of languages. But the contrast between true Christianity and Christendom continues till now to be exposed by the faithful anointed remnant and the associated "great crowd" of God's "men of good will." More and more people see it!

"AN EAGLE"

The people who were adversely affected might have thought that the fulfillment of the tableaus that followed the blowing of the first four trumpets by the heavenly angels was woeful enough. But more and worse things of this kind were to come, and they did, according to the full purpose of God. This was pictured by the interruption that the apostle John saw take place between the sounding of the fourth trumpet and that of the fifth. He writes: "And I saw, and I heard an eagle flying in midheaven say with a loud voice: 'Woe, woe, woe to those dwelling on the earth because of the rest of the trumpet blasts of the three angels who are about to blow their trumpets!' "—Revelation 8:13.

As an eagle flies so high, it can be seen by people over a large area above which it flies and can also be heard widely. It being far-visioned, it could see well ahead of itself with sharp distinctness. (Job 39: 29) It will be remembered that one of the "four living creatures" that John saw about God's heavenly throne included one, the fourth one, "like a flying eagle." (Revelation 4:6, 7) This eagle-like "fourth living creature" invited John to come and see the fourth apocalyptic horseman, Death, riding on a pale horse and followed by Ha'des. (Revelation 6:7, 8) Whether the symbolic "eagle" that John saw flying in midheaven pictured one of God's heavenly cherubs making an announcement of world importance, we cannot be sure. At least, this eagle represents some servant or servant class whom God favors with a prevision of things immediately ahead and who informs the anointed remnant on earth, just as the "eagle" advised the apostle John in advance. The remnant was thus reminded that three more trumpets were yet to be blown, preceding the bold disclosure of further woeful things. This meant more work for the remnant, calling for great courage. Accordingly, further international assemblies were planned and announced by the Watch Tower Bible & Tract Society.

CHAPTER 17

The Blowing
of the Fifth
and Sixth Trumpets

WHAT unfolded itself to the vision of the apostle John after the fifth heavenly angel blew his trumpet reminds us very much of the frightful plague of locusts that was prophetically described in Joel 2:1-11. In fact, a number of the ideas and comparisons in Joel's prophecy correspond with those in John's description. In vivid terms the apostle John writes:

"And the fifth angel blew his trumpet. And I saw a star that had fallen from heaven to the earth, and the key of the pit of the abyss was given him. And he opened the pit of the abyss, and smoke ascended out of the pit as the smoke of a great furnace, and the sun was darkened, also the air, by the smoke of the pit. And out of the smoke locusts came forth upon the earth; and authority was given them, the same authority as the scorpions of the earth have. And they were told to harm no vegetation of the earth nor any green thing nor any tree, but only those men who do not have the seal of God on their foreheads.

"And it was granted the locusts, not to kill them, but that these should be tormented five months, and the torment upon them was as torment by a scorpion when it strikes a man. And in those days the men will seek death but will by no means find it, and they will desire to die but death keeps fleeing from them.

"And the likenesses of the locusts resembled horses

prepared for battle; and upon their heads were what seemed to be crowns like gold, and their faces were as men's faces, but they had hair as women's hair. And their teeth were as those of lions; and they had breastplates like iron breastplates. And the sound of their wings was as the sound of chariots of many horses running into battle. Also, they have tails and stings like scorpions; and in their tails is their authority to hurt the men five months. They have over them a king, the angel of the abyss. In Hebrew his name is Abaddon, but in Greek he has the name Apollyon."—Revelation 9:1-11.

The star now seen by the apostle John is different from the "great star burning as a lamp" seen falling from heaven after the third angel blew his trumpet. (Revelation 8:10) Who, then, is this "star that had fallen from heaven" that John saw after the blowing of the fifth trumpet? We are helped to identify him, for "the key of the pit of the abyss" was given to him, and he unlocked this place. Also, he is "the angel of the abyss," and he is king over the terrible swarm of locusts that fly out of the abyss. In Hebrew his name is Abaddon, meaning "Destruction"; and in Greek it is Apollyon, meaning "Destroyer." All this plainly identifies the "angel" as picturing Jesus Christ, the Son of Jehovah God.

About a century before John's vision this Son of God had descended from heaven to earth to be born as the man-child Jesus. At his sacrificial death and burial he descended into the abyss. (Philippians 2: 5-8; Ephesians 4:7-10; Romans 10:6, 7) On the third day of his death God brought him up from the abyss and gave him the key of the abyss, which here corresponds with Ha'des, the common grave of dead mankind. He thus has power over dead mankind.

This is why, in Revelation 1:17, 18, the resurrected Jesus Christ says that he is now forever alive from the dead and "I have the keys of death and of Ha'des." He is also the "angel" of Revelation 20: 1-3 who comes down and binds Satan the Devil and his demons and throws them into the abyss and shuts them up in it for a thousand years. After the end of his thousand-year reign over mankind, he will destroy Satan the Devil and his demons following their release from the abyss for a little while. In this way he will fulfill God's prophecy in Genesis 3:15. At the approaching battle of Armageddon he will also destroy the earthly enemies who then fight against God's Messianic kingdom. (Revelation 19:11-21; 20: 7-10) He will fulfill his name "Destroyer."

Who, now, are the symbolic locusts that he releases from the "pit of the abyss"? Insect locusts do not have a king over them (Proverbs 30:27); but Jesus Christ is king over these symbolic "locusts," for which reason they must be the present-day anointed remnant of his disciples who are joint heirs with him for the heavenly kingdom. That is why upon the heads of these "locusts" there were "what seemed to be crowns like gold." (Revelation 9:7) During the first world war (1914-1918 C.E.) Jehovah God had permitted them to be put by their religious, political and military enemies into the deathlike, inactive spiritual condition like that inside the "pit of the abyss"; but after World War I God used the reigning King Jesus Christ to release these symbolic locusts from this "pit of the abyss." How? By revitalizing them for worldwide Kingdom work foretold in Matthew 24:14 and Mark 13:10.

These symbolic locusts are subject to the glorified Jesus Christ as their King and as Head of the Christian congregation. To point up this fact, the "locusts" are pictured as having "hair as women's hair," although "their faces were as men's faces." Women's hair, being naturally long, is a sign of having authority upon her head or exercised over her. (1 Corinthians 11:7-15; Ephesians 5:21-32; 1:22, 23) As they are followers of the "Lion that is of the tribe of Judah, the root of David," the teeth of these "locusts" are "as those of lions." Spiritually speaking, they are able as mature Christians to devour the hard, solid food found in God's Word, particularly the truths about God's kingdom as ruled by this "Lion that is of the tribe of Judah," Jesus Christ. (Hebrews 5:14 to 6:3; 1 Corinthians 3:1, 2) Like Christ, they have a love for God's righteousness, and this love of righteousness is like a breastplate to protect their hearts.

Quite fittingly, then, the "locusts" were pictured as having "breastplates like iron breastplates." In fact, they have on the "complete suit of armor from God," and this enables them to accept their part in suffering evil as 'fine soldiers of Christ.' (Ephesians 6:11-18; 2 Timothy 2:3, 4) Like an army of Christian soldiers, they are ready to do spiritual battle with weapons that are from God against false religious reasonings and "every lofty thing raised up against the knowledge of God." (2 Corinthians 10:3-5) No wonder those locusts "resembled horses prepared for battle"!—Revelation 9:7-9.

Unlike natural locusts, these symbolic locusts were told not to devour with their lionlike teeth any vegetation, green thing or tree. They were to harm "only those men who do not have the seal of God on their foreheads." These particular men would therefore not be of the 144,000 spiritual Israelites who are sealed with the "seal of the living God" before the "four winds" are let loose from the "four corners of the earth." (Revelation 7:1-8) Evidently, because "those men" make religious professions of being spiritual Israelites in God's new covenant, people would expect these to be the sealed ones. Among all the professors of the Christian religion, such "men" who do not have the seal would be the ordained clergy, Catholic, Orthodox and Protestant, together with the commercial profiteers, politicians and military officers who are prominent members of their churches. Their not being really "sealed" proves that they are false to their claims.

How were these to be 'harmed'? The symbolic locusts were instructed "not to kill them," but to torment them. This would be in a religious sense. How? As with scorpions' stings. In their tails the locusts had "stings like scorpions," with which to strike the unsealed men of Christendom. For how long? For "five months." This would mean for their lifetime as symbolic locusts, for the insect locust gets born in springtime and dies at the end of summer, thus after about five months of life. (Revelation 9:5, 10) Now to the question, When did this tormenting begin?

THE "LOCUST" ATTACK BEGINS

In the apostle John's vision, this tormenting operation began after the fifth angel blew his trumpet. In modern fulfillment, the symbolical trumpet blowing that heralded the locust attack occurred in the spring of 1926. On May 25-31 of this year the International Bible Students Association held an international convention in London, England, the famous Royal Albert Hall being used for the two public meetings the last two days and the Alexandra Palace for the other sessions. Friday afternoon, May 28, after the speech on "The Servant and Service" based on chapter forty-nine of Isaiah, the Association's president introduced the resolution entitled "A Testimony to the Rulers of the World." Enthusiastically the convention adopted this. Also, the newly published 384-page book *Deliverance* was released to the convention. Sunday night, May 30, the same resolution was first read to the packed-out Royal Albert Hall, after which the president, in support of the resolution, gave the thrilling public talk on "Why World Powers Are Tottering—The Remedy." Did this get publicity?

The next morning a London newspaper with a regular circulation of 800,000 copies came out with a full presentation of the resolution "A Testimony" and the supporting public speech, and by extra copies being printed a million or more copies reached the reading public. The speech pointed to the Devilish origin of the League of Nations, which was promoted and supported by the British Government and religiously advocated by the clergy of Britain and all of Christendom. According to Bible prophecy, it boldly declared the ultimate failure of such an international organization for world peace and security. The failure of the clergy to support God's true Messianic kingdom was forthrightly pointed out. The new book *Deliverance* called attention to similar world-important things. Likewise, the new booklet *The Standard for the People*, 110,000 copies of which the conventioners offered on Saturday on the streets of London on a small contribution. Later upward of fifty million copies of the resolution "A Testimony" were distributed free in tract form, in many languages, all around the globe.

The reaction that followed, in Britain, in America and elsewhere, made it manifest that the symbolic "locusts" were tormenting the foremost professing Christians "who do not have the seal of God on their foreheads." The exposure of human schemes that were devised in the name of religion and against God's kingdom stung like the sting from the tail of a scorpion. Figuratively speaking, such "men" would have liked to die in order to get away from this torment that stung their religious pride, but the "death" that they sought kept "fleeing from them." The great publicity that was being given to the stinging truths by radio, public lecture and printed literature was something they could not get away from. As the symbolic locusts winged their way about, a loud sound of publicity went along, "as the sound of chariots of many horses running into battle." The "locusts," in fact, were engaged in a real spiritual battle.—Revelation 9:5, 6, 9, 10.

Just as the insect locusts carry on their devastating work like a plague for the length of their lifetime, "five months," so the symbolic locusts carry on in this tormenting work for as long as they live and have this divine commission to do tormenting. When the deathblow was given to the League of Nations by World War II, this did not mean an end to their commission to torment religiously the unsealed men of Christendom. The world's peace and security organization reappeared in the form of the United Nations in 1945. This called for further stinging of the unsealed "Christians" who favor and hope in the United Nations instead of the heavenly kingdom of Jehovah God by Jesus Christ.

The "locusts" had come out of the "pit of the abyss," where they had been subjected to forced inactivity during World War I, and now they were determined to make the most of their dedicated Christian lives. The opening of the abyss for them by the "angel of the abyss" meant nothing good for the unsealed "men" of Christendom. As if out of a smoking "great furnace" the symbolic locusts came up against them and were all fired up, heated up with zeal for God's kingdom.

The rising smoke was a signal in advance of the woe that was to come upon the unsealed "men" of the professed Christian world. It portended that their day was not to be brightened, for by the smoke "the sun was darkened." In the case of a very heavy swarm of locusts, "sun and moon themselves have become dark," to persons on the ground underneath the flying locust swarm.

The apostle John reports that "also the air" was darkened by the smoke from the pit of the abyss. Like smoke thickening the atmosphere that one tries to breathe, so, too, the air close to the ground could be "darkened" or be thick with flying locusts in a dense moving swarm. (Revelation 9:2; Joel 2:10) If a literal, natural locust plague could be so woeful, a plague of symbolic locusts would be no less woeful, especially when the locusts have something like a scorpion's tail with a sting and persistently go after certain men to torment them to the point of their wanting to die! Good reason there was, then, for the onlooking apostle John to call it a "woe," when he said after seeing the tableau that followed the fifth trumpet: "The one woe is past. Look! Two more woes are coming after these things."

This was in agreement with what the eagle flying in midheaven had forewarned. (Revelation 9:12; 8:13) Just as the locust plague down in ancient Egypt in Moses' days had not harmed God's chosen people of Israel, so the first "woe" had not hurt the remnant of the 144,000 sealed ones of spiritual Israel, neither any of the "great crowd" of God-fearing persons who worship Jehovah God at his spiritual temple. (Revelation 7:2-15) It would be expected, then, that the remaining two "woes" would not hurtfully affect these two groups either.—Exodus 8:22, 23; 9:3-19.

THE SIXTH ANGEL BLOWS HIS TRUMPET

What form would the second "woe" take to afflict "those dwelling on the earth"? The apostle John informs us as he writes: "And the sixth angel blew his trumpet. And I heard one voice out of the horns of the golden altar that is before God say to the sixth angel, who had the trumpet: 'Untie the four angels that are bound at the great river Euphrates.' And the four angels were untied, who have been prepared for the hour and day and month and year, to kill a third of the men." (Revelation 9:13-15) The expression "the hour and day and month and year" would mark a precisely definite time, and this would indicate that Jehovah God is a strict Timekeeper.

Likewise, the "voice out of the horns of the golden altar" must be speaking just at the right time, in advance of the loosing of the "four angels." Since this golden altar was used by God's angel in conjunction with offering up the incense along "with the prayers of the holy ones before God," this "voice" evidently offers a prayer, instead of a command, to the sixth angelic trumpeter for the loosing of the "four angels." (Revelation 8:3, 4) Such a voice from the four altar horns properly symbolizes prayers for a release as offered by the anointed remnant as if with "one voice" and with full strength, the power pictured by the 'four horns.' They would pray, not for "four angels" in the invisible spirit realm to be released, but for themselves. Hence the word "angels" here takes its basic meaning of *messengers*.

In the apostle John's day the "great river Euphrates" was the eastern border of the Roman Empire. It was also the northeastern border of the land that Jehovah God promised to the patriarch Abraham. (Genesis 15:18, 19) However, in the Bible the principal association of this river was with ancient Babylon as founded by the "mighty hunter" Nimrod. (Genesis 10:8-10) In the year 607 B.C.E. the Babylonian Empire destroyed Jerusalem and its glorious temple and carried off most of the surviving Jews into exile in Babylon. Thereafter these Jews and their descendants were held bound in exile at the Euphrates River for seventy years. The prayers of the faithful, God-fearing ones ascended to Jehovah God for release at his due time, in the appointed year, the seventieth year of the utter desolation of the territory of Judah and Jerusalem. At the foretold seventieth year, 537 B.C.E., God answered their prayers and released them by the new Aryan king of Babylon, Cyrus the Conqueror. (Psalms 102:13-22; 126:1-4; 137:1-9; 2 Chronicles 36:20-23; Daniel 9:1-4) An experience similar to this was had by modern-day spiritual Israel.

During World War I the remnant of spiritual Israel was brought into bondage to Babylon the Great, the world empire of false religion, and her political and military paramours. After the end of the first world war on November 11, 1918, the faithful anointed remnant, held "bound" at the antitypical "great river Euphrates," prayed for release. To their surprise and joy, their being loosed or untied came in the first postwar year, 1919. In grateful devotion to the great God of their deliverance they now presented themselves as ready to do His will and work at any hour, day, month and year whatsoever. When the time came for Him to have the sixth trumpet sounded, to be followed by any action then due, they showed themselves ready and willing. They were indeed "prepared for the hour and day and month and year, to kill a third of the men."—Revelation 9:14, 15.

KILLING THE "THIRD OF THE MEN"

At the time for the killing to take place the mass of mankind was expected to be worshiping demons, idolizing images of various materials, committing murders, carrying on spiritistic practices and indulging in sexual immorality. (Revelation 9:20, 21) Yet not all of these were to be "killed," only a "third of the men." Population calculators figure that in the first century of our era, in the apostle John's day, the population of the whole world was 250,000,000, or only 50,000,000 more than the number of "horses" that John next saw. Today the world population is calculated as over 3,419,420,000 persons, whereas by the year 1930 it had reached only 2,000,000,000. A third of these would be a large number, but that is about the number of those who profess to be members of the churches of Christendom, Catholic, Orthodox, Protestant and other sectarians. No war of human history down to this very year has killed off so many persons, not even all human wars put together. So it is apparent that the killing of a "third of the men" is a symbolic or spiritual kind of killing. How was it done?

The "four angels" that were loosed from their bonds at the "great river Euphrates" appear to be the leaders of the 'killers.' The apostle John describes them after telling of the loosing of the "four angels," saying: "And the number of the armies of cavalry was two myriads of myriads: I heard the number of them. And this is how I saw the horses in the vision, and those seated on them: they had fire-red and hyacinth-blue and sulphur-yellow breastplates; and the heads of the horses were as heads of lions, and out of their mouths fire and smoke and sulphur issued forth. By these three plagues a third of the men were killed, from the fire and the smoke and the sulphur which issued forth from their mouths. For the authority of the horses is in their mouths and in their tails; for their tails are like serpents and have heads, and with these they do harm."—Revelation 9:16-19.

The number of the horsemen that the apostle John heard was "two myriads of myriads," that is to say, two hundred million, or twenty thousand times ten thousand. That was only 50,000,000 short of the estimated world population of John's day. And yet these 200,000,000 horsemen would kill only "a third of the men" by means of the plagues! Of course, a third of the world population by the year 1930 would be around 700,000,000. What, then, is pictured by these 200,000,000 horses and their riders? They were indeed a tremendous reinforcement to the "four angels" who had been released from bondage at the "great river Euphrates" to accomplish this tremendous killing in a spiritual sense. And evidently the "horses" were directed against the great world empire of false religion, Babylon the Great, prefigured by ancient Babylon on the river Euphrates. (Revelation 16:12-19) At the time of the blowing of the sixth trumpet the dominant part of Babylon the Great was under attack, namely, Christendom. Quite properly so, for Christendom is most hypocritical religiously, most reprehensible.

In the language in which the apostle John wrote (the common Greek) the expression "they had . . . breastplates" could apply both to the horses and to "those seated on them." Probably, though, it applies to only the riders, in which case this is the only feature that is described about those seated on the horses. The most description is given to the horses themselves. As the horses were pictured as having riders, this would indicate that these symbolic horses had human intellect controlling them and guiding them. Since the riders acted for or under the loosed "four angels" who are commissioned "to kill a third of the men," this signifies that the symbolic horses are under the intellectual control and guidance of these four "angels" or messengers, namely, the anointed remnant that was released from Babylon the Great in the year 1919. Only their "breastplates" come foremost to view.

"They had fire-red and hyacinth-blue and sulphur-yellow breastplates." Their breastplates in having such colors suggest three destructive things, fire, dark smoke, and sulphur. Thus these messengers or "four angels" would have a message of destruction in their hearts for the "third of the men" who were to be killed. It was a message of destruction like that which anciently befell Sodom and Gomorrah, upon which cities God rained down fire and sulphur from heaven and from the burning of which a smoke ascended "like the thick smoke of a kiln." (Genesis 19:23-28; Luke 17:28-30) Like Sodom and Gomorrah, so ancient Babylon was foretold to become a deserted ruin. —Jeremiah 50:40.

As foretold in Revelation 14:9-11, in the present "time of the end" of this system of things those persons who worship and serve the Devil's earthly political institutions are being tormented with fire and sulphur to the death and are having the "smoke of their torment" ascend forever and ever. Those political systems themselves will be thrown into the "fiery lake that burns with sulphur," which lake symbolizes destruction, "the second death." (Revelation 19:20; 20:10, 14, 15; 21:8) The divine message setting forth such destructive elements as these is what the anointed remnant keep to the front like a breastplate. In this way, just like the released "four angels," the released remnant forewarn the "third of the men" of their impending destruction at the coming execution of God's just judgment. They can pronounce such Babylonish "men" of Christendom to be already spiritually dead, awaiting destruction at God's hands. Thus these messengers like the "four angels" kill such "third of the men."

PUBLICITY "HORSES"

However, more attention is devoted to the horses than to their riders. More description is made of the horses as being the main thing in this prophetic tableau. Well, now, what do such symbolic "horses" picture? Symbolic cavalrymen rode these horses. So, too, the anointed remnant of messengers use symbolic horses, namely, the vehicles by means of which the remnant present their terrifying message. It is the vehicle that bears them to the people. (Esther 8: 10, 14) Armed with it they proceed against the "third of the men" who are to be "killed," spiritually speaking. That is to say, the symbolic "horses" picture the means of publicizing the judgment message that the anointed remnant use, particularly the printed page. Since in the Revelation (6:2, 4; 9:9; 19:11-21) as well as in the rest of the Bible horses imply warfare (except in Isaiah 28:28), the means of publicity used by the breastplated remnant have to do with spiritual warfare.

"And the heads of the horses were as heads of lions." This fact recalls that the first of the four living creatures that John saw around God's throne was like a lion, which pictured courageous justice. Also, the self-sacrificing Lamb of God was called "the Lion that is of the tribe of Judah, the root of David." (Revelation 4:6, 7; 5:5) Accordingly, the publicity means used by the anointed remnant since the blowing of the sixth trumpet show great courage and are justly used. Also, they have to do with the established heavenly kingdom of Jesus Christ, the symbolic Lion of the tribe of Judah, to which his forefather David belonged. That kingdom is God's agency by which he deals out destruction to the "third of the men" in His due time. That is why the description of the symbolic horses says: "Out of their mouths fire and smoke and sulphur issued forth. By these three plagues a third of the men were killed, from the fire and the smoke and the sulphur which issued forth from their mouths."—Revelation 9:17, 18.

This multitudinous means of publishing the destruction coming to the foes of God's Messianic kingdom also has a painful sting. This feature of the symbolic horses is called attention to in the words: "For the authority of the horses is in their mouths and in their tails; for their tails are like serpents and have heads, and with these they do harm." (Revelation 9:19) The serpentlike tail was thus just as destructive as what issued out of the mouths of the symbolic horses. The bite from such a serpentlike tail was poisonous, and it produced a burning sensation preliminary to the death of the one bitten. The symbolic horses had death-dealing power in a double way, both when approaching and when leaving their victims behind. There was no escaping it; the deadly message was bound to take effect, to indicate that the execution of God's judgment of destruction on the Kingdom's enemies is sure. What is announced by the symbolic horses of Kingdom publicity is certain to be carried out. What a woe such publicity is to the enemies! It is nothing invisible in the spirit world! It is visible, tangible!

Such symbolic horses were sent into action in modern times after the sounding of the sixth trumpet. This action began with the notable public event of importance to God's kingdom in the year 1927 C.E. On July 18-25 an international assembly was held in Toronto, Ontario, Canada, by the International Bible Students Association. On Sunday, August 24, 1927, the high point of this convention was reached, at the widely advertised public meeting. A visible public audience of 15,000 gathered to the convention auditorium, but there was an invisible audience of countless millions tied in with the speaker's stand by a radio network of fifty-three stations. This was the greatest radio chain ever forged up to that time, through the agency of the National Broadcasting Company of America. The subject of the hour's public address was "Freedom for the Peoples." First the speaker, the then president of the International Bible Students Association, read a resolution of ten paragraphs addressed "To the Peoples of Christendom." In the public address that followed he spoke in elucidation and support of the stirring resolution.

Listening supporters of Christendom must have felt the fiery, sulphurous heat when the opening resolution said:

> . . . Therefore God has decreed and declared that there shall come upon the world a time of tribulation such as never was known and that during that trouble "Christendom" or "organized Christianity," so-called, and all of Satan's organization shall be destroyed; and that Christ Jesus, the righteous King, will assume complete authority and control and will bless the peoples of earth.

> SIXTH: That it must be now apparent to all thoughtful peoples that relief, comfort and blessings so much desired by them can never come from the unrighteous system of "Christendom" or "organized Christianity," and that there is no reason to give further support to that hypocritical and oppressive system. In this hour of perplexity Jehovah God bids the peoples to abandon and for ever forsake "Christendom" or "organized Christianity" and to turn completely away from it, because it is the Devil's organization, and to give it no support whatsoever; and that the peoples give their heart's devotion and allegiance wholly to Jehovah God and to his King and kingdom and receive full freedom and the blessings God has in store for them. . . .

At the close of the public address that enlarged upon the resolution the visible audience rose to its feet in support of the resolution, and doubtless many of the invisible audience of millions did the same, except those of the "third of the men" who were to be killed, spiritually speaking. To these latter ones it was the beginning of a frightful "woe."

Now for the first time such an international convention resolution and its supporting speech were printed in booklet form for distribution, this booklet being entitled "Freedom for the Peoples." It was also translated into a number of languages.

On October 1, 1927, distribution of this *Freedom* booklet began. In course of time millions of copies were placed in the hands of the common people as well as their rulers. To use the symbolic illustration of Revelation 9:16-19, myriads of "horses" having lions' heads and breathing out fire, smoke and sulphur began dashing out, especially against Christendom, and under the intellectual driving and control of the anointed remnant, the released "four angels." These myriads of "horses" were only forerunners of what was to come. On March 1, 1927, the printing establishment of the Watch Tower Bible & Tract Society had moved into its new and larger eight-story factory in Brooklyn, New York, to carry on a greater offensive against the foes of God's kingdom by publishing and shipping out more Bibles, books, booklets, magazines and tracts, like sending out charging "horses."

But what about "two myriads of myriads" of such "horses"? Well, this new factory built and owned by the Watchtower Society, Incorporated, of New York, printed and shipped out millions of pieces of Bible literature during its first year, hundreds of myriads of copies of such. However, this factory became the nucleus of a grand factory complex that today occupies four city blocks, the latest addition being a ten-story factory that was dedicated January 31, 1968. To all this there have been added printing establishments connected with a number of the ninety-four branches of the Watch Tower Bible & Tract Society of Pennsylvania around the globe. These are all turning out enormous quantities of Bible literature. Together, throughout the years since 1927, they have printed and shipped out "two myriads of myriads" of pieces of Bible literature, and then some. The charging of these symbolic "horses" increased greatly when the Watch Tower's magazines began to be offered on the streets, from house to house, from store to store. Today 5,800,000 copies of each issue of *The Watchtower* are printed, twice a month. In 1968 there were 138,615,041 copies printed in 72 languages. Its companion magazine *Awake!* had a printing of 135,-689,298 in 26 languages. This sums up to 274,304,339 magazines printed in just one year.

Thus the charge of these symbolic "horses" against the doomed "third of the men" has increased from year to year, all such "horses" being under the guidance of the anointed remnant, the released "four angels." That is why all these hundreds of millions of pieces of Bible literature are not handled by and distributed through commercial bookstores, but are circulated by Jehovah's Christian witnesses, who go from house to house. From a spiritual standpoint, these symbolic "horses" continue killing off the "third of the men," but what about all the rest of mankind? Have they responded to the call to liberty, to Christian freedom from religious Babylon the Great?

A "great crowd" of God-fearing persons have done so throughout the earth, as foretold at Revelation 7:9-17. To them the religious priests and clergy of Babylon the Great have become as dead, without religious domination over these freed members of the "great crowd." But otherwise, comparatively speaking, it has been as the apostle John foresaw: "But the rest of the men who were not killed by these plagues did not repent of the works of their hands, so that they should not worship the demons and the idols of gold and silver and copper and stone and wood, which can neither see nor hear nor walk; and they did not repent of their murders nor of their spiritistic practices nor of their fornication nor of their thefts." (Revelation 9:20, 21) The hopes of the "third of the men" for world conversion to Christendom's religion are therefore doomed. The fiery-sulphurous, plaguing messages of the symbolic "horses" continue to point out the coming disaster to Christendom as the dominant part of Babylon the Great. The second "woe" must continue to its full realization!

CHAPTER 18

"There Will Be No Delay Any Longer"

THE SECOND woe that had been announced by the blowing of the sixth trumpet was not declared to be past until it is so stated at Revelation 11:14: "The second woe is past. Look! The third woe is coming quickly." In the meantime the apostle John in exile as a prisoner on the Isle of Patmos sees a new series of visions that seem to depart from the order of events but that must be shown in the Revelation before the blowing of the seventh trumpet. (Revelation 10:1 to 11:14) This new series involves him personally, bringing him into the action. In the vision John was still inside the "opened door in heaven," standing there and watching.

John sees what follows upon the opening of the seals of the scroll by the Lamb, "the Lion that is of the tribe of Judah, the root of David," that is, the glorified Jesus Christ. (Revelation 4:1, 2; 5:1-10) John has just seen the loosing of the "four angels" that were held bound at the great river Euphrates and then the appearance of frightful-looking horses with riders on them, 200,000,000 strong, dashing forward to kill "a third of the men" on the earth. (Revelation 9:13-20) Now the scene changes and John sees come down from heaven a "strong angel" of God, a special messenger of tremendous size, able to stand astride sea and dry land. John describes him as follows (Revelation 10:1-3):

"And I saw another strong angel descending from heaven, arrayed with a cloud, and a rainbow was

248

upon his head, and his face was as the sun, and his feet were as fiery pillars, and he had in his hand a little scroll opened. And he set his right foot upon the sea, but his left one upon the earth, and he cried out with a loud voice just as when a lion roars. And when he cried out, the seven thunders uttered their own voices."

The features as noted about this "strong angel" combine to indicate that he represents or stands for the glorified Lord Jesus Christ, who before his human birth was the archangel Michael. (Daniel 10:21; 12:1; Jude 9; Revelation 12:7) He is here described as being "arrayed with a cloud," wrapped in a cloud. Cloud is a feature associated with the glorified Jesus Christ, as in Revelation 1:7, where John writes of him, saying: "Look! He is coming with the clouds, and every eye will see him, and those who pierced him; and all the tribes of the earth will beat themselves in grief because of him. Yes, Amen." (Compare Daniel 7:13; Matthew 24:30, 31; 1 Thessalonians 4:17.) The cloud in which the "strong angel" is arrayed would conceal or make invisible his body except his arms and his lower legs. This reminds us that the second coming and second presence of Jesus Christ will be invisible to eyes of men on earth, because now he is a glorious heavenly spirit, and men on earth "see" him by discerning from the manifestations of his power that he is invisibly present, exercising his authority in heaven and on earth.—Matthew 25:31-46; 28:18.

The rainbow that was "upon his head" suggests that he is a special representative of Jehovah, "the God of peace," for the apostle John had seen in his earlier vision of the enthroned Jehovah God that "round about the throne there is a rainbow like an emerald in appearance." (Revelation 4:3; compare Ezekiel 1:28.) After the global flood of the prophet Noah's day the rainbow that Jehovah God caused to appear in the cloud betokened peace after storm and that His covenant toward mankind is peaceful, barring another inundation of the whole earth with water. (Genesis 9:8-17; Isaiah 54:9) How appropriate, then, for a rainbow to be upon the head of the "strong angel" who pictures Jesus Christ, inasmuch as he was foretold to become "Prince of Peace."—Isaiah 9:6, 7.

As regards this "strong angel," the fact that "his face was as the sun" corresponds with what the apostle John says concerning his earlier vision of Jesus Christ at the divine temple, that "his countenance was as the sun when it shines in its power." (Revelation 1:16) This may have reminded John of when he saw Jesus transfigured on a "lofty mountain" in the Middle East, that "his face shone as the sun, and his outer garments became brilliant as the light." (Matthew 17:1, 2) Such a sun could shine forth "with healing in its wings" or in its rays for those who are restored to God's favor. (Malachi 4:2) Here in this vision of the "strong angel" we see a happy combination of cloud, sun and rainbow. The cloud does not conceal the angel's lower legs.

So John could say of the "strong angel" that "his feet were as fiery pillars." The angel's feet were glorious as well as his head, just as in the vision of Revelation 1:14, 15. Whatever would come under his power, control and authority would come, as it were, under glorious feet, sturdy like pillars, no more to be tampered with than fire is. If the "sea" upon which he set his right foot was the Aegean Sea in which the Isle of Patmos lay, and the "earth" upon which he set his left foot was the nearby land of Asia Minor, then the "strong angel" was facing southward. Or, if the sea and earth were, so to speak, the Mediterranean Sea and ancient Palestine, he would still be facing south. This would picture how the whole earth, its seas and dry land, have now been put under the feet of the glorified Jesus Christ, that is to say, have been put in subjection to him by the Almighty God Jehovah. The fish of the sea and the living creatures on the dry land, including the birds who roost at the earth, are now all subject to the resurrected, glorified heavenly Jesus Christ. (Hebrews 2:5-9; Psalm 8:4-8) Especially so since 1914 C.E.

Thus the vision that the apostle John here sees of the "strong angel" applies since the year 1914 C.E. But why especially since then? Because in that year at the close of the appointed times of the Gentile nations the Lord Jesus Christ was enthroned in the heavens by his heavenly Father to reign and go subduing in the midst of his enemies. (Luke 21:24; Psalm 110:1-6; Acts 2:34-36) This meant that the "time of the end" had begun for the earthly system of things that was completely opposed to God's Messianic kingdom. The way was now cleared, all time requirements had been met, for the fulfilling of the things that were prophetically set forth by signs in the book of Revelation.—Daniel 11:35, 40.

In the hand of the "strong angel," evidently in his left hand, there was a "little scroll opened." This "little scroll" (Greek, *biblarídion*) would seem very small in the hand of such a large-size angel who could stand astride sea and earth, but it could contain much information. Its contents were not to be kept secret, for it was an opened scroll, so that the apostle John could read it. In fact, the scroll was meant for John's use.

The fact that the angel "cried out with a loud voice just as when a lion roars" comports with the role that the angel plays. He represents "the Lion that is of the tribe of Judah," the glorified Jesus Christ now clothed with kingly power in the heavens. (Proverbs 19:12; 20:2) The lionlike cry of the angel touches off a series of thunders: "When he cried out, the seven thunders uttered their own voices." (Revelation 10:1-3) It was a complete number (7) of thunders, and they symbolized expressions from Jehovah God, evidently as of storm warnings. In Psalm 29:3 it is written: "The voice of Jehovah is over the waters; the glorious God himself has thundered." For seven times in this psalm the expression "the voice of Jehovah" as being thunderous occurs. (Psalm 29:3, 4, 4, 5, 7, 8, 9) The "seven thunders" were not just a rumbling noise but they carried a message that John understood. That nothing of importance might be lost, he was about to begin writing down the thunderous message.

However, a voice, not from the "strong angel," but from heaven, stopped him from doing so. John says: "Now when the seven thunders spoke, I was at the point of writing; but I heard a voice out of heaven say: 'Seal up the things the seven thunders spoke, and do not write them down.'" It was not then the time for writing, but was, rather, the time for the apostle John to absorb the contents of the "little scroll opened." It is well known that a frequent commentator on the book of Revelation, namely, the first president of the Watch Tower Bible & Tract Society, Charles Taze Russell, was looked to by many to write his explanation of the complete book of Revelation. But before he could do so, he died two years after the end of the Gentile Times, or on October 31, 1916. The following year, in July of 1917, the Society under its second president, Joseph F. Rutherford, published the book *The Finished Mystery,* which set out a commentary on the whole of Revelation, as largely based on the previous writings of C. T. Russell.

In course of time *The Finished Mystery* proved to be unsatisfactory, because it had been written and published before many critical parts of the book of Revelation were fulfilled to make possible a correct understanding. So, although an attempt was made to write down things heard, *The Finished Mystery* did not break the secret of any "seven thunders" that had "uttered their own voices." (Revelation 10: 3) It was therefore a time to wait for accurate understanding to be made possible, and in the meanwhile to absorb spiritual knowledge from the hand of Jehovah God by means of his glorified Son Jesus Christ. This was done.

SWORN TO IN THE CREATOR'S NAME

Stopped from writing the message of the "seven thunders," the apostle John again focused his attention on the glorious "strong angel," and he hears some most encouraging words. He says: "And the angel that I saw standing on the sea and on the earth raised his right hand to heaven, and by the One who lives forever and ever, who created the heaven and the things in it and the earth and the things in it and the sea and the things in it, he swore: 'There will be no delay any longer; but in the days of the sounding of the seventh angel, when he is about to blow his trumpet, the sacred secret of God according to the good news which he declared to his own slaves the prophets is indeed brought to a finish.'"—Revelation 10:5-7.

Doubtless the apostle John saw the likeness in some respects between this vision and that of the prophet Daniel of the sixth century B.C.E., who wrote: "And I began to hear the man clothed with the linen, who was up above the waters of the stream, as he proceeded to raise his right hand and his left hand to the heavens and to swear by the One who is alive for time indefinite: 'It will be for an appointed time, appointed times and a half. And as soon as there will have been a finishing of the dashing of the power of the holy people to pieces, all these things will come to their finish.'"—Daniel 12:7.*

The "strong angel" of John's vision did not swear by himself or in his own name, but swore by someone higher, by the immortal Creator of heaven, earth and sea and of all things in them. So, too, the glorified Jesus Christ, the archangel Michael, recognized Jehovah God as the Creator of all things and as being higher and greater than his only-begotten Son. (John 14:28; 1 Corinthians 11:3; Revelation 3:14) In due recognition of this, the Lord Jesus Christ swore by

---

* See the book *"Your Will Be Done on Earth,"* pages 329-333, as published in 1958 by the Watch Tower Bible & Tract Society of Pennsylvania.

the Most High God Jehovah the Creator of all. Thus he assured John and all fellow Christians down till today that there will be no further delay on God's part.—Hebrews 6:16, 17.

The original Bible word here translated "delay" is the Greek word *khrónos,* which simply means "time" in an indefinite sense, so that the Authorized or King James Version Bible (of 1611) rendered the phrase: "There should be time no longer." This does not, of course, mean that time, which figures as a "fourth dimension" in Doctor Einstein's relativity theory, would be no more.* Rather, it means that there should be no further grant of time, in other words, no more "delay" as to the matter involved.

Why did this reference to "delay" come up for comment by the "strong angel"? Was it in answer to the question, raised by the martyred Christian souls after the Lamb opened the fifth seal of God's scroll: "Until when, Sovereign Lord holy and true, are you refraining from judging and avenging our blood upon those who dwell on the earth?" (Revelation 6:9, 10) Not altogether, and yet the answer to this question "Until when?" would be connected with the finishing of the "sacred secret of God," or, "the mystery of God." (Revelation 10:7, *NW,* margin, 1950 edition) The Creator of the sun, moon and stars has a fixed time for each feature in the outworking of his unchangeable purpose; and when the appointed time comes for a particular feature to be fulfilled, there is no grant of time given beyond that. This strict timekeeping holds true also regarding the "sacred secret of God."

What is that "sacred secret of God"?† The things that the apostle John sees following the sounding

---

* For an interesting comment on Revelation 10:6 according to the *Authorized (King James) Version* see *The Watch Tower* as of August 15, 1925, page 247, paragraph 33. Also, the book *Light,* Volume One, pages 178-180, under "Time No Longer," published in 1930.

† For an interesting suggestion on this see *The Watch Tower* as of April 15, 1919, pages 120, 121, under "The Finished Mystery," particularly the final two paragraphs. A reprint of July 1882.

of the trumpet of the seventh angel supply the information to clear up the mystery of it. According to the American Standard Version Bible, published in 1901, Revelation 10:7 reads: "But in the days of the voice of the seventh angel, when he is about to sound, then is finished the mystery of God, according to the good tidings which he declared to his servants the prophets." The "mystery of God" proves to be the Messianic kingdom of God in which the mysterious "seed" of "the woman" spoken of prophetically in Genesis 3:15 must reign. By means of this woman's "seed" Jehovah God must eventually "bruise" the symbolic serpent, Satan the Devil, in the head. (Romans 16:20, 25, 26) As a man on earth, Jesus Christ said to his disciples: "unto you is given the mystery of the kingdom of God." (Mark 4:11, *AS; AV*) Naturally there are mysterious features about this "mystery of God," such as to who compose this "seed" of God's "woman," and also who make up the congregation over which the Messiah or Christ is the Head.—Matthew 13:11; Luke 8:10; Ephesians 3: 3-9; Colossians 1:26, 27; 2:2; 4:3; 1 Timothy 3: 16, *AV; AS.*

This mystery or "sacred secret of God" is "according to the good news which he declared to his own slaves the prophets." The declaration of this mystery of God began with his own prophecy in the Garden of Eden as recorded by his slave the prophet Moses in Genesis 3:15. This information that God continued to declare to his slaves the prophets for them to proclaim to mankind is really "good news." God's greatest human prophet, Jesus Christ, foretold that "this good news of the kingdom" would be preached or heralded earth wide to all the nations before the "end" of the system of things came. (Matthew 24:14) Nevertheless, the proclamation of the Messianic kingdom of God is bad news, woeful news, to the vast majority of mankind in the "time of the end." That is why this "mystery of God" is rightly associated with the blowing of the seventh trumpet, the one that introduces the last of the three woes. (Revelation 8:13) To these it is a woe because the finishing of the "mystery of God" brings about the destruction of the entire visible organization of Satan the Devil on earth.

THE EATING OF THE "LITTLE SCROLL"

While the apostle John waited for the seventh angel to blow his trumpet to introduce the "third woe" (Revelation 11:14), he was given another assignment or was reminded of another assignment of service in addition to that of writing special letters to the "angels" or overseers of the "seven congregations that are in the district of Asia." (Revelation 1:4, 20; 2: 1 to 3:22) John was now quite an aged man, and during his exile or imprisonment on the penal isle of Patmos he was not able to do extensive witnessing. (John 21:20-23; Revelation 1:9) He was here like the "faithful and discreet slave" class of his fellow Christians in the years 1914-1918 of World War I. However, his earthly ministry as an apostle of Jesus Christ was not yet over. He was assured of this by what now occurred, of which he writes:

"And the voice that I heard out of heaven is speaking again with me and saying: 'Go, take the opened scroll that is in the hand of the angel who is standing on the sea and on the earth.' And I went away to the angel and told him to give me the little scroll. And he said to me: 'Take it and eat it up, and it will make your belly bitter, but in your mouth it will be sweet as honey.' And I took the little scroll out of the hand of the angel and ate it up, and in my mouth it was sweet as honey; but when I had eaten it up, my belly was made bitter. And they said to me: 'You must prophesy again with regard to peoples and nations and tongues and many kings.'" —Revelation 10:8-11.

This experience of the apostle John somewhat resembled that of the prophet Ezekiel in exile in the land of Babylonia in the year 613 B.C.E. Jehovah

God in vision told Ezekiel to open his mouth and eat what He was giving to the prophet. A hand was extended to him and it spread out the roll of a book before him so that he could see that it was written upon on front and back. When he ate the unrolled book it was in his mouth "like honey for sweetness." Having eaten it, he was now under command to "speak to the house of Israel." He tells us that a spirit bore him along and took him, "so that I went bitterly in the rage of my spirit, and the hand of Jehovah upon me was strong." (Ezekiel 2:8 to 3:14) Feeding on God's Word was sweet to the prophet Ezekiel, but this qualified him and made him responsible to say to the rebellious house of Israel messages that foretold bitter things for them.

The opened little book that the glorified Jesus Christ gave to his apostle John was evidently meant to be published by him. To feed upon this written word from God was sweet to John's spiritual taste, although that word expressed bitter things for rebellious mankind. John's belly was made bitter by eating it, but his own personal spirit was not embittered. Rather, the written word that John found bitter to digest foretold bitter things in store for rebellious mankind. John did not refuse to eat the written word because it would make his belly bitter and it would entail upon him the presenting of a message bitter for men.

The ones who told John that he must prophesy again were doubtless Jehovah God and the Lord Jesus Christ as pictured by the "strong angel" who gave John the book. They said that John must prophesy again, not before peoples, nations, tongues and kings, but "with regard to" them. By what John had already recorded in the first nine chapters of the Revelation he had prophesied regarding peoples, nations, tongues and kings. So the word "again" meant that he must write and publish the further part of the prophetic Revelation. This did not necessarily mean that John would be released from prison exile on the Isle of Patmos, for doubtless he finished writing all the Revelation there. According to tradition he was released, and thereafter he wrote his Gospel account of the life of Jesus Christ and his three letters, all of which are contained in the Holy Bible. But these last writings of John were not specifically prophesyings with regard to peoples, nations, tongues and kings. We are glad that John obeyed and did what he was told to do, for, as a result, we have today the full number (twenty-two) of chapters of the Revelation.

In harmony with the experience of the apostle John, the usefulness of the aged Christian congregation did not end during 1914-1918, when the activities of the anointed remnant were put under restrictions as on a penal island, like John on Patmos. Jehovah God had work for the remnant to do after World War I. The fulfillment of the prophecies of the Revelation had yet to take place to the full, and this implicated the anointed remnant. God had used them to make history in connection with the modern-day fulfillment of the Revelation. Hence any record of such fulfillment must, in order to be complete and true, include mention of the remnant of anointed Christians. It has been sweet to the spiritual taste of the remnant to feed upon the prophetic book of the Revelation. During World War I they did, by means of the book *The Finished Mystery*, feed on a commentary on the whole book of Revelation despite its being put under ban by the governments of some lands. The records show that they courageously endeavored to circulate this commentary on Revelation with all its bitter prophecies for rebellious mankind. They did not shrink back from publicizing those bitter prophecies.

CHAPTER 19

Death and Resurrection of the "Two Witnesses"

SUDDENLY, after the apostle John is told that he must prophesy again with regard to peoples, nations, tongues and kings, a temple appears before him. It is not the temple that was built by King Herod the Great at Jerusalem in Judea; that temple along with the holy city of Jerusalem was destroyed by the Roman armies under General Titus in the year 70 C.E. and had now lain in ruin for twenty-six years. Since the apostle John, in the vision, was near the "opened door in heaven" through which he had been invited to enter, this temple must have been a visionary one.—Revelation 4:1-3; 10:9-11.

This temple could remind John of the visionary temple that the prophet Ezekiel saw in the year 593 B.C.E., or in the fourteenth year after Jerusalem and its temple as built by King Solomon had been destroyed by the Babylonians. (Ezekiel 40:1-5) In Ezekiel's vision a manlike person of coppery appearance took the prophet on a tour of the temple as he explained it, measuring it with a flaxen cord and a six-cubit-long measuring reed. But in John's vision he himself was given a rodlike reed and was told to measure the visionary temple:

"And a reed like a rod was given me as he said: 'Get up and measure the temple sanctuary of God and the altar and those worshiping in it. But as for the courtyard that is outside the temple sanctuary, cast it clear out and do not measure it, because it has been given to the nations, and they will trample the holy city underfoot for forty-two months. And I will cause my two witnesses to prophesy a thousand two hundred and sixty days dressed in sackcloth.' These are symbolized by the two olive trees and the two lampstands and are standing before the Lord of the earth."—Revelation 11:1-4.

The temple sanctuary or *naós* (Greek) occupied only part of the temple area; and as for "those worshiping in it," these would be the 144,000 spiritual Israelites. (Revelation 7:1-8) As is suggested by the measuring operations described in Zechariah's prophecy (2:1-4), the measuring of the spiritual temple would be for finding out how many it would hold. Also, how many would minister at the golden incense altar by offering acceptable prayer to God through his mediator Jesus Christ? Even before the end of the Gentile Times in early fall of 1914 C.E., the anointed remnant as pictured by the apostle John had measured the final membership of the spiritual temple class and had found it Scripturally to be 144,-000.—Revelation 14:1-3; 1 Peter 2:5, 9; Ephesians 2:20-22; see *Zion's Watch Tower* as of November 1880, under "Gathering to Christ," paragraph 12.

However, why was the "courtyard that is outside the temple sanctuary" cast clear out and left unmeasured? This was because the courtyard was "given" to the Gentile nations, who were to trample the "holy city" underfoot for forty-two months. The courtyard therefore pictures those spiritual Israelites who were then yet on earth. They were in line for membership in the heavenly spiritual temple but had not yet measured up in a final, decisive way to all the requirements for membership in that temple. That was the state of the anointed remnant yet on earth at the end of the Gentile Times in 1914 C.E. They had not yet finally conquered this world so as to be worthy of the promise made in Revelation 3:12: "I will make him a pillar in the temple of my God, and he will by no means go out from it any more." Therefore, for a disciplinary test, this symbolic "courtyard" was cast clear out and left for the Gentile nations to profane along with trampling the holy city underfoot for forty-two months. When did it occur?

"FOR FORTY-TWO MONTHS"

History establishes that this occurred during World War I of 1914-1918 C.E. Forty-two months would not include the whole length of that first world war. According to the thirty-day length of a prophetic month, forty-two months would, at twelve months to a year, equal three and one-half years, or one thousand two hundred and sixty (30 x 42) days. This calculation would correspond with another way of measuring the same time period as given in Daniel 7:25. There it is said that the holy ones of the Most High God were to be given into the hand of the worldly political elements "for a time, and times and half a time." That means three and one-half times, each "time" being equivalent to a solar year of $365\frac{1}{4}$ days.

Being a Jew by birth, the apostle John would calculate the time according to the Jewish lunar calendar system. Since the Gentile Times began about the middle of the seventh Jewish lunar month (Tishri), they began about Tishri 15 (October 4/5) in the year 1914. Tishri 15 was also the date for the starting of the Jewish Feast of the Booths (Tabernacles, or Ingathering). For most of the years, from the start of the Feast of the Booths on Tishri 15 to the following Passover on Nisan 14 (after sundown) this time would be six lunar months, whereas only seven times out of every nineteen years an intercalary month known as VeAdar (or Second Adar) would be inserted in order to adjust the Jewish lunar calendar to the Gentile solar calendar.* But from Passover of one year to the Passover of the next year, the time would be one full lunar year (sometimes including thirteen lunar months because of the inserting of the intercalary month or VeAdar or Second Adar).

Accordingly, from the starting day of the Feast of the Booths in 1914 (the end of the Gentile Times) to the Passover of the year 1915 was six lunar months. From the Passover of the year 1915 to the Passover of the year 1918 was three years, there being only one intercalary month (VeAdar; Second Adar) duly inserted in 1916. The time being thus measured, from the starting day of the Feast of the Booths in 1914 (end of the Gentile Times) to the Passover of 1918 was three and a half years. Biblically speaking, this was three and a half "times," or "forty-two months," or, "a thousand two hundred and sixty days." This

---

* DIAGRAM OF THE YEAR 1916 C.E. WITH A COMPARISON OF THE LUNAR CALENDAR AND THE SOLAR CALENDAR

JEWISH CALENDAR	SECULAR (GREGORIAN) CALENDAR
Tebeth 25 (5676 A.M.)	January 1, 1916
Shebat 1	January 6
Adar 1	February 5
Adar Sheni 1 (Intercalary)	March 6
Nisan 1	April 4
Iyar 1	May 4
Sivan 1	June 2
Tammuz 1	July 2
Ab 1	July 31
Elul 1	August 30
Tishri 1 (5677 A.M.)	September 28
Heshvan 1	October 28
Kislev 1	November 26
Tebeth 1	December 26
Tebeth 6	December 31

NOTE: The Jewish day always begins at sundown of the day previous to the one indicated on the secular calendar.

See *The Universal Jewish Encyclopedia,* under the heading "Jewish Calendar for 200 Years."

time period, by beginning on Tishri 15, or on October 4/5, of 1914, ended on Nisan 14, or March 26/27, of 1918.*

In violation of the ending of the Gentile Times around October 4/5, 1914, the Gentile nations were fighting for world domination in World War I. At that time the kingdom of Jesus Christ, "the Lion that is of the tribe of Judah," was born in the heavens and enthroned at God's right hand. Then the newly crowned Messiah Jesus rode forth to conquer his earthly enemies, the Gentile nations, who had trampled on his Kingdom rights that King David's family had exercised in the land of Judah until ancient Babylon caused its desolation in 607 B.C.E. This was accomplished by about the middle of the lunar month Tishri (the seventh Jewish month), and then it was that the "seven times" of the "appointed times of the [Gentile] nations" began.—Luke 21:24; Daniel 4:16, 23, 25; Revelation 6:1, 2; Psalm 110:1-6.

As those Gentile Times began around the fifteenth day of the Jews' seventh lunar month (Tishri) in 607 B.C.E., their end would be around the middle of that same month (Tishri 15) or on October 4/5 in 1914 C.E.† Three and a half years from then according to the Jewish calendar would be around Passover time of the year 1918, or at sunset of March 27, 1918, the end of Passover day.

During World War I of 1914-1918 the anointed remnant were trying to care for the interests of the Messianic kingdom that had anciently been associated with earthly Jerusalem. Hence they represented and were ambassadors on earth of that "holy city." In fulfillment of Revelation 11:2, they had to be trampled by the Gentile nations "for forty-two months," or three and a half years or "times." They were

* The members of the International Bible Students Association celebrated the Memorial of Christ's death after sundown of March 26, 1918. The Orthodox Jews celebrated their Passover on Nisan 15 or March 27, 1918, after sundown.

† This dating well agrees with what is stated in *The Watch Tower* as of November 1, 1914, page 325, top six lines of column 1.

indeed trampled upon during the above-mentioned period in 1914-1918, the first world war being seized upon by the Gentile nations to do this trampling. But what was to happen to the anointed remnant after the forty-two months ended?

"MY TWO WITNESSES"

Today those remaining of this anointed remnant are known world wide as Jehovah's witnesses. They were also his witnesses back there in 1918. They are the ones designated in Revelation 11:3 as "my two witnesses." Till early in that year, in Canada up till February 12, 1918, and in America up till March 14, 1918, the anointed remnant were publishing and circulating that commentary on the entire book of Revelation, *The Finished Mystery,* besides Bibles and six volumes of *Studies in the Scriptures* that discussed the entire Bible. So what is said in Revelation, chapter eleven, about "my two witnesses" should well apply to this anointed remnant; and facts show that it does. Revelation 11:3 quotes God as saying: "I will cause my two witnesses to prophesy a thousand two hundred and sixty days dressed in sackcloth."

This has been explained to designate the period from the first half of November of 1914 down till May 7, 1918. This explanation has been given because the 1,260 days were understood to refer to a period of self-centered, personal mourning on the part of the anointed remnant, sackcloth being a symbol of mourning during a black period. Revelation 6:12, for instance, uses the expression "black as sackcloth of hair."* However, the being dressed in sackcloth may not refer to private, personal mourning because of disappointment of one's hopes and aspirations. Rather, it may refer to the nature of the prophecy that "my two witnesses" prophesy. They are gloomy prophets, prophets with a gloomy message

---

* See the book *Light,* Volume One, pages 194-200, as published by the Watch Tower Bible & Tract Society in 1930. Also, *"Your Will Be Done on Earth,"* pages 180-182, as published in 1958.

for others, and not concerned about their own personal affairs. We recall that the prophet Isaiah was commanded by Jehovah God to walk about absolutely naked and barefoot for three years, why? "As a sign and a portent against Egypt and against Ethiopia," as a portent that soon the world power of Assyria would lead away captives and exiles from Egypt and Ethiopia "naked and barefoot."—Isaiah 20:1-6.

Likewise, for the "two witnesses" to prophesy in sackcloth for a thousand two hundred and sixty days might well signify that during this period of time they proclaimed a gloomy, mournful message for the nations. Certainly when, after October 4/5, 1914, the anointed remnant proclaimed world wide that the Gentile Times had ended and that the nations were approaching their destruction at the battle of Armageddon, it was a darksome, mournful message for the Gentile nations, inside and outside of Christendom. So whereas the Gentile nations were trampling upon them as prospective heirs of the Kingdom in the heavenly Jerusalem "for forty-two months," the anointed remnant were at the same time (or, for the one thousand two hundred and sixty days) tormenting them. How? By declaring the doom of those Gentile nations in the "war of the great day of God the Almighty." God caused these witnesses to prophesy, for He gave them the message from his written Word and from the fulfillment of its prophecies.—Revelation 16:14-16; see *The Watch Tower* as of November 1, 1914, and its leading article entitled "Making Ready for the Reign of Righteousness." Also articles in subsequent issues of *The Watch Tower* through March 15, 1918.

The unnamed "my two witnesses" are given some identification by God's words: "These are symbolized by the two olive trees and the two lampstands and are standing before the Lord of the earth." (Revelation 11:4) These descriptive words are a direct reference to the prophecy of Zechariah 4:1-14, where

Governor Zerubbabel of Judah and the high priest Joshua are symbolized by "two olive trees" that furnish oil for the lampstand. Governor Zerubbabel and High Priest Joshua were of the remnant that returned from Babylonian exile in 537 B.C.E., and they supervised the rebuilding of Jerusalem and of its temple and the restoration of Jehovah's worship there. (Zechariah 3:1-10) Hence, in being like the "two lampstands" that burned olive oil, the anointed remnant that prophesied in sackcloth for 1,260 days were yet to do a reconstructive work, a restoration of Jehovah's worship in the earth, a letting of the light of God's Bible truth shine forth in all the earth.

The anointed remnant, "my two witnesses," are like other Bible prophets, namely, Elijah of the tenth century B.C.E. and Moses of the sixteenth century B.C.E. This becomes evident when the enemies try to harm them during the 1,260 days during which they are prophesying "dressed in sackcloth." God says: "And if anyone wants to harm them, fire issues forth from their mouths and devours their enemies; and if anyone should want to harm them, in this manner he must be killed. These have the authority to shut up heaven that no rain should fall during the days of their prophesying, and they have authority over the waters to turn them into blood and to strike the earth with every sort of plague as often as they wish."—Revelation 11:5, 6.

When unfaithful Baal-worshiping King Ahaziah of Israel sent bands of troops out to arrest the prophet Elijah and to bring him back because of his threatening prophecy, Elijah called down fire from heaven upon two bands of such troops. As it were, fire came out of Elijah's mouth. (2 Kings 1:1-12) During World War I of 1914-1918 the religious leaders of Christendom were fomenting great persecution upon the International Bible Students Association, to stop their public activities. But the courageous anointed remnant breathed out fiery destruction against them by publishing and circulating the exposure of the false doctrines and unchristian practices of the apostate Christians, for example, the book *The Finished Mystery* in July of 1917, followed shortly by issue No. 99 of *Bible Students Monthly* containing the feature article "The Fall of Babylon." After the American government banned *The Finished Mystery* the anointed remnant brought out a new large two-page tract headed *Kingdom News* and issued and circulated three successive issues of this with its fiery messages. All such Bible messages fairly consumed the enemies, religious and political.—Jeremiah 5:14.

According to the word of Elijah a devastating drought befell the kingdom of Israel. For three and a half years there was neither rain nor dew, and famine raged. (1 Kings 17:1 to 18:45; Luke 4:25, 26; James 5:17, 18) Like Elijah, God's "two witnesses," the anointed remnant, had the "authority to shut up heaven that no rain should fall during the days of their prophesying" (during the "thousand two hundred and sixty days" or three and a half years). An example of how the anointed remnant did this is set out in the issue of October 15, 1914, of *The Watch Tower,* pages 307, 308, paragraphs 7, 8, which we here quote:

PRAYING FOR PEACE IN EUROPE: Our Honorable President [Woodrow Wilson] with praiseworthy intent requested all Christian people to make October 4 a day of prayer for peace in Europe. However, we cannot concur with our Worthy President in this matter. Much as we appreciate peace—and we have all our life labored to be a peacemaker—we cannot pray the Almighty to change His plans to conform to those of our Honored President.

For twenty-five hundred years God, through the Bible Prophets, has been telling His people about this great war and concerning the more terrible Armageddon which will follow it; and can we expect Him to reverse the program at our behest?

The prayers of these millions praying for the prosperity of the Germans and the extermination of the Allies, and the prayers of other millions for the success of the Allies and the annihilation of the Germans, and the prayers of the Pope and of our President and other good people that this awful war shall promptly cease will all go unanswered, if we read our Bible aright. The war will proceed and will eventuate in no glorious victory for any nation, but in the horrible mutilation and impoverishment of all. Next will follow the awful Armageddon of Anarchy.

The anointed remnant could not Scripturally pray for Jehovah God to open the windows of heaven and rain down blessings upon the war-mad world and spare them from suffering the "beginning of pangs of distress" that his Son Jesus Christ had foretold in Matthew 24:7, 8 and Revelation 6:3-8. Thus, in effect, the anointed remnant took courage to "shut up heaven that no rain should fall." No wonder that, to the nations, they looked like prophets "dressed in sackcloth."

Six centuries before Elijah, the prophet Moses was used by Jehovah God to strike oppressive Egypt with ten plagues in order to force Pharaoh to let the Israelites go free. The first plague with which Moses struck Egypt was the turning of all its waters into blood, so that the fishes died and the Egyptians could not drink water from the regular sources of it. (Exodus 7:14-25) As shed blood is a symbol of death, the anointed remnant, when prophesying in sackcloth, showed from the Scriptures that the waters of which Christendom had been drinking in the form of religious teachings and philosophies were really death-dealing, like blood, and therefore not to be drunk by true Christians. (Genesis 9:4; Acts 15:20, 29) The anointed remnant struck other spiritual blows against the doctrines, practices and organization of Christendom just as the remnant saw it appropriate to deal to that apostate religious system. All such proving that Christendom is unchristian, pagan, tormented Christendom very much and also the politicians and militarists who were friends, members and supporters of her.

KILLING AND REVIVING

The political system of this world, being a good friend of the religious leaders of Christendom, felt that it could endure such activities of God's "two witnesses," the anointed remnant, no longer. By God's permission, even as foretold by God's Word, it took action against them. Revelation 11:7-10 foretold it, saying:

"And when they have finished their witnessing, the wild beast that ascends out of the abyss will make war with them and conquer them and kill them. And their corpses will be on the broad way of the great city which is in a spiritual sense called Sodom and Egypt, where their Lord was also impaled. And those of the peoples and tribes and tongues and nations will look at their corpses for three and a half days, and they do not let their corpses be laid in a tomb. And those dwelling on the earth rejoice over them and enjoy themselves, and they will send gifts to one another, because these two prophets tormented those dwelling on the earth."

As calculated in paragraph 1, page 262, the 1,260 days that these "two prophets" prophesied "dressed in sackcloth" ended on March 26/27, 1918. The symbolic "wild beast" did not ascend out of the abyss first after that date. This "wild beast" is the same one described in Revelation 13:1, 2 as ascending out of the abyss of the sea. Its ascent really took place in the century following the great flood of Noah's day and it became the Devil's worldwide system of politics. This beastly political system, which had ascended out of the symbolic abyss away back there, took action against God's "two witnesses" after March 26/27, 1918.

How did it make war against them, conquer them and at last kill them? It took advantage of martial law and other emergency measures during World War I. On Friday, April 6, 1917, President Woodrow Wilson, who had requested nationwide prayers for peace on October 4, 1914, declared war on Germany and thus America got into the first world war. Three months later, in July of 1917, the Watch Tower Bible & Tract Society published the 608-page book *The*

Finished Mystery, which specially tormented the clergy of Christendom. Just prior to this, on June 15, 1917, America enacted its military conscription and espionage laws, these being patterned after like laws of the then existing British Empire. So now the means were at hand for the religious clergy to use in inducing the symbolic "wild beast" to war on God's "two witnesses."

Already on February 12, 1918, the Canadian Secretary of State had banned *The Finished Mystery* and the series of tracts entitled "Bible Students Monthly," number 99 of which had featured "The Fall of Babylon." Following suit, on March 14, 1918, the United States Department of Justice at Washington, D.C., termed the distribution of *The Finished Mystery* to be a violation of the Espionage Act. Promptly the *Watch Tower* issue of March 15, 1918, announced the preparation and shipping of a new series of large-size two-page tracts entitled "Kingdom News," which would set forth the reason for the suppression of *The Finished Mystery* and the responsibility of the religious clergy in connection therewith. The third and last issue of *Kingdom News* appeared in May of 1918.

On Tuesday, March 26, 1918, the International Bible Students celebrated the annual Memorial of Christ's death world wide, at the end of the foretold "thousand two hundred and sixty days." (Revelation 11: 3) The *Watch Tower* issue of April 15, 1918, advised the Bible students to "colporteur" for the six volumes of *Studies in the Scriptures,* especially volume four entitled "The Battle of Armageddon" and to pursue the Pastoral Work in private homes.

In addition to action taken by the symbolic "wild beast" against God's "two witnesses" throughout the war-torn world, the political "wild beast" bared its teeth and claws against the headquarters of the witness work, in Brooklyn, New York. On May 7, 1918, it brought about the arrest of the president and the secretary-treasurer of the Watch Tower Bible & Tract

Society and of the two coauthors of *The Finished Mystery*, a fourth member of the editorial staff of the *Watch Tower* magazine, and three other members of the Society's office staff at Brooklyn headquarters. Then followed the disrupting of the connections between the Brooklyn headquarters and its branches and agencies throughout the earth. Thursday night, June 20, 1918, after a fifteen-day trial, the jury rendered its verdict of "Guilty!" and about 1:30 o'clock on Friday afternoon, June 21, the Federal judge handed down the sentence against these representative men of God's "two witnesses" class. Twenty years' imprisonment on each of four counts was dealt to seven of these accused ones, all twenty-year terms to run concurrently, and for the eighth accused the judge decided on ten years of imprisonment.

On America's Independence Day, July 4, 1918, these eight sentenced Christian witnesses of the Most High God were started on their railroad trip to the United States Federal penitentiary in Atlanta, Georgia. The political "wild beast" had relentlessly carried on its war upon God's "two witnesses" class and apparently had conquered. This culmination of its warfare was, figuratively speaking, a deathblow; it killed God's "two witnesses," the anointed remnant, as far as their tormenting prophesying "in sackcloth" was concerned. What a relief this was to their enemies, religious, political, judicial and military! All the evidence available at the time is to the effect that, despite World War I troubles, they 'rejoiced' over the killing of God's "two witnesses" and enjoyed themselves in that connection. They were disposed to "send gifts" to one another by congratulating one another for what part they had played in gaining this victory over religious tormentors, just as Revelation 11:10 had foretold.

Those of the various peoples, tribes, languages and nations belonging to Christendom tried to bring as much reproach and shame as possible upon these "two witnesses" of God. They wanted the popular reputation of the witnesses to stink. Revelation 11:9 says that they "will look at their corpses for three and a half days, and they do not let their corpses be laid in a tomb." In the Middle Eastern countries, where the apostle John worked, it was the custom to bury the corpse on the very day of the person's death. So the letting of corpses lie around publicly exposed for three and a half days in a warm climate would result in their beginning to rot and become a stench. (Compare John 11:39.) It also exposed them to being devoured by scavenger dogs or carrion birds. It heaped indignity upon the dead. The not laying of the two corpses "in a tomb" meant that the gloating on-lookers did not consider God's "two witnesses" as deserving of a resurrection from the dead. Christendom did not want them ever to be revived!

IN THE SPIRITUALLY CALLED SODOM AND EGYPT

Where was it that the corpses were let lying exposed, unburied? Revelation 11:8 says that "their corpses will be on the broad way of the great city which is in a spiritual sense called Sodom and Egypt, where their Lord was also impaled." What was or is the name of "the great city"? It was not Sodom, nor was it Egypt, but in God's written Word it is "in a spiritual sense called Sodom and Egypt." However, there is another feature that marks "the great city"; it is the place "where their Lord was also impaled." The quoted subordinate clause modifies, not Egypt, but "the great city." The "Lord" of the two dead witnesses who was "also impaled" was the Lord Jesus Christ, and he was impaled in 33 C.E., not in Egypt, but at unfaithful Jerusalem. (Luke 13:33, 34) In Isaiah 1:8-10 Zion or Jerusalem is prophetically spoken to as a Sodom. In Ezekiel 16:46, 55, 56 Sodom is spoken of as being the younger "sister" of Jerusalem and as being less culpable than Jerusalem.

Because of its religious oppression and enslavement of Jehovah's own people, unfaithful Jerusalem could "in a spiritual sense" be called Egypt. Just as the first Passover lamb was slain down in Egypt in the prophet Moses' day, so Jesus Christ, as the antitypical Passover Lamb, was killed at unfaithful Jerusalem. —John 1:29, 36; 1 Corinthians 5:7; 1 Peter 1:19.

However, unfaithful Jerusalem as the spiritual Sodom and Egypt was not existing in the time of the Revelation to John (in 96 C.E.), and God's "two witnesses" could not have been killed by the symbolic "wild beast" at ancient unfaithful Jerusalem. It had already been destroyed in the year 70 C.E. and had not yet been rebuilt by the pagan Romans. The Jewish Christians had got out of Jerusalem and out of all Judea considerably before 70 C.E. The modern city of Jerusalem was in the hands of the Moslem Turks until the British army captured it in December of 1917; and there were no members of the anointed remnant there during all of World War I. Hence the expression "the great city" must mean the antitypical unfaithful Jerusalem, namely, Christendom. Certainly "in a spiritual sense" she can be called "Sodom and Egypt," and it was primarily in the midst of her that God's "two witnesses" were 'killed' in 1918 C.E. Just as "their Lord," Jesus Christ, was killed on a stake at unfaithful Jerusalem in 33 C.E., so his followers, God's "two witnesses," the anointed remnant, were 'killed' in Christendom.

ARISING FROM THE DEAD

Of course, the anointed remnant who were then known as International Bible Students were not literally 'killed' by what took place in 1918 C.E. because of the war waged upon them by the symbolic "wild beast," although some members may have been actually killed during the persecution that raged. Because of wartime conditions in militarily divided Christendom, including submarine warfare, the international organization of the anointed remnant was quite broken up. Because of the pressure that was unjustly applied by the persecutors, the offices of the Watch Tower Bible & Tract Society began to be transferred, on August 26, 1918, from Brooklyn, New York, to Pittsburgh, Pennsylvania, not to be moved back to Brooklyn until September of 1919, but the magazine *The Watch Tower* continued to be published semimonthly without an issue being missed.

Despite the government ban on *The Finished Mystery* that had been imposed just two weeks before, the anointed remnant met on March 26, 1918, and celebrated the annual Memorial of Christ's death. War conditions prevented a world report thereon. Yet at the next such celebration, April 13, 1919, a partial report for the Americas (plus 4 places in Great Britain and 1 in France) showed that 17,961 had partaken of the emblematic bread and wine. To the end of World War I on November 11, 1918, there were fifteen traveling speakers, "pilgrims," that visited and addressed the congregations and the public throughout the United States. There were 225 full-time book distributors, "colporteurs," placing in the homes of the people the six volumes of *Studies in the Scriptures*. In a summary of the work for that critical year of 1918, *The Watch Tower* as of December 15, 1918, page 372, reported (from its then Pittsburgh address):

. . . For several reasons it is not possible to report accurately on some things; . . . the number of STUDIES IN THE SCRIPTURES sold include only those sold by Colporteurs, and not those sent out to classes and individuals by our Shipping Department. It is also impossible even to approximate the amount of volunteer work done [with the tracts]. On the other hand, the friends seem to have appreciated the convention privileges to a wonderful degree. Over forty conventions of a general character have been held during the year, besides probably as many more of a local character. Glowing reports have been received from all these conventions. . . . every month in the year has its conventions. Several large conventions are announced for the near future.

At the Milwaukee, Wisconsin, convention from August 30 to September 2, 1918, about 850 attended, and there on the last day ("Kingdom Day") the Federal officers interrupted the 3 p.m. Bible talk by "pilgrim" J. A. Bohnet, barred the doors and then required all young men to show their draft registration cards. After that rude interruption the Bible talk was resumed by the speaker. Concerning that convention the *Watch Tower* issue of October 15, 1918, page 319, said: "To realize that we are three and a half years into the great time of trouble and then to note the smiling faces of all present was a most wonderful evidence of our precious Master's promise: 'Lo, I am with you alway'; and again, the assurance: 'I will never leave thee nor forsake thee.' "

In view of the foregoing facts concerning the year 1918 C.E., how could it be said that God's "two witnesses," "these two prophets," the anointed remnant, were 'killed' and their dead bodies were lying unburied in the broad way of antitypical unfaithful Jerusalem, Christendom? Well, note that Revelation 11: 7 says that, "when they have finished their witnessing," the symbolic "wild beast" would war upon them to the death. This indicates that it was their "witnessing" or prophesying work that was killed. This was the special "witnessing" that had been done during the "thousand two hundred and sixty days" with the special literature that was then used. For instance, a supplement was inserted in all copies mailed out of *The Watch Tower,* dated September 1, 1918, reading as follows:

IMPORTANT NOTICE TO ALL WATCH TOWER
SUBSCRIBERS AND BIBLE STUDENTS

The circulation of the following books and papers is completely suspended during the period of the war:

THE FINISHED MYSTERY
Special Edition, March 1st, WATCH TOWER (ZG)
All BIBLE STUDENTS' MONTHLIES
All KINGDOM NEWS

Any classes or individuals holding any of the above literature belonging to THE WATCH TOWER BIBLE AND TRACT SOCIETY are hereby instructed to hold the same, subject to our orders. This is a confirmation of notice sent you last March.

WATCH TOWER BIBLE AND TRACT SOCIETY

Along with the foregoing, since being unjustly sentenced in court on June 21, 1918, the leading members of the governing body of the anointed remnant all around the earth were lying in prison as if they were criminal felons, much to the discredit of the "witnessing" work of God's anointed remnant who were heirs of the heavenly kingdom with Christ. The vicious action of the symbolic "wild beast" left no room for surprise that all the anointed remnant throughout the earth suffered great persecution, this badly crippling their public activities as witnesses of the Most High God, Jehovah. They were "objects of hatred by all the nations on account of my name." —Matthew 24:9.

Making a brief reference to the situation during World War I, the article "For the Elect's Sake" in the *Watch Tower* issue of May 1, 1925, said on page 135, paragraph 67:

It is a well-known fact that during the World War the opportunity for proclaiming the message of the kingdom was restrained and limited up to the Spring of 1919. In the warring nations many of the brethren were forced into the army. Circulation of the truth literature was prohibited; and many brethren in different countries were imprisoned. Persecution began especially in 1917; and in the Spring of 1918 officers of the SOCIETY were imprisoned, Bethel dismantled, the Tabernacle sold, and the headquarters removed to small quarters in Pittsburgh. For some time thereafter little or no witnessing was done. The conditions were such at that time that had the World War progressed and not come to an end there would have been no more public witnesses of any consequence given on earth. . . .

Contrary to the expectation of the International Bible Students Association, the 'battle of Armageddon' did not immediately follow World War I. On November 11, 1918, an armistice was signed between the warring nations, and yet the anointed remnant had not been taken to heaven but had been left on the earth, and in disgrace, like the corpses of the "two witnesses" lying unburied on the broad way of "the great city," Christendom. But not for long. What was foretold in Revelation 11:11-13 was due to take place at God's due time, as we read:

"And after the three and a half days spirit of life from God entered into them, and they stood upon their feet, and great fear fell upon those beholding them. And they heard a loud voice out of heaven say to them: 'Come on up here.' And they went up into heaven in the cloud, and their enemies beheld them. And in that hour a great earthquake occurred, and a tenth of the city fell; and seven thousand persons were killed by the earthquake, and the rest became frightened and gave glory to the God of heaven."

Three and a half was the number of the years that the "two witnesses" had prophesied "dressed in sackcloth." But we are not to understand the "three and a half days" of their lying dead in the city's broad way to mean three and a half years, each day to be symbolic of a year, as in Ezekiel 4:6. The "three and a half days" specified in Revelation 11:9-11 stand for only a short period of time of public-witnessing inactivity on the part of the anointed remnant and of malicious gloating on the part of their enemies. Those "three and a half days" ended in March of 1919. A petition was being circulated for signers in behalf of the release of the eight representative men of the Watch Tower Bible & Tract Society. Before the petition was completed by those of the anointed remnant in the United States, the eight Federal prisoners were admitted to bail, on March 21, 1919.

Four days later the eight prisoners were released from the Federal penitentiary in Atlanta, Georgia, and taken on the train to New York city. The next day, March 26, 1919, the Federal Court in Brooklyn, New York, let them go free on bail. Then, indeed, "spirit of life from God" entered into the symbolic corpses of the "two witnesses," and they became alive to the "witnessing" activity that now lay ahead of them. They no longer stayed lying inactive in the broad way of Christendom, but "they stood upon their feet," ready again for God's public service with all the means that he would supply for this. The language here used with regard to them corresponds with the phraseology used in Ezekiel's vision of the valley of dry bones of Israel that were reunited, clothed upon with flesh and made to live again.—Ezekiel 37:5, 10.

They were further strengthened in standing on their feet when, on May 15, 1919, the conviction of the eight ex-prisoners from Atlanta penitentiary was reversed by the majority decision in the United States Circuit Court of Appeals for the New York District. (On May 5, 1920, despite strenuous efforts of the enemies to have the case retried, the Federal District Court dismissed the case, thereby completely exonerating these eight representatives of the Watch Tower Society.) When the anointed remnant thus got back on their feet again, fully alive, "great fear fell upon those beholding them."—Revelation 11:11.

How, though, did the anointed remnant hear a "loud voice out of heaven say to them: 'Come on up here'"? This was especially by means of the first general convention of the International Bible Students Association held at Cedar Point, Ohio, September 1-8, 1919. Here on September 5 the Watch Tower Society's president, now released from prison, spoke on the subject "Announcing the Kingdom," based on Revelation 15:2 and Isaiah 52:7. After this the publication of a new magazine subsidiary to *The Watch Tower* was announced, namely, *The Golden Age*. The first issue was to appear on October 1, 1919, and a great campaign for securing subscriptions for the magazine from the general public was to be carried on. This information was received with tremendous enthusiasm by the thousands of conventioners. As an encouragement to the anointed remnant throughout the earth to reanimate, revitalize the organization for this new Kingdom work, the *Watch Tower* issue of September 15, 1919, under the caption "Announcing the Kingdom," page 281, said, in part:

> . . . We believe the new magazine, THE GOLDEN AGE, is the very thing that the people will desire, and let us pray that if it be the Lord's will he will favor it with

his great blessing. Every reader of THE WATCH TOWER has wanted to pass on the message of glad tidings. Now will you avail yourself of this opportunity?

HOW TO PROCEED

The organization that handled the Seventh Volume work proved a wonderful success. Seven thousand of the friends were engaged in that special work. We are asking the classes everywhere to revive that organization and put it in proper form. . . . In the present work we desire that every one of the consecrated who has a great love and burning zeal for the Lord and his cause shall participate.

The Lord Jehovah God did favor the new magazine with his great blessing, and today that magazine, now known as *Awake!* has a semimonthly printing of 5,650,000 copies in 26 languages, whereas *The Watchtower* has a semimonthly printing of 5,800,000 copies in 72 languages.

In September of 1919, before *The Golden Age* began to circulate, the headquarters of the Watch Tower Society were moved back to their original location in Brooklyn, New York. This Society established its own printing factory in Brooklyn and itself began printing the magazine *The Watch Tower* with the issue of February 1, 1920. At the same factory *The Golden Age* began to be printed with the issue of April 14, 1920, No. 15. Soon afterward *The Watch Tower* in its issue of June 1, 1920, began advertising again *The Finished Mystery,* and on June 21 a great campaign was begun of placing the magazine edition of this book by calling on the public from house to house. Next, the leading article entitled "Gospel of the Kingdom" in the *Watch Tower* issue of July 1, 1920, explained that the Kingdom work foretold in Matthew 24:14 had special application to us since 1914, in which year the Messianic kingdom of God had been established.

ASCENT TO HEAVEN

The faithful ones of the anointed remnant livelily responded to the call and the opportunities for the service of God's kingdom that was established in the heavens at the close of the Gentile Times in 1914. Figuratively, according to Revelation 11:12, "they went up into heaven in the cloud, and their enemies beheld them." From a deathlike condition to the active service of the heavenly Kingdom was indeed an ascent for the anointed "two witnesses" class, and it was attended with spiritual glory as symbolized by "the cloud." This ascent was attended with such publicity and impressiveness that "their enemies," particularly those in Christendom, could not do otherwise than behold them. Sackcloth upon these "two witnesses" was offset by glory in this exalted spiritual state of serving as ambassadors of the reigning heavenly kingdom of God by Christ. Their vicious enemy, the symbolic "wild beast" out of the abyss, could no more "kill" them as the "two witnesses" class. To this very date the worldwide political system of Satan the Devil has been unable to do this. The "witnesses" have "spirit of life from God," and they are determined to keep alive spiritually.

At this critical time a great upheaval took place in Christendom, especially over the issue of God's established Messianic kingdom and the man-made substitute, the League of Nations. The churches of Christendom decided in favor of the political League of Nations, the Federal Council of Churches of Christ in America even hailing this organization for world peace and security as "the political expression of the Kingdom of God on earth."* What was the effect of this symbolic earthquake in Christendom? Revelation 11:13 answers: "And in that hour a great earthquake occurred, and a tenth of the city fell; and seven thousand persons [Greek, names] were killed by the earthquake, and the rest became frightened and gave glory to the God of heaven."

The "city" that is the victim of the earthquake

---

* See the book "Your Will Be Done on Earth," page 204, paragraph 27, through page 209, paragraph 35. This book was published by the Watch Tower Bible & Tract Society of Pennsylvania in 1958.

is, of course, antitypical unfaithful Jerusalem, modern Christendom. Not all of this symbolic city fell in ruin; only a symbolic "tenth" of it. The structure of Christendom has continued till today, but did it suffer any loss from the earthquake at the beginning of the postwar period back in 1919? What it did lose to itself was called "a tenth." This reminds us that, when the prophet Isaiah was told about the destruction coming upon Jerusalem and its Kingdom of Judah, "there will still be in it a tenth, and it must again become . . . like a massive tree in which, when there is a cutting down of them, there is a stump; a holy seed will be the stump of it." (Isaiah 6:13) This stump or "holy seed" proved to be the faithful remnant that survived the exile in Babylon and returned home to rebuild the holy temple at Jerusalem. In 1919 neither the war-surviving members of the anointed remnant nor those who came out of Christendom to become a part of the anointed remnant joined Christendom in supporting the League of Nations, as against God's kingdom. Thus Christendom lost this symbolic "tenth" part.

When the prophet Elijah fled from the face of the threatening queen Jezebel of Israel into the mountainous region of Horeb, Jehovah God told Elijah:

"I have let seven thousand remain in Israel, all the knees that have not bent down to Baal, and every mouth that has not kissed him." (1 Kings 19:1-18) The apostle Paul applied this to the remnant of Israel that did not stick to Jerusalem in rejecting Jesus Christ as Jehovah's Messiah but forsook her, leaving her to the consequences of her antichristian course. (Romans 11:1-5) Similarly, in the symbolic "earthquake" over God's Messianic kingdom in 1919 there was a remnant faithful to God's kingdom by Christ, a symbolic "seven thousand persons [names]," that died to Christendom. They ceased to exist to her. No longer could she retain their "names" on her church registries. They were no longer alive and active in her.

In what way, then, was it that "the rest became frightened and gave glory to the God of heaven"? Well, do frightened people give sincere "glory to the God of heaven" for an earthquake that causes a "tenth" of their city to fall and the loss of "seven thousand" lives? Did "the rest" of Christendom repent over what they had done against the "two witnesses" class, the "two prophets," and join them after they were revived from the death state?

History down to this date denies that such a thing has taken place. Rather, "the rest" of Christendom got frightened at what had happened to the "tenth" part and the "seven thousand persons" and did not want that to happen to them. So, in their fright, "the rest" held onto their own religious sects in Christendom and "gave glory to the God of heaven" according to their own sectarian religious ways. They never turned to supporting the Messianic kingdom of God that had been established in the heavens. They turned to the League of Nations. When, after World War II, this was replaced by the United Nations, they adopted this. But as for God's revived "two witnesses," these continued to proclaim God's Messianic kingdom as mankind's only hope for lasting peace and security.

CHAPTER 20

The Seventh Angel Blows His Trumpet

NINETEEN centuries ago the apostle John saw in symbols ("signs") what happened after the sixth heavenly angel blew his trumpet. What followed the trumpet blowing was declared to be the second of a series of three woes. The "second woe" came about through the loosing of the "four angels that are bound at the great river Euphrates."—Revelation 9:13-15.

Just after the loosing of the "four angels" two hundred million fierce-looking horses, under riders, charged against a "third of the men" to kill them. Similarly, after God's revived "two witnesses" ascended to heaven and "the city" was damaged by the great "earthquake," hundreds of millions of pieces of Bible literature in favor of God's heavenly kingdom and against the League of Nations and the United Nations were circulated under the guidance of the "two witnesses" class. What a woe that was to Christendom!

Quite properly, then, after the apostle John had reported on the "great earthquake," he could write: "The second woe is past. Look! The third woe is coming quickly." (Revelation 11:14) This "third woe" was left for announcement by the only remaining angel with an unblown trumpet, "the seventh angel." What kind of woe will he announce?

"And the seventh angel blew his trumpet. And loud voices occurred in heaven, saying: 'The kingdom of the world has become the kingdom of our Lord and of his Christ, and he will rule as king forever and ever.' "—Revelation 11:15.

The expression "the kingdom of our Lord and of his Christ" identifies this government as the Messianic kingdom established by the Lord God Jehovah, for "his Christ" or his Messiah shares in it. By this kingdom Jehovah "will rule as king forever and ever."

Kingdom of the world of mankind rightly belongs to Jehovah God. But from 607 B.C.E. onward he had allowed his kingship of the world by means of an anointed descendant of the royal family of King David to lapse, to be interrupted. For how long? For a period of "seven times," seven symbolic "times," or two thousand five hundred and twenty years. (Daniel 4:16, 23, 25) Those "seven times" of unchallenged, uninterrupted rule of the world by Gentile world powers ended around October 4/5 in 1914 C.E. It was then that the kingdom of the world of mankind legitimately did "become the kingdom of our Lord and of his Christ." Then Jesus the Christ or Messiah in heaven did accept kingship from the Source of all rightful kingship, Jehovah.

Back in the year 29 C.E., in the mountain of temptation, Jesus had refused to accept kingship when Satan the Tempter said to him: "I will give you all this authority and the glory of them [the kingdoms of the inhabited earth], because it has been delivered to me, and to whomever I wish I give it. You, therefore, if you do an act of worship before me, it will all be yours." Unhesitatingly Jesus Christ made his choice against Satan the Devil and for Jehovah God, saying in reply to the Devil: "It is written, 'It is Jehovah your God you must worship, and it is to him alone you must render sacred service.' " (Luke 4:5-8; Matthew 4:8-10) Three and a half years later, shortly before being put to death on a stake, this Jesus said to the Roman governor, Pontius Pilate, at Jerusalem: "My kingdom is no part of this world. . . . But, as it is, my kingdom is not from this source." (John 18:36) He died because of refusing to accept kingship over earth at the hands of Satan the Devil, that he might accept kingship in 1914 C.E. at the hands of the Lord God Jehovah, who had made a covenant with him for such kingdom.—Luke 22:28-30; Daniel 7:13, 14.

THE MYSTERY FINISHED

But hold on there! At Revelation 10:7 God's angel solemnly, on oath, declared: "In the days of the sounding of the seventh angel, when he is about to blow his trumpet, the sacred secret of God according to the good news which he declared to his own slaves the prophets is indeed brought to a finish." Or, according to the *American Standard Version:* "In the days of the voice of the seventh angel, when he is about to sound, then is finished the mystery of God, according to the good tidings which he declared to his servants the prophets." What now, at the blowing of the seventh trumpet, is this "mystery of God" proved to be?

Well, when the seventh angel did begin to sound, heavenly voices were heard to say with a loud voice: "The kingdom [the kingship, the right and title to reign] of the world has become the kingdom of our Lord and of his Christ [his Messiah]." This proves that the "mystery of God" is the kingdom of the Lord God Jehovah, his ruling as King, by means of his Messiah or Christ. In ancient Israel, during the years 1077 to 607 B.C.E., Jehovah God ruled as king by means of his anointed ones, David and his royal descendants, who sat "upon Jehovah's throne" at Jerusalem. (1 Chronicles 29:23) But now he reigns by his antitypical David, his beloved Son Jesus Christ.

So, then, when and how was this royal "mystery of God" finished? It was finished at the end of the Gentile Times in 1914 and by Jehovah's beginning this kingdom of Himself by means of his Messiah or Christ, the resurrected, glorified Jesus Christ. Thus at last he put his secret purpose into action. His power to rule as King over the world of mankind was rightfully taken up by himself as the Universal Sovereign. In expression of this he crowned and enthroned his Messiah or Christ in the heavens and at his right hand. (Psalm 110:1, 2) Since then the power to rule as king over the world of mankind has belonged to the Lord God Almighty, Jehovah, and his Messiah or Christ acts for him. From now on Jehovah God the Almighty will rule as King forever and ever, and never again will he permit his rule as King over the earth to be interrupted by the domination of the Gentile nations. This enthronement of his Son Jesus Christ did not have to wait for the completing and resurrecting and glorifying of the true church, the congregation of the 144,000 faithful, spirit-begotten followers of Jesus Christ. In 1914 none of these were as yet in heaven.

After the binding of Satan the Devil and his demons, the enthroned Jesus as the Messiah of Jehovah God will reign for a thousand years. Never again will Satan the Devil be able to establish Gentile domination over the earth, even though he is given the opportunity to do so at the end of the thousand-year reign of Jesus Christ and his glorified congregation.—Revelation 20:1-10.

But how is it that this Messianic kingdom of God is a woe, "the third woe"? Is not this Messianic kingdom meant for the blessing of all the families of the earth? (Genesis 12:1-3; 22:18) Yes, indeed. However, to some this finishing of the royal "mystery of God" is a cause of woe, whereas to others it is a cause for thanksgiving to God. This fact was well prefigured by what the apostle John saw after he heard the loud voices in heaven announce that the kingdom of the world had become the kingdom of the Lord God and of his Messiah or Christ and that from then on the Lord God would reign forever and ever by means of his Christ. In Revelation 11:16-18 the apostle John writes:

"And the twenty-four older persons who were seated before God upon their thrones fell upon their faces and worshiped God, saying: 'We thank you, Jehovah God, the Almighty, the one who is and who was, because you have taken your great power and begun ruling as king. But the nations became wrathful, and your own wrath came, and the appointed time for the dead to be judged, and to give their reward to your slaves the prophets and to the holy ones and to those fearing your name, the small and the great, and to bring to ruin those ruining the earth.' "

According to this vision, the ones that thank Jehovah God the Almighty for making a show of his all-power and taking over the kingship of the world of mankind are the symbolic "twenty-four older persons" who sat on thrones before God. These picture the 144,000 Kingdom joint heirs of Jesus Christ. Only a remnant of these were on earth when Jehovah God took his power to rule as King in 1914. The vast majority of them were still asleep in death, awaiting his coming to the spiritual temple with his Messianic Messenger and then resurrecting them from the dead. (Malachi 3:1; 2 Timothy 4:1) When, in heaven, these resurrected ones learn that Jehovah God the Almighty has taken his great power to reign, they cannot but fall upon their faces and worship him as their God and Supreme King and then thank him for finishing the "mystery of God," his Messianic kingdom, and reigning. As for the faithful anointed remnant yet on earth in the flesh, even now before their coming glorification, they fall in worship before Jehovah God and thank him for beginning his reign by means of his Christ.

On the other hand, the blowing of the seventh trumpet and the finishing of the "mystery of God" is a climactic woe to the nations of the world. Rather than becoming thankful and rendering allegiance to the reigning Sovereign of the Universe, these nations "grew wrathful." How? By imitating the "god of this system of things," Satan the Devil, who expresses his wrath by persecuting. (Revelation 12:13, 17) So in wrath the Gentile nations began persecuting the earthly ambassadors of the newly begun Messianic kingdom of God. They trampled the "holy city underfoot for forty-two months," from the end of the Gentile Times in 1914 to the spring of 1918. (Revelation 11:2) They used the circumstances of World War I for persecuting God's "two witnesses," during the "thousand two hundred and sixty days" when these were prophesying "dressed in sackcloth." The Gentile nations tried to harm "these two prophets" of Jehovah God. They warred upon these Christian "prophets" until they had conquered them and killed them, figuratively speaking. (Revelation 11:5-8) Thus the nations began giving vent to their wrath at God's kingdom.

To this very day the nations continue wrathful and reveal it by keeping on opposing, oppressing and persecuting the revived "two witnesses," as these courageously continue preaching "this good news of the kingdom," now the good news of the finished "mystery of God." (Matthew 24:14) This, in turn, arouses the wrath of Jehovah God, and shortly now the time will arrive for him to express his own wrath in the "war of the great day of God the Almighty" at the place called in the Hebrew language Har–Magedon (Armageddon, *AV*). (Revelation 16:14, 16) In that war Jesus Christ as the Messianic King will tread those nations in the "winepress of the anger of the wrath of God the Almighty." (Revelation 19:11-16) For the nations that will be the woe of woes.

THE TIME FOR JUDGING AND GIVING REWARD

Besides woe for the enemy nations, the finishing of the "mystery of God" ushers in "the appointed time for the dead to be judged, and to give their reward to your slaves the prophets and to the holy ones and to those fearing your name, the small and the great." (Revelation 11:18) That means resurrection from the dead!

But when? Not accidentally, the time of the ministry of Jesus Christ from his baptism in water to his resurrection from the dead corresponds with "forty-two months," or a "thousand two hundred and sixty days," from about Tishri 15 of the year 29 C.E. to Nisan 16 of the year 33 C.E. (Daniel 9:24-27) Just six days before his resurrection, or on Monday, Nisan 10, Jesus entered into the temple at Jerusalem and executed God's judgment there by cleansing the temple of those doing commercial business and making money there. (Matthew 21:12, 13; Mark 11:11, 15-17) In a similar manner, forty-two months or a thousand two hundred and sixty days from the end of the Gentile Times in 1914 C.E., the glorified Jesus Christ accompanied his heavenly Father Jehovah God to the spiritual temple to start a judgment work. (Malachi 3:1-5) Then would come "the appointed time for the dead to be judged." Since the proper order of things is "for the judgment to start with the house of God," the first ones to be resurrected would be "the holy ones," that is, those of the 144,000 Kingdom joint heirs "who have fallen asleep in death through Jesus."—1 Peter 4:17; 1 Thessalonians 4: 14-16.

Many of those who were thus sleeping in death through Jesus at the time that he came to the temple in 1918 C.E. were Christian prophets. So these could be included within the expression "your slaves the prophets," to whom reward was to be given. Remember how the anointed remnant, the "two witnesses" of God, prophesied "dressed in sackcloth" and were called "these two prophets." (Revelation 11:3, 10) From the time that those who had "fallen asleep in death through Jesus" were resurrected to life as divine spirit creatures in heaven, the happiness spoken of in Revelation 14:13 applies to those of the anointed remnant who "die in union with the Lord from this time onward." Those of the anointed remnant thus dying faithful are "happy" because they do not have to sleep for any length of time in death but are instantaneously resurrected to heavenly life as spirit creatures clothed with the "divine nature." Once this fact was a mystery or "sacred secret."—1 Corinthians 15:50-54; 2 Peter 1:4.

Thus in due time after the finishing of the "mystery of God" the "first resurrection" of the 144,000 anointed followers of Jesus the Messiah begins to take place, and it will not be completed until the last one of these faithful ones has ended his earthly course in human death and is instantaneously raised to heavenly spirit life. (1 Corinthians 15:42-49; Revelation 20:4-6) However, at God's chosen time after his victory at Armageddon and after the binding and abyssing of Satan the Devil and his demons, the resurrection of the world of mankind will begin. Then there will take place the resurrection of those who were God's dedicated "slaves" and who served as his inspired prophets before the death and resurrection of Jesus Christ. But these are not the only ones to be resurrected to human life on earth under the Messianic kingdom of Jesus the Son of God. Jesus died as the propitiatory sacrifice for the sins of the whole world, and at the proper time those to whom the benefit of this sacrifice applies will be raised from death to life on earth. (1 John 2:1, 2; John 1:29, 36; 1 Timothy 2:5, 6) This will include "the small and the great."

In that wonderful time of resurrection "those fearing your name, the small and the great," will be given their reward. The divine judgment will be expressed toward these resurrected ones on earth. Their having been small or great in power, position or influence in this present life will not be what will count in their behalf or against them. What will merit the glorious reward of everlasting life in an earthly paradise home will be their fearing God's name, Jehovah.—Revelation 20:11, 12.

Particularly since the year 1914 C.E. the world of mankind has patently been transforming its earthly home into no earth-wide paradise of pleasure, no Garden of Eden. Since that year fallen mankind has been acting more ruinously toward the earth than ever before, more and more making it unfit to live in and more and more dangerous to live in. Men high in commercial, political and military circles of the nations act as if they owned the earth. But the earth really belongs to no man or group of men or bloc of nations. It belongs to Jehovah God. He is its Creator. (Revelation 4:11) He is its rightful Ruler. (Psalm 24:1, 2, 7-10) When he created and settled perfect man upon this earth, he instructed the perfect man and his wife to subdue the earth and make it everywhere like the Garden of Eden in which He had created them. (Genesis 1:26-28; 2:7-24) Almighty God still holds to that original purpose, but, outrageously since 1914, selfish, sinful mankind has foolhardily been working against God's purpose.

Since Jehovah God has taken to himself his great power to rule as King through his Messiah, the time has come for Him to reverse matters. His unchanged purpose to have a paradise home for men who fear his name must be realized at his due time, which is steadily getting nearer. How will he proceed? By expressing his wrath toward the ruiners of the earth. His time has come, not only to reward his "holy ones" and his slaves, the prophets, and all those fearing his name, but also "to bring to ruin those ruining the earth." (Revelation 11:18) This will mean the everlasting ruin of such ones. The "war of the great day of God the Almighty" will accomplish this needed cleansing of the earth of all those ruinous ones. Thereafter, under the Messianic kingdom of God, all those fearing his name will be colaborers with Him in bringing to never-fading Paradise beauty all the inhabited earth.

TRUMPETLIKE ANNOUNCEMENT WORLD WIDE

Wonderfully good news all this! But when was the appropriate time to give worldwide publication to this as by the pealing of a trumpet? When, in these modern days, was it the time for the "seventh angel" to blow his trumpet and loud voices to announce that the Lord God had come to power as King?—Revelation 11:15.

In the year 1928 C.E. the beginning was made, not of the marvelous things announced, but of the worldwide announcement of such things. To a marked degree, it began with the seventh of a series of annual Bible Student conventions at which resolutions of world importance were adopted and other Christian exploits were performed. This seventh and last of those annual conventions was held in Detroit, Michigan, July 30 through August 6, 1928. On the morning of Sunday, August 5, the public lecture "Ruler for the People" was delivered by the then president of the International Bible Students Association. This was heard, not only by the immediately visible audience of 12,000, but by a countless invisible audience listening in on the till then largest network of radio stations ever linked together in mankind's history, 107 of them, requiring 33,500 miles of telephone lines and 91,400 miles of telegraph lines. This message about divine government for the people was even beamed by shortwave to "the land down under," Australia, and New Zealand.

This speech having such an extensive audible coverage of the earth was delivered really in support of a resolution that was first read at the appointed hour to that vast listening body. It was entitled "Declaration Against Satan and for Jehovah." In its eight paragraphs it stated that Jehovah God is the King of Eternity and true Friend and Benefactor of all creation; that because Satan will not give up his wicked rule over mankind, Jehovah God with his executive officer Jesus Christ will wage the war of Armageddon and destroy the visible organization of Satan and will establish righteousness on earth by Christ and bring everlasting blessings to all men; and that therefore the due time had come for lovers of righteousness to take their stand for Jehovah God and serve him that they might receive his boundless blessings.

At the close of the supporting public address this resolution was heartily adopted by a rousing voice vote. Not only were lengthy reports of this resolution and supporting speech later published in the magazines *The Golden Age* and *The Watch Tower,* but the resolution and speech were circulated in millions of copies of the booklet *The People's Friend,* in a number of languages.

In precise harmony with the meaning of this historic event, on Friday, August 3, at this Detroit convention there was released to the public the 368-page book entitled "Government." In a matter of fourteen years this Bible-study aid was to reach a circulation of 2,680,747 copies in 19 languages. Stressing the meaning of this significant time, the opening words of the opening chapter were: "The year 1914 marked the turning point in the affairs of men. Since then, as never before, the people have appreciated the necessity for a stable government." In its chapter 8 on the subject "Theocracy" the book *Government* said: "What form of government will then control the peoples of earth? That government will be a pure theocracy. For centuries the whole creation has groaned and suffered in pain, waiting for the manifestation of that government. (Romans 8:19) . . . It was in 1914 that God began to exercise his authority over the affairs of the world through his beloved Son whom he then placed upon his holy throne."—Pages 242, 247, 248.

That challenging message, in defiance of Satan's world rule, which then was trumpeted forth, has continued to peal throughout the years till now and its volume is increasing. By printed page and by public lectures it has sounded throughout the whole earth. Hundreds of millions have heard and read about it. Thirty years after the momentous year of 1914 there was published the book *"The Kingdom Is at Hand."* In 1963 in an around-the-world international assembly there was released the book *"Babylon the Great Has Fallen!" God's Kingdom Rules!* These books and other Kingdom literature are increasingly being presented to the people at their homes in at least 200 lands and in 165 languages, for use in home Bible study regarding God's Messianic kingdom. No wonder the nations have become wrathful, to the extent of persecuting the Kingdom proclaimers! Let them vent their wrath in this way! The time is now almost upon us for God's own wrath to explode. Then he will forever ruin those who are ruining the earth, after which his will shall come to be done in earth as it is in heaven.

GOD RULES AS KING

In this time of disquieting turbulence of the nations one stabilizing fact of universal importance must never be lost from sight: God Almighty rules on his throne of universal sovereignty! This fact was put on view by what the apostle John saw in vision at this juncture after the seventh angel blew his trumpet. Describing it, John writes: "And the temple sanctuary of God that is in heaven was opened, and the ark of his covenant was seen in his temple sanctuary. And there occurred lightnings and voices and thunders and an earthquake and a great hail."—Revelation 11:19.

A wonderful sight was this! The "ark of the covenant" of Jehovah God had not been seen by a high priest of Israel in the Most Holy of the temple since the destruction of earthly Jerusalem and her temple by the Babylonians in the year 607 B.C.E. (Numbers 10:33-36; 14:44; 1 Kings 3:15; 6:19; 8:1-21; 2 Chronicles 35:1-3; 36:17-21) At that time the ark of the covenant disappeared and its whereabouts became unknown. It was not transported to heaven, for it was made of acacia wood and gold, material things, and it was symbolic of heavenly realities, whereas heaven itself is the location of those very realities. (Hebrews 9:1-5, 23-26; 10:1) When that material ark of the covenant disappeared at the temple's destruction, Jehovah God ceased to reign over

Israel by means of his anointed kings of the royal family of David. His kingdom in the line of David was ruined.—Ezekiel 21:24-27.

Fittingly, the ark's top cover, surmounted by two golden cherubs, pictured the throne of Jehovah God the King. From there Jehovah God spoke to his prophet Moses. (Numbers 7:89) Before it Israel's high priest sprinkled the blood of the Atonement Day sacrifices, Jehovah God then appearing in a cloud over the ark's cover. (Leviticus 16:1-3, 14, 15) The four sides of the Most Holy of the temple sanctuary were decorated with figures of cherubs. (Exodus 26:1, 31-33; 36:8, 35; 1 Kings 6:23-35) True to these pictorial things, Jehovah God was said to sit upon the cherubs (Psalms 80:1; 99:1; Isaiah 37:16) This matches the vision that the apostle John had of Jehovah God seated upon his heavenly throne. (Revelation 4:6-8) Since the golden lid of the ancient ark of the covenant had such a royal meaning, the appearing of God's ark of the covenant in the heavenly temple sanctuary after the seventh angel blew his trumpet meant that Jehovah God was once more reigning

by means of his Messiah, the Anointed One.

The temple sanctuary of God that was opened to John's view to show his ark therein was not the spiritual temple which is made up of the 144,000 living stones built up on Jesus Christ as the chief cornerstone. (1 Peter 2:5-9; Ephesians 2:20-22) No, but it is the temple sanctuary that Jehovah God put up, and into which Jesus Christ the High Priest entered before ever he founded his Christian congregation on Pentecost of 33 C.E. (Hebrews 8:2; 9: 11-14) It is the exclusive holy area of the heaven of the heavens where Jehovah sits enthroned, surrounded by his official cherubs.

Two thousand five hundred and twenty years from when the golden ark of the covenant vanished as a sign of terminating God's reign over the kingdom of Israel, the end of the Gentile Times came, namely, in 1914 C.E. At that time the antitypical "ark of his covenant" was set forth in the opened temple sanctuary of God in heaven. Thus he pictured that he reigned again by means of his Messianic Priest-King, Jesus Christ. This was in magnificent agreement with what loud voices were saying after the seventh angel blew his trumpet: "The kingdom of the world has become the kingdom of our Lord and of his Christ." (Revelation 11:15) The mystery of God was indeed finished!

In John's vision the proof of God's reigning in his heavenly temple was evidenced by the awesome display of more than human forces such as lightnings and superhuman voices, thunders, an earthquake and a great hailstorm. Since 1914 C.E., the things symbolized by such earthly phenomena occurred through the agency of Jehovah's visible organization, his faithful anointed remnant. Such phenomenal things as accomplished by means of these anointed Christians could only have God's wondrous power as an explanation for them. All these spectacular things verify that Jehovah is in his heavenly throne reigning.

CHAPTER 21

The Heavenly Birth of God's Messianic Kingdom

NOW FOR the first time a "woman" appears in heaven in the procession of visions given to the apostle John on the Isle of Patmos. This mysterious figure is not "that woman Jezebel" mentioned earlier in Revelation 2:20, in connection with the earthly congregation of Thyatira. She is an approved "woman," honorably married and bringing forth the good fruitage of her marriage tie. The mystery of who she really is can be solved by means of what the apostle John tells us about her. Before telling us about her, John has heard the seventh angel sound his trumpet, and the "mystery of God" has been shown to him to be finished, and he has seen the evidence that Jehovah God the Almighty is reigning in his heavenly temple sanctuary. After that, as John tells us, "a great sign was seen in heaven, a woman arrayed with the sun, and the moon was beneath her feet, and on her head was a crown of twelve stars, and she was pregnant. And she cries out in her pains and in her agony to give birth."—Revelation 12:1, 2.

No aid is given toward identifying this heavenly "woman" by giving her a name. She is not called Zion—that is the name of the mountain upon which the Lamb of God is seen standing with his 144,000 faithful followers who have his name and the name of his Father written on their foreheads, according to Revelation 14:1-4. She is not called Jerusalem, or New Jerusalem, for that is the name of the Lamb's wife, who is made up of those 144,000 followers. (Revelation 21:2, 9-14) But whoever it is that accepts the child to which this "woman" gives birth reveals himself thereby to be her husband and identifies her as his wife. That One is the Creator of the symbolic sun with which she is arrayed and Creator of the symbolic moon beneath her feet and of the twelve symbolic stars with which her head is crowned. Just as a husband is responsible to provide raiment, adornment and guidance for his wife, so the Creator provided heavenly spiritual light for his "woman," to be arrayed with it and to shine with it by day and to walk by means of it through the night, being crowned with it by night for her beautification.

Stars shine by night. The fact that the number of stars with which the woman was crowned was twelve indicates that this light is organizational light, twelve being a symbol of organizational completeness or governmental perfection. This meaning is to be seen in that there are twelve tribes of spiritual Israel, also twelve apostles of the Lamb; and the holy city, New Jerusalem, has twelve gates, three on each of its four sides, the city being based on twelve foundations bearing the names of the apostles. (Revelation 7: 4-8; 21:12-14, 19-21) There is organizational light for the heavenly "woman," no less so than for the "twelve tribes" of spiritual Israel here on earth.—James 1:1.

This woman in heaven is a "sign" woman, a "great sign" or symbol of something. Of what? Of the Creator's enlightened heavenly organization in the sense of its being his "woman" or wife. The idea of God's having such an organizational "wife" is nothing new, because for more than eight centuries before the apostle John was given the Revelation the prophet Isaiah was inspired to write to a womanlike city: "Your grand Maker is your husbandly owner, Jehovah of armies being his name; . . . And all your sons will be persons taught by Jehovah, and the peace of your sons will be abundant." (Isaiah 54:5, 6, 13) Jesus Christ himself quoted from those words and applied them to his faithful followers. (John 6:44, 45) It was thus indicated that the heavenly "woman" of Jehovah God would have children, sons. The faithful holy angels of heaven would be members composing that "sign" woman.

The reproach of barrenness does not attach to Jehovah's "woman." The apostle John saw that "she was pregnant." But what does he mean by saying that "she cries out in her pains and in her agony to give birth"? (Revelation 12:1, 2) The organizational "woman" knew that the time for her to deliver a child was near, for her pains and agony were already upon her. The time of human birth is usually foreknown, it being nine months or thirty-six weeks from the time of the conception of an offspring. So, too, God's heavenly womanlike organization knew the approximate time for the impending birth to take place; even the enemies in heaven also knew this. The heavenly birth meant the beginning of a new system of things for all of God's holy angels, even for his only-begotten Son Jesus Christ. This definitely meant a great change in the heavenly administration of things, a sweeping change in the organization of heavenly things. This would stir up things.

In ancient Israel in the days of the prophet Samuel, when there was a change of administration from that of the judges raised up by Jehovah God to that of a visible earthly king under Jehovah God, it meant a drastic change for the twelve tribes of Israel. The prophet Samuel forewarned the nation of the restricting changes that this change of administration would mean. Although such changes were agreed to by the people who wanted the change and were eager to have the change, yet in actuality it doubtless caused many national pains, as forewarned of by Samuel. (1 Samuel 8:7-22; 12:1 to 13:2) Thereafter no longer was it allowed for each man to do just what was right in his own eyes; each one had to line up with the royal government.—Judges 21:25.

In close resemblance to that ancient picture, a

changeover in the type of administration in heaven would call for needed changes in the structure and running of things. The time when the Gentile Times, "the appointed times of the nations," were due to end was foreknown to the very year. This was even foreknown for decades in advance down here on earth from the study of God's Word and its time schedule. (Luke 21:24) As the time for the end of the Gentile Times got closer, to introduce a change in the administration of things in heaven as well as on earth, due preparation would be made up there for this changeover. (Ephesians 1:8-11) The decision as to whether to submit to it or not would have to be made on the part of those who would come under this new administration.

It could not be expected that a new administration could go into operation in an orderly way without due prearrangements having been made for this. There was to be no political coup, no snatching of the reins of government by an ambitious upstart or by a power-greedy group of conspirators, no usurpation. As Jehovah is a "God, not of disorder," this was to be a formal, duly provided for, duly arranged for installation of a new administration. The time for this installation being at the end of the Gentile Times, which had begun with the overthrow of God's anointed king in ancient Israel, this fact called for putting back, for reinstalling the administration by God's anointed king, his Christ. This would bring about a tremendous test for all those affected. Hence the preparations for the formal, official birth of the new administration caused great stirrings in the invisible, angelic heavens. For God's heavenly wifelike organization this experience was like undergoing birth pains, an agony to get over with the birth of the new administration, to have the thing definitely settled.

"ANOTHER SIGN"

From all the attending circumstances, someone else outside God's wifely organization in heaven foreknew and expected that the birth of a new administration was due to come and was at hand. The apostle John describes that one in these words: "And another sign was seen in heaven, and, look! a great fiery-colored dragon, with seven heads and ten horns and upon its heads seven diadems; and its tail drags a third of the stars of heaven, and it hurled them down to the earth. And the dragon kept standing before the woman who was about to give birth, that, when she did give birth, it might devour her child."—Revelation 12:3, 4.

This terrible-looking creature is a "sign" dragon, a sign or symbol of something. It is like a monstrous sea serpent. (Isaiah 27:1) Its very attitude shows it to be an enemy of God, for it is an enemy of God's "woman" and of her child even before its birth. The dragon puts itself in the same position as the serpent to which Jehovah God referred when he made his mysterious prophecy, stated in Genesis 3:15, in these words: "I shall put enmity between you and the woman and between your seed and her seed. He will bruise you in the head and you will bruise him in the heel." Like a dragon, it is a Swallower Down, but in a sevenfold sense, for it has seven heads. (Jeremiah 51:34) Its being fiery colored indicates that it is destructive, consuming like fire. It is a "sign" symbol of Satan the Devil.

What do the "seven heads" of the dragon signify? This, namely, that Satan the Devil would exercise headship over and through seven successive political world powers on earth, as these are reported in their historic order in God's written Word, the Holy Bible. These world powers, all of them enemies and oppressors of Jehovah's people, are (1) ancient Egypt, (2) Assyria, (3) Babylonia, (4) Medo-Persia, (5) Greece (Macedon), (6) Rome, and (7) a world power unnamed in the Bible but which later history proved to be the dual world power of Great Britain and the United States of America (of the northern hemisphere). There being "seven" such symbolic

302 "THEN IS FINISHED THE MYSTERY OF GOD"   Revelation 12:3, 4

"heads" intelligently controlling the corresponding world powers, it bespeaks the completeness of Satan the Devil's political control over the world of mankind by means of this series of seven successive world powers.

In the Sacred Scriptures a horn is used to symbolize power, both offensive and defensive. The dragon's having ten symbolic horns pictures the completeness of invisible power that Satan the Devil has exercised through political governments on earth. Jesus called him "the ruler of this world."—John 16:11.

The tail of this symbolic dragon is also mighty: "its tail drags a third of the stars of heaven, and it hurled them down to the earth." (Revelation 12:4) These "stars of heaven" not unreasonably stand for bright-shining angels that belonged to Jehovah's holy heavenly organization, heavenly spirit sons of God. (Job 38:7) The proper place of physical stars is up in the skies, in the heavens; but the symbolic dragon with its mighty tail hurled these symbolic stars down from their proper heavenly place to the earth. Apparently, then, these "stars of heaven" picture those particular angels who for selfish reasons "did not keep their original position" in God's holy heavens but who "forsook their own proper dwelling place" up there in order to cohabit sensuously with beautiful daughters of men here below. Thus these angels "sinned" against Jehovah God and put themselves on the side of the symbolic dragon (Jude 6; 2 Peter 2:4; 1 Peter 3:19, 20; Genesis 6:1-4) Doubtless Satan the Devil used his influence like a "tail" to do this. By this means he hurled them to the earth, separating them from God's holy organization.

In this way the symbolic dragon, Satan the Devil, gained "angels" for himself, as his "seed." He did not swallow them down like a dragon to devour or destroy them, but hurled them down with his mighty tail. This he did before the flood of Noah's day, and hence before the formation of the seven world powers over which he was to exercise supervision by means of his "seven heads," upon which are his "seven diadems" of royalty. Logically, when the dragon kept standing before God's "woman" as the Gentile Times drew near to their end in 1914, those angels of the dragon were also standing lined up behind him to aid him in trying to "devour" or swallow down her "child" at its birth so as to prevent a new administration.

These opposing angels included a "third of the stars of heaven," a minority of the stars and yet a considerable number of them, forasmuch as the fraction "third" is used as a symbol of emphasis. So there could be tens of thousands, legions, of these demons, under the control of the "great fiery-colored dragon," who is "the ruler of the demons."—Mark 5:9-15; Matthew 12:24.

BIRTH OF A CHILD FOR THE THRONE

Regardless of the dragon on the *qui vive* to thwart the divine purpose for the birth, there was a perfect birth at the due time in heaven, for the Father of the expected offspring was perfect, and so was his wife, the mother organization. But—who got the child—God the kingly Father or the voracious jaws of the "seven heads" of the symbolic dragon? The apostle John's record, in Revelation 12:5, 6, gives us the bulletin of events: "And she gave birth to a son, a male, who is to shepherd all the nations with an iron rod. And her child was caught away to God and to his throne. And the woman fled into the wilderness, where she has a place prepared by God, that they should feed her there a thousand two hundred and sixty days." The mother escapes from the dragon, so too the child.

No cause for surprise that the dragon was eager to "devour" or swallow down that "son, a male," for it was God's purpose that it should "shepherd all the nations with an iron rod," finally dashing them all to pieces therewith! The Satanic dragon was determined not to be deprived of his "seven diadems," which symbolized his complete spiritual kingship over the seven successive world powers. He was not interested in having "all the nations," of which he was the invisible ruler and "god," dashed to shivers by God's new administration. So he set himself to devour the woman's "child" as soon as it was born and when it would reasonably be at its weakest. To his chagrin he failed!

The woman's child was, not a queen, but "a son, a male." Whom or what does it represent? Not Jesus Christ, but God's Messianic kingdom. That is why it was caught up to God and to his throne, God thus acknowledging it as his offspring by his "woman."

However, this Messianic kingdom is not something merely theoretical, a mere governmental formula. For it to exist and come into power it must be made a living reality in a living person, a "male" who could bear kingdom titles and responsibilities and take action, really reigning. That person was God's only-begotten Son, the glorified Jesus who is the Christ or Messiah of God. So the birth of the symbolic "son, a male," took place when God's wifely organization brought forth or furnished the right member of the organization for the royal office. The kingdom of God's Messiah was actually installed in the heavens after the woman's "child" was caught away to God and to his throne, by Jehovah's enthroning his anointed Son in order to make the kingdom a working reality. This occurred in 1914 C.E. at the end of the Gentile Times. Then and there, at this enthronement or clothing of the Messiah with full usable Kingdom authority, was finished the "mystery of God."—Revelation 10:7, AS.

Why, though, was it that, after this successful birth, God's "woman" "fled into the wilderness" to be fed there for one thousand two hundred and sixty days? The reason why becomes plain when we learn what happened after the birth and enthronement of the heavenly Messianic kingdom. After the Bible's account of what happened (in Revelation 12:7-12) the flight of God's woman into the wilderness is again referred to and thus becomes explainable. What, then, was it that also followed the enthronement of her "child"?

WAR IN HEAVEN

The apostle John reports it, saying: "And war broke out in heaven: Michael and his angels battled with the dragon, and the dragon and its angels battled but it did not prevail, neither was a place found for them any longer in heaven. So down the great dragon was hurled, the original serpent, the one called Devil and Satan, who is misleading the entire inhabited earth; he was hurled down to the earth, and his angels were hurled down with him. And I heard a loud voice in heaven say:

"'Now have come to pass the salvation and the power and the kingdom of our God and the authority of his Christ, because the accuser of our brothers has been hurled down, who accuses them day and night before our God! And they conquered him because of the blood of the Lamb and because of the word of their witnessing, and they did not love their souls even in the face of death. On this account be glad, you heavens and you who reside in them! Woe for the earth and for the sea, because the Devil has come down to you, having great anger, knowing he has a short period of time.'"—Revelation 12:7-12.

Here is the first and only mention of that heavenly warrior Michael in the Revelation to John. But he has been known by name since the days of the prophet Daniel, in the sixth century before our Common Era. An angel appeared to Daniel in the third year of the reign of Cyrus the Great, the king of Persia, and he told of how "Michael, one of the foremost princes," came to help him and how this same Michael, who was the spirit prince of Daniel's people, held strongly with this angel in his difficulty. Then, after telling of the final movements of the "king of the north" and the "king of the south," the angel said: "And during that time Michael will stand up, the great prince who is standing in behalf of the sons of your people. And there will certainly occur a time of distress such as has not been made to occur since there came to be a nation until that time. And during that time your people will escape, every one who is found written down in the book."—Daniel 10:13, 21; 12:1.

Moreover, before ever the war broke out in heaven, Michael, the heavenly prince of Jehovah's people, had confronted Satan the Devil in the invisible realm. This was immediately after the death of the prophet Moses in the year 1473 B.C.E. The inspired disciple Jude reports on this strange confrontation, saying: "But when Michael the archangel had a difference with the Devil and was disputing about Moses' body, he did not dare to bring a judgment against him in abusive terms, but said: 'May Jehovah rebuke you.'" (Jude 9) Nevertheless, in that dispute the archangel Michael won out, for it turned out to be Jehovah God that buried the body of Moses his servant at a place that not even the Devil Satan has been able to reveal to anybody on earth. (Deuteronomy 34:5, 6) But now after the birth and enthronement of God's Messianic kingdom in 1914 C.E., it was no longer a case in which Michael waited upon Jehovah to rebuke Satan the Devil, but Jehovah used Michael in warring against Satan the Devil and his demon angels, hurling them out of heaven. What a "salvation" or victory that was!

Is there any question as to who is this Michael the archangel? He is no one else but Jesus Christ the only-begotten Son of God! He is the one who, before our Common Era began, was the heavenly prince of Jehovah's people, including Daniel. Never did he renounce the right to that heavenly name, even when he became a perfect man here on earth in order to work for the interests of God's Messianic kingdom and to ransom all mankind by offering himself to God for a perfect human sacrifice. (John 18:36, 37; Matthew 20:28) After his resurrection from the dead and his return to heaven, he resumed that heavenly name.

Since he has his angels, of whom he frequently spoke while on earth, he is rightly "the archangel" of God. He being "the beginning of the creation by God," he was produced before any other heavenly angels were created with whom to form a wifely organization for Jehovah God. (Revelation 3:14) In the year 1914 C.E., after the "time of the end" began for the "king of the north" and the "king of the south," he stood up in royal Messianic power. His standing up thus was to lead to a "time of distress such as has not been made to occur since there came to be a nation until that time." (Daniel 11:40 to 12:1) He is the principal seed or offspring of God's "woman" (wifely organization) for bruising the Serpent in the head and hence for hurling him down from heaven.—Genesis 3:15.

The name Jesus (shortened form for Jehoshua) means "Salvation of Jehovah." The meaning of the name Michael is in the form of a question, namely, "Who Is Like Jehovah?" He is a Champion, a Challenger for Jehovah against anybody, against Satan the Devil and his demon angels. Just how Michael and his angels battled against the dragon and his angels, and with what weapons, is not Scripturally stated; probably, like with many other scientific things, we could not even understand it. How long the battle kept on we are not told. Only the decisive result is reported to us: the dragon and his angels were deposed from the heavens. There was no further proper place for them up there in those heavens. The dragon's accusations before God day and night had all proved to be false, and there was no need, toward the settlement of the great controversy, for the dragon to remain that close to God's presence and audience so as to press his accusations any farther.—Proverbs 27:11.

This great accuser is given a foursquare set of names, Dragon, meaning Swallower Down; Serpent, which has taken on the meaning of Seducer, Deceiver,

Misleader; Satan, meaning "Resister"; and Devil, meaning "Slanderer." (Jeremiah 51:34; Genesis 3:4, 5; 2 Corinthians 11:3; 1 Timothy 3:11; 2 Timothy 3:3) With regard to the heavens it is said that the dragon's tail dragged only a third part of the stars of heaven and hurled them down to the earth; but with regard to the earth he has better success, for he "is misleading the entire inhabited earth."—Revelation 12:4, 9.

Those angels who belong to the symbolic dragon and who battled with him against Michael and his angels, doubtless included the spirit princes mentioned in Daniel 10:13, 20, namely, "the prince of the royal realm of Persia" and "the prince of Greece." This implies that there were also spirit princes for the other five of the seven world powers, that is, the spirit princes of Egypt, Assyria, Babylonia, Rome and the Anglo-American dual world power. These "princes" and all the other lesser angels were hurled down with the "dragon" to the earth, never to get back to heaven.

What a relief this was for the holy angels to have the dragon and his demon angels ousted from heaven and confined to the vicinity of this earth! For excellent reason the "loud voice in heaven" could say: "Now have come to pass the salvation and the power and the kingdom of our God and the authority of his Christ." (Revelation 12:10) The ouster of the dragon and his angels meant a "salvation," that is, a victory, and it was due to the exercise of triumphant power on God's part. This victory over the dragon and his angels was an initial expression of "the kingdom of our God and the authority of his Christ." The ouster showed that God's kingdom had come into power and that "his Christ," his anointed King, had begun to exercise his God-given authority.

This fact proves that the birth and enthronement of the male child of the "woman" pictured the birth and inauguration of God's Messianic kingdom, the finishing of the "mystery of God." At its very birth and inauguration this Messianic kingdom of God showed itself, not weak like a newborn babe, but most powerful. How so? Because by it "the accuser of our brothers has been hurled down," that is to say, the chief enemy of Jehovah God and of his holy universal organization has been hurled down.

THE ACCUSED "BROTHERS"

Who are the accused ones, and what does the accusation leveled against them by Satan the Devil say? The faithful angels in heaven call the accused ones "our brothers." Yet the accused are not heavenly angels, but they are the ones who "conquered him [the accuser] because of the blood of the Lamb and because of the word of their witnessing, and they did not love their souls even in the face of death." —Revelation 12:10, 11.

This description makes it certain that the accused are the dedicated, baptized, anointed followers of the Lamb Jesus Christ. They need the sin-removing benefits of the blood of his perfect human sacrifice. They are the ones who, on earth, give the witness, not only concerning the Lamb sacrificed, but also concerning the God who provided the Lamb and to whom the sacrifice of the Lamb was offered in behalf of all mankind. They, and not the angels of heaven, are the ones that are faced with a martyr's death for being active, obedient followers of the Lamb of God.

What does the Devilish accusation against them charge? This, that Almighty God cannot put Christians on earth who, if fully exposed to temptation and resistance by the accusing Satan the Devil, will live up to Christian rules of conduct, hating sin and imitating Jesus Christ and obeying Jehovah God as Ruler rather than men. Satan the Devil would be too powerful for them; they could not overcome such a wily, pressure-using person as *he* is.

So, for them to die as true Bible Christians having the approval of God would mean for them to conquer Satan the Devil, proving him to be a false accuser and God to be the Creator and Ruler whom creatures love so much as to obey him fully at all costs. God's victory, therefore, would be, not only by battle against the dragon and his demon angels, but also by proving the love from Christ's followers to be so strong that they would lay down their lives as Jesus Christ did for obeying Him above all. This would be a moral victory for Jehovah God, proving Satan a liar.

Did the Devil accuse the anointed Christians of being sinners? According to the flesh, yes, they were sinners, for they were born such by descent from the fallen Adam. But they accepted the ransom sacrifice of Jesus Christ. They trusted that by the sin-atoning value of Christ's blood they would be cleansed from the stain of sin and be counted as righteous in God's eyes. Hence concerning them it is written: "Who will file accusation against God's chosen ones? God is the One who declares them righteous. Who is he that will condemn? Christ Jesus is the one who died, yes, rather the one who was raised up from the dead." (Romans 8:33, 34) By repenting of their unwilling sins, they evidence their hatred of sin, and obtain God's forgiveness through Christ's blood. In this way those Christians who faithfully finished their earthly course conquered Satan the Devil "because of the blood of the Lamb." Satan's accusation on this score is false!

The accuser before God charged further that they could be frightened or intimidated into denying Jehovah God and his Christ or Messiah. But down till the birth of God's Messianic kingdom in 1914 and the outbreak of the war in heaven there were faithful Christians who refused to disown God and his Christ under any circumstances produced by the great accuser. Like the aged apostle John on the Isle of Patmos they persisted to the end of their earthly lives in "speaking about God and bearing witness to Jesus." —Revelation 1:9.

Even as far back as 1877 C.E. there were those who were pointing forward to the end of the Gentile Times in 1914 and who gave a wide witness concerning the full establishment of God's Messianic kingdom to occur at that time.* Right on into the throes of World War I of 1914-1918 the International Bible Students were proclaiming these things by much printed literature in many languages and by word of mouth privately and in public lectures and by the free exhibition of the famous Photo-Drama of Creation illustrated with Biblical color slides and motion pictures. Thus after the ouster of Satan and his demons from heaven it could be said by the loud voice in heaven that faithful Christian "brothers" from the first century onward had conquered the great dragon "because of the word of their witnessing." On this score also the great accuser before God was proved to be a liar.

These Christian "brothers" considered it to be the main thing of their lives to prove their faithfulness and loyalty to God and his Christ. As respects them the loud voice in heaven was true in testifying that "they did not love their souls even in the face of death." They proved to be like the apostle Paul, who said, a few years before his martyrdom: "I do not make my soul of any account as dear to me, if only I may finish my course and the ministry that I received of the Lord Jesus, to bear thorough witness to the good news of the undeserved kindness of God." (Acts 20:24) They were willing to surrender their earthly soul as the price for holding true to God and his Christ. They proved their faith in Jesus' words: "Whoever loses his soul for my sake will find it." (Matthew 16:25) Hence Satan the Devil lost out in his wicked efforts to silence them by threatening them

---

* For example, see the book entitled "Three Worlds, Or, Plan of Redemption" (on front cover), as published by N. H. Barbour and C. T. Russell in 1877 at Rochester, N.Y. The two-page chart at the beginning of the book says in its second-last column: " 'Times of the Gentiles' began B.C. 606 when Nebuchadnezzar received universal dominion. They continue during *seven times.*' Seven prophetic times is 7 multiplied by 360; or two thousand five hundred and twenty. And will therefore end *forty years* after A.D. 1874; that is, in A.D. 1914." In confirmation of this, note, for instance, page 129, paragraph 3, under the page heading "The Harvest."

with death. On the other hand, Jehovah God was vindicated by the unswerving, unbreakable loyalty of these faithful followers of his Christ.

In response to the loud voice in heaven, the angels who reside in the invisible heavens where no further place is found for the dragon did rejoice over the ouster of the great dragon and his demonic angels. But what about our earth and sea? It began a time of special "woe" for the people inhabiting these, "because the Devil has come down to you, having great anger, knowing he has a short period of time." (Revelation 12:12) His defeat in the war in heaven was a strong portent that his remaining time now before being bound as with chains and imprisoned in the abyss had a limit and was short. He had long been "misleading the entire inhabited earth." Now he was determined to force the destruction of everybody on land and sea at God's hands at the coming destruction of Babylon the Great (the world empire of false religion) and the following 'battle of Armageddon.' This he would bring about by causing all the trouble and false propaganda that he and his demons could, in order to turn all mankind away from the victorious kingdom of God. He would fight against the preaching of the "good news of the kingdom." All this he has since attempted.

DEMONIC PERSECUTION

What, now, was the reaction on the part of the "great dragon" and his demon angels at their being forever ousted from the holy heavens? Twentieth-century history answers the question in agreement with what the apostle John saw take place in vision. John wrote: "Now when the dragon saw that it was hurled down to the earth, it persecuted the woman that gave birth to the male child. But the two wings of the great eagle were given the woman, that she might fly into the wilderness to her place; there is where she is fed for a time and times and half a time away from the face of the serpent." (Revelation

12:13, 14) How is this being fulfilled in the history of our century?

One way of expressing his "great anger" at his being ousted from heaven was for the "dragon" to persecute God's "woman." As she had given birth to the "male child," God's Messianic kingdom, she had a large share in the responsibility for the dragon's ouster, and so he would persecute her. Although he was debarred now forever from heaven, the dragon and his demons at their abased earthly location would try to make it as hard as possible for the angels who make up the symbolic "woman" whenever these intervened in earth's affairs in behalf of the interests of God's established kingdom. Furthermore, the remnant of the 'woman's' seed or offspring on earth were also a part of her, coming forth as it were from her womb; and thus by persecuting this remnant of Christ's anointed followers yet on this earth, the dragon and his demons would be persecuting God's "woman," the mother of the Kingdom. The apostle John's further account of the earthly activities of the dragon and his demons verifies that this is what they did.

Apparently after the dragon's ouster the "woman" left her position in heaven where she was arrayed with the sun and with the moon under her feet and with a crown of twelve stars about her head, for Revelation 12:6 says that "the woman fled into the wilderness, where she has a place prepared by God." When did the woman's flight to the wilderness and the feeding of her there take place, away from the serpent?

To get to the wilderness, the "two wings of the great eagle" were given to her. This mode of flight bears a resemblance to something in ancient time, in the sixteenth century B.C.E. After the first Passover supper, that one held down in Egypt in 1513 B.C.E., Jehovah God brought the twelve tribes of Israel miraculously through the waters of the Red Sea and into the wilderness of Mount Sinai, where they stayed for more than nine months. Later referring to this in the song of the prophet Moses, Jehovah God said: "Just as an eagle stirs up its nest, hovers over its fledglings, spreads out its wings, takes them, carries them on its pinions, Jehovah alone kept leading him, and there was no foreign god along with him." (Deuteronomy 31:30; 32:11, 12) At Mount Sinai itself, before giving to the Israelites the Ten Commandments, Jehovah God said to them through Moses: "You yourselves have seen what I did to the Egyptians, that I might carry you on wings of eagles and bring you to myself." (Exodus 19:1-4) Likewise, symbolically, "two wings of the great eagle" helped God's "woman," under threat of persecution, to fly into the wilderness after Satan's ouster.

The ouster of the "great dragon" and his demons from heaven was apparently fully accomplished by the end of World War I. According to Revelation 11:1, 2, the "holy city" was trampled on by the Gentile nations "for forty-two months," from autumn of 1914 to spring of 1918. During this same period, spoken of as 1,260 days, God's "two witnesses" prophesied, "dressed in sackcloth," despite the efforts to harm them. After this these "two prophets" were killed by the "wild beast" out of the abyss. But after a short time, like three and a half days, they were raised from the death state and exalted to heavenly service. At that time there came the release of the anointed remnant. (Revelation 11:3-13) This release occurred in the spring of 1919 C.E. By then the persecution of the anointed remnant during World War I was past, and postwar persecution of this faithful remnant was now ahead. For this they needed to be strengthened with spiritual food. This, then, would be the suitable time for God's "woman," as represented by the remnant of her seed on earth, to flee into the wilderness to be fed.

Ancient Israel's flight from Egypt in 1513 B.C.E. was immediately after the Passover of Nisan 14 of that year. Correspondingly Passover time becomes the starting point in the year 1919 C.E. According to the Jewish calendar, Nisan 1, 1919, began on the night of March 31. Hence Nisan 14 would start on the night of Sunday, April 13, 1919, which time is when the International Bible Students celebrated the annual Lord's supper or evening meal. (*The Watch Tower,* as of May 15, 1919, page 151) The president and the secretary-treasurer of the Watch Tower Bible & Tract Society, released along with their six fellow prisoners from Atlanta Federal penitentiary on March 25, 1919, and set at liberty next day on bail, partook of this celebration of the Lord's supper. Partial reports received during that first postwar year showed that more than eighteen thousand attended that Memorial. Right afterward, in its issue of April 15, 1919, the official magazine *The Watch Tower and Herald of Christ's Presence* began giving timely spiritual food in its leading article "Liberty in Christ" and in other Bible material of that issue. When did this feeding program, thus begun, end?

According to Revelation 12:6, 14, God's "woman" was to be at God's prepared place for her in the wilderness for "a thousand two hundred and sixty days," or "a time and times and half a time," or three and a half times.* This means that each "time" corresponded with 360 days, or twelve months of thirty days each. This shows that these three and a half years are prophetic years. They therefore correspond with three and a half years according to the Jewish lunar calendar, which at times has intercalary or lunisolar years of thirteen lunar months.

According to the Jewish lunar calendar, three and a half years from Passover day, Nisan 14, 1919, would end on Tishri 13, 1922, or on October 5, 1922, at

---

* Since three and a half "times" equal 1,260 days, seven (2 x 3 1/2) "times" equal 2,520 days. Accordingly, the "seven times" for Gentile domination of the earth equal 2,520 units of time, that is, 2,520 symbolic "days," or 2,520 years, from early autumn of the year 607 B.C.E. to the early autumn of the year 1914 C.E.—Daniel 4:16, 23, 25; Luke 21:24.

The number 2,520 is remarkable in that it is a multiple of any one of the numerical digits from 1 to 9, and, of course, is thus divisible by any one of them, and also by ten (10).

sundown. (In the solar calendar this included one leap year [1920], and in the Jewish lunar calendar it included one thirteen-month or lunisolar year [1921].) So this period of special feeding in the symbolic wilderness "away from the face of the serpent" began at Passover time, April 13/14, 1919, and ended the thirteenth day from the Jewish New Year (Rosh Hashanah), or on October 4/5, 1922. This was indeed a time of spiritual feeding.

Toward the beginning of this feeding period came the first Cedar Point, Ohio, convention of the International Bible Students Association, on September 1-8, 1919, at which the projected publishing of a new magazine, *The Golden Age,* was announced on Friday, September 5. The following October 1, 1919, *The Golden Age* (today known as *Awake!*) began to be published in addition to *The Watch Tower*. In its issue of October 1, 1919, *The Watch Tower* published a nine-page report on that international assembly. Also, bans on all or various publications of the Watch Tower Bible & Tract Society began to be lifted in certain lands.

Quite appropriately in March 1920, the Watch Tower Society published the book entitled "Talking with the Dead" (later changed to "Can the Living Talk with the Dead?") This was a well-documented exposé of spiritism, demonism, as it was rampant then throughout the earth. Shortly afterward the *Watch Tower* issue of July 1, 1920, set forth that Matthew 24:14 concerning the preaching of "this good news of the kingdom" had special application since the Kingdom's birth in 1914. Six months later the January 1, 1921, issue of *The Watch Tower,* in its second article identified the mysterious "image of the wild beast" of Revelation 13:14, 15, as symbolizing the then-existing League of Nations for world peace and security, succeeded now by the United Nations.

Toward the end of 1921 the new Bible-study aid entitled "The Harp of God" was published in October, and shipments of it to those ordering it began on

December 1, 1921. This book of 384 pages, which was meant to be an epitome of the seven volumes of *Studies in the Scriptures,* finally attained a circulation of 5,819,037 copies in 22 languages. This and other means of supplying the needed spiritual food continued to be published and distributed.

Then, toward the close of the three and a half "times" or 1,260 days, came the grand climax. This was in the form of the second international convention at Cedar Point, Ohio, held by the International Bible Students Association on September 5-13, 1922. (The entire issue of *The Watch Tower* under date of November 1, 1922, was taken up by the report of this outstanding assembly of Jehovah's anointed remnant.) Shortly thereafter, on September 22, 1922, the Jewish lunar year ended. Then came Tishri 13, or October 4/5, 1922, which is just before the time of the year for the Jewish "festival of booths" and which marked the end of the special feeding of God's "woman" in the wilderness condition. This date found the anointed remnant of her seed on earth well nourished, spiritually strengthened for God's work ahead. Just twenty-six days later (on October 31, 1922) they began distributing world wide 45,000,000 copies of the Cedar Point convention resolution, "The Challenge."

ATTEMPT TO ENGULF THE "WOMAN"

With the holding of the second international convention at Cedar Point, Ohio, in September of 1922, the series of "seven trumpets" began to be blown. (Revelation 8:1-7) It was time for the dragon, angry at being abased, to take action. Not being able to swallow down God's "woman" any more than he had been able to swallow down her "male child" in 1914, the great dragon belched out something after the "woman." It was not his diabolical propaganda such as was pictured by one of the "three unclean inspired expressions that looked like frogs." Such propaganda as that he would use to gather the "kings of the entire inhabited earth" to the "war of the great day of God the Almighty" at Armageddon. (Revelation 16:13-16) But after the thousand two hundred and sixty days (three and a half "times"), the thing that the dragon belched out was, rather, something to do away with the now well-fed remnant of the 'woman's' seed yet on the earth. Was he successful in this?

The apostle John tells us the vision that he saw of this, saying: "And the serpent disgorged water like a river from its mouth after the woman, to cause her to be drowned by the river. But the earth came to the woman's help, and the earth opened its mouth and swallowed up the river that the dragon disgorged from its mouth."—Revelation 12:15, 16.

The symbolic serpent, the dragon, tried something that is like what is called a "human sea" attack against God's "woman" as represented on earth by the anointed remnant of her seed. The "water like a river" that the serpent-dragon belched out was composed of humankind, or masses of men and women who become noisy for their cause "just like the noise of many waters." (Isaiah 17:12, 13) There were "flash floods of good-for-nothing men" that tried to terrify the anointed remnant of the 'woman's' seed with the prospects of violent death and Sheol, the grave. (Psalm 18:4, 5, 16, 17) Thus the anointed remnant became menaced by the symbolic waters of fanatical Fascists, Communists and Nazis and Catholic Actionists, religionists who were eager for reestablishing the Holy Roman Empire by means of Fascism and Nazism; also "waters" of militarists, nationalistic patrioteers and aggressive imperialists. The "waters" became like a "river."

In October of 1922 Benito Mussolini led his Black Shirts in a march on Rome and established a Fascist government in Italy to last for more than twenty years. In the same year Catholic Action was organized by Pope Pius XI for advancing papal rulership.

The death of Lenin in Communist Russia on January 21, 1924, led to the rise of the brutal dictatorship of Stalin and Communist aggressions. In 1931 the Japanese imperialists started on their way toward taking over much of the mainland of Asia. In 1933 Adolf Hitler took over the government of Germany and soon posed the threat of Nazi domination of the whole world. In 1936 came the nationalist "Movement" against republican government in Spain, leading to the totalitarian dictatorship of a Caudillo or "Leader." Dictatorship was also established in neighboring Portugal even earlier, in 1934. Peacetime military conscription was introduced into the United States of America and fanatical patrioteers gained wide influence. Thus in wave after wave the symbolic "waters" poured forth from the serpent-dragon's mouth with one main objective, to 'drown' God's "woman" who had brought forth God's Messianic kingdom, the "male child."

Certainly those waves of ambitious, violent men were not in favor of God's Messianic kingdom, and so they could issue forth only from God's chief enemy, from the symbolic serpent-dragon, Satan the Devil. So these human "waters" were part of the "woe" that was to come because the Devil had been ousted from heaven and had come down to the vicinity of our earth and was so angry, knowing that he had a short period of time left. Many of the peoples of the earth found those symbolic "waters" to be a woe and hence resisted them. Quite to be expected, this led to World War II. The outcome of the war brought a defeat to the effort of the serpent-dragon to sweep over the whole earth with these "waters" in order to drown God's "woman." This is what the apostle John foresaw under symbolic imagery, in that "the earth came to the woman's help, and the earth opened its mouth and swallowed up the river that the dragon disgorged from its mouth."—Revelation 12:16.

The "earth" symbolized the more stable, democratic, conservative part of human society, that tried to preserve its rights, its liberties, its constitutional or traditional forms of governments, its cherished culture.

Of course, this "earth" was not directly interested in helping God's "woman" any more than it was in favor of her "male child," God's Messianic kingdom. It was resisting and so it was counteracting the onrush of the "waters" in order to protect its own earthly interests. This action of the "earth" really produced a hot war and a cold war between the totalitarian, authoritarian "king of the north" and the democratic "king of the south," the movements of both of whom during the "time of the end" are foretold in Daniel 11:27 to 12:4. Nevertheless, many of the measures that the stabilized "earth" took and its defeat of the aggressive "waters" served for the benefit of God's "woman," and in this way this "earth" came to the "woman's" aid to keep her from being drowned.

To the chagrin of the serpent-dragon, the anointed remnant of the 'woman's' seed yet on earth came out of World War II stronger than ever before. How so? In that at the close of World War II in 1945 they had been joined by tens of thousands of the "great crowd" of earthly subjects of God's Messianic kingdom. Particularly since 1935 C.E. these had cast in their lot with the anointed remnant regardless of the persecution that had to be undergone. The *1946 Yearbook of Jehovah's Witnesses* (page 218) was able to report despite the disrupted world conditions: "The report shows that in one month during 1945 there were 141,606 publishers engaged in field service, to compare with the monthly average of 127,478 for the whole service year." In the prewar year of 1938 there had been only 47,143 such Kingdom publishers. Thus the "dragon" was frustrated in this fashion, in addition to its being permanently ejected from the holy heavens. What was the effect of all this upon the serpent-dragon, Satan the Devil, together with his demon angels? The apostle John says:

"And the dragon grew wrathful at the woman, and went off to wage war with the remaining ones of her seed, who observe the commandments of God and have the work of bearing witness to Jesus."—Revelation 12:17, *NW; NEB*.

Unable to destroy God's "woman," the dragonlike Satan the Devil could vent his increased wrath at

her by taking it out on the anointed remnant who really belonged to the "woman" because they were the "remaining ones of her seed" yet on earth. Let no true Christian lose sight of this significant fact: The main target of Satan the Devil today is this anointed remnant who represent God's "woman" on earth! These distinguish themselves, not merely by going under the name of Jehovah's Christian witnesses, but especially because they "observe the commandments of God" for Christians in this "time of the end." Even in a clash between the "commandments of God" and those of the political "superior authorities" of earth they take the position of the apostles of Jesus Christ when before the Supreme

Court of Jerusalem in the first century C.E.: "We must obey God as ruler rather than men."—Acts 5:27-32.

The anointed remnant are also distinguished by their God-given privilege of having "the work of bearing witness to Jesus." Despite mounting religious persecution, they press on with this "work of bearing witness to Jesus," especially to Jesus as now being God's Messianic King reigning since the Gentile Times ended in 1914.

The dragonlike Satan the Devil and his demons are waging a losing war against the anointed "remaining ones" of the seed of God's "woman." No pressure from the dragon's world makes them break off from observing "the commandments of God" and extending their "work of bearing witness to Jesus." In further proof of this continuous defeat of the warring dragon is the noteworthy fact that the "great crowd" that takes its stand for God and his reigning Christ alongside the anointed remnant increases steadily. (Revelation 7:9-17) The early field service reports of 1969 showed there were 1,229,016 who regularly each month were actively taking part in the "work of bearing witness to Jesus" in 200 lands and island groups of the sea. Included among these were 82,842 that were baptized in water during the 1968 service year.

Very manifestly Jehovah God is blessing and protecting his dedicated servants on earth. So, then, let the angry serpent-dragon continue to war against the anointed remnant and the growing "great crowd" of their dedicated fellow witnesses. Instead of seeing these destroyed in the "war of the great day of God the Almighty" at Armageddon, the dragon will see them survive. It is they who thereafter will see the great dragon and his demons hurled into the abyss after Armageddon.—Revelation 20:1-3.

Earthly Foes of "The Mystery of God"

SATAN THE DEVIL is the arch-foe of "the mystery of God," that is to say, the Messianic kingdom of God in the hands of the glorified Jesus Christ. From the day of God's prophetic notice given to him in the garden of Eden and recorded in Genesis 3:15, "the original serpent" has tried to prevent this "mystery of God" from being finished and fully disclosed before the gaze of all heaven and earth. Indisputably, then, any ruling elements on earth that are foes of this "mystery of God" must be on the side of the symbolic "great dragon," "the original serpent." Their origin must have come from him and not from the God of the Messianic mystery. This is the plain meaning of the vision that the apostle John next saw after beholding the ouster of the "great dragon" and his demon angels from heaven down to the earth and their going to war against God's anointed remnant on earth, "the remaining ones" of the seed of His "woman." John says:

"And it stood still upon the sand of the sea. And I saw a wild beast ascending out of the sea, with ten horns and seven heads, and upon its horns ten diadems, but upon its heads blasphemous names. Now the wild beast that I saw was like a leopard, but its feet were as those of a bear, and its mouth was as a lion's mouth. And the dragon gave to the beast its power and its throne and great authority."—Revelation 13:1, 2.

It was not first after the symbolic dragon and its

demon angels were hurled out of heaven that the dragon, standing still upon the sand of the sea, saw the wild beast ascend out of the sea. Actually this symbolic "wild beast" was in existence and was displaying its beastliness long before God's Messianic kingdom was born in the heavens in the year 1914 and thereafter the dragon and his demon angels were hurled out and down to this earth. Being now in the vicinity of our earth, the "dragon" is well pictured as standing upon the sand of the sea and watching to see how his visible earthly organization functions, operates as his agent or tool. The sea is symbolic, of course, and it pictures a vast portion of mankind ("peoples and crowds and nations"), this portion being rebellious at God's sovereignty and estranged from him and producing its own preferred style of government. (Revelation 17:15) In agreement with this, God's prophet says, in Isaiah 57:20, 21:

" 'The wicked are like the sea that is being tossed, when it is unable to calm down, the waters of which keep tossing up seaweed and mire. There is no peace,' my God has said, 'for the wicked ones.' "

The natural sea is a great deep, an abyss. (Genesis 1:2; 7:11; 8:2; Deuteronomy 8:7; 33:13, *LXX*) So the "wild beast that ascends out of the abyss" and kills God's "two prophets" is the same as the "wild beast" that the dragon sees "ascending out of the sea." (Revelation 11:7) Under the invisible influence of the "dragon" this symbolic wild beast emerges from the "sea" of tossed-about humankind, not having the peace of God and not hoping for his Messianic kingdom. The emergence of this "wild beast" from the sea reminds one of the prophet Daniel's night vision of the sixth century B.C.E., in which he saw "four huge beasts" coming up out of the wind-tossed sea. The four beasts are explained by God's angel to symbolize four successive political world powers, the first one being like a lion, the second one like a bear, and the third one like a leopard. (Daniel 7:1-26) As in the case of them, the wild beast that the dragon sees ascend out of the sea symbolizes a human political organization.

Its being like a leopard made the sea beast somewhat like the third beast that Daniel saw, which pictured the Grecian (Macedonian) World Power. Its having feet like those of a bear gave it a feature of the second beast seen by Daniel, which pictured the Medo-Persian World Power. Its mouth being like that of a lion gave it a feature of the first beast in Daniel's vision, which pictured the Babylonian World Power. This suggests that this symbolic "wild beast" was already in existence or under formation away back in the days of the lionlike Babylonian World Power of the seventh and sixth centuries B.C.E.

But the "wild beast" has seven heads. This indicates that it was in existence or under formation even earlier than that Babylonian World Power. How much earlier? As early as the first world power that had to do with Jehovah's chosen people in Bible history. That was the Egyptian World Power, prior to the eighth century B.C.E. and extending still farther back into the seventeenth century B.C.E., after the death of the Hebrew Joseph as prime minister of Egypt (1657 B.C.E.). So this is a composite wild beast, a composite political organization that has comprised seven world powers, from ancient Egypt to the Anglo-American World Power.

The seven heads of this sea beast find their counterpart in the seven heads of the dragon; they are a reflection of the dragon's seven heads. (Revelation 12:3) This correspondency betokens that the "great dragon," Satan the Devil, exercises invisible headship over these seven successive world powers and that he has appointed invisible demon princes over them, as, for instance, "the prince of Persia" and "the prince of Greece." (Daniel 10:13, 20) As the identity of this sea beast is examined, it becomes more and more apparent that it pictures the entire worldwide political organization of Satan the Devil from its start in the second century after the flood of Noah's day until now.

The symbolic "wild beast" out of the sea really got started in the days of Nimrod, the great-grandson of the patriarch Noah, and while Noah was still alive after the flood. Genesis 10:8-12 describes this, saying: "And Cush became father to Nimrod. He made the start in becoming a mighty one in the earth. He displayed himself a mighty hunter in opposition to Jehovah. That is why there is a saying: 'Just like Nimrod a mighty hunter in opposition to Jehovah.' And the beginning of his kingdom came to be Babel [Babylon] and Erech and Accad and Calneh, in the land of Shinar. Out of that land he went forth into Assyria and set himself to building Nineveh and Rehoboth-Ir and Calah and Resen between Nineveh and Calah: this is the great city."

From those facts it is plain that the "dragon," Satan the Devil, not Jehovah God, gave to the wild beast out of the sea "its power and its throne and great authority." (Revelation 13:2) Its power, throne and great authority it has constantly used against Jehovah God and his purpose to finish "the mystery of God."

It has more horns than heads. Hence some of the heads may have had two horns, to represent dual world powers, such as Medo-Persia, the Roman World Power in its Eastern Empire and Western Empire, and the Anglo-American World Power. The "horns" pictured "kings" or ruling elements. This fact is emphasized in that each horn had a diadem upon it, whereas in the case of the "dragon" each of its seven heads wore a diadem. But in the case of the reigning Jesus Christ, it is said that "upon his head are many diadems," whether seven or ten or even more not being stated. These "many diadems" mark him as "King of kings and Lord of lords." (Revelation 19: 12, 16; 17:12-14; Daniel 8:20-22) Hence the ten royal "horns" of the wild beast out of the sea will be unable to resist the King of kings during God's war at Ar-

mageddon but will be shorn of their royal power
and authority and lose their thrones. Inasmuch as
the ten diademed horns are upon the seven heads, it
adds to the argument that the wild beast that ascended out of the sea pictures Satan's agelong, worldwide political organization on the earth, from Nimrod's
days in the twenty-third century B.C.E. till now.

The Devilish nature of this political "wild beast"
is further shown in that it has "upon its heads blasphemous names." (Revelation 13:1) In using the word
"blasphemous," the apostle John likely knew that the
word "blasphemy" in Greek is derived from roots
conveying the thought of "hurting (blasting) the reputation (or, credit)," "throwing words or reports at"
so as to smite.

So, "to blaspheme" came to mean "to speak with
impious irreverence concerning God himself, or what
stands in some peculiar relation to him." (Parkhurst's
A Greek and English Lexicon to the New Testament,
page 97) For example, the Pharaohs of the Egyptian
World Power ranked themselves as gods and their
attitude toward Jehovah God is voiced in Pharaoh's
defiant retort to the prophet Moses: "Who is Jehovah,
so that I should obey his voice to send Israel away?
I do not know Jehovah at all and, what is more, I
am not going to send Israel away." (Exodus 5:2) So
in their dealings with Jehovah's true people all seven
headlike world powers of Satan's political organization have blasphemed the true God. They have taken
to themselves "blasphemous names."

"DEATH-STROKE" HEALED

Within this twentieth century the life of the "wild
beast" out of the sea seemed threatened. The apostle
John saw this prophetically portrayed in vision and
wrote: "And I saw one of its heads as though slaughtered to death, but its death-stroke got healed, and
all the earth followed the wild beast with admiration."
(Revelation 13:3) This stroke of death, or stroke
that leads to death, was administered by the sword

of war, so that the symbolic 'head' looked as if "slaughtered to death."—Revelation 13:14.

The overturning of one world power by its successor is not likened to giving a "death-stroke" to a head of the wild beast; otherwise, there would finally have to be seven such slaughterings of a head to death. But the vision shows only one of the seven heads wounded "as though slaughtered to death." The overthrow of the Egyptian World Power by the Assyrian World Power did not endanger the existence of the whole 'sea beast.' Neither did the overthrow of Assyria by Babylon, nor that of Babylon by Medo-Persia, nor that of Medo-Persia by Greece (Macedonia), nor that of Greece by Rome, nor that of Rome by the British Empire. Those six overthrows did not produce a "death-stroke."

Later, in Revelation 13:14, the stroke is called "the sword-stroke." So, then, the "death-stroke" pictures World War I of 1914-1918 C.E., and it was inflicted by the seventh 'head' (the Anglo-American World Power) upon the sixth 'head,' the Roman World Power (both the Eastern Empire and the Western Empire).

It was after two centuries of fighting with the Spanish, Dutch and French (remnants of the Roman Empire) that Great Britain (with its thirteen American colonies) emerged in the year 1763 C.E. as the "foremost commercial and colonial power in the world." She thus took world domination away from what remained of the Roman Empire and thus became the Seventh World Power foretold in Bible prophecy.* But it was in the year 1914 that the British Empire went to war against the German Empire, the Austro-Hungarian Empire and the Turkish Empire and, in 1915, against Bulgaria. This World War I finally involved twenty-eight nations and empires including the United States of North America in 1917. It inflicted a terrible defeat on what were the remnants of the Holy Roman Empire of the German

---

* See *Modern Europe to 1870,* by Carlton J. H. Hayes, pages 330-346, in chapter 8, entitled "British Expansion."

Nation. Territories, as well as colonies, were lost by these, their own territories being carved up.

The Turkish Empire lost Palestine, including Jerusalem, once part of the Roman Empire, the Sixth World Power. The Germanic or Teutonic remnants of that world power seemed to be "slaughtered to death" as far as exercising further challenging world influence is concerned. The very life of the whole "wild beast" out of the sea seemed threatened. So devastating was the first world war that it was generally felt that if another war like it on a global scale came, the world of mankind would not be able to endure it.

However, the worldwide political organization of Satan the Devil, namely, the symbolic sea beast, survived the effects of World War I. Its sixth head, as represented chiefly by Germany, recovered so well that on September 8, 1926, republican Germany was admitted to the League of Nations. Later, through the establishment of the dictatorship of the Nazi Fuehrer Adolf Hitler, in 1933, it defied the League of Nations and proceeded to the building up of the Third German Reich (Empire). Hitlerite Germany willfully provoked World War II in September 1939. Unmistakably, to judge matters by the recovery of the sixth head, the "death-stroke" got healed.

Did all of this create or enhance in the world of mankind the yearning desire for God's established Messianic kingdom, the finished "mystery of God"? Revelation 13:3 answers correctly, saying prophetically: "And all the earth followed the wild beast with admiration." (*NW*) "The whole world went after the beast in wondering admiration." (*NEB*) This means that the world of mankind had their confidence renewed as to the ability of the Devil's worldwide political organization to recover and heal itself. They gave no serious consideration to the fact that in 1914 C.E. the end had come to the seven Gentile Times for the worldwide rulership by that symbolic "wild beast" without interference from God's Messianic kingdom. The preaching of "this good news of the kingdom," as foretold by Jesus Christ in Matthew 24:14, did not cause the postwar world of mankind to admire God's Messianic kingdom and to seek it "first." (Matthew 6:33) The spirit of nationalism took hold of the national groups as never before, and they continued to follow admiringly their own political governments. This was unavoidably bound to lead to World War II in 1939-1945.

The world of mankind, even the people of Christendom, refused to believe that for them to follow the symbolic "wild beast" with wondering admiration was the same as Devil worship. They resented being told this by the International Bible Students Association and the publications of the Watch Tower Bible & Tract Society. But the language of the apostle John is unequivocal regarding this fact, for he goes on to say regarding the people on earth: "And they worshiped the dragon because it gave the authority to the wild beast, and they worshiped the wild beast with the words: 'Who is like the wild beast, and who can do battle with it?' "—Revelation 13:4.

Such questions were a direct challenge to God the Almighty and his Christ. What if the Gentile Times had expired in 1914 C.E.? The people felt that nevertheless Jehovah God had not then ousted the political "wild beast" from its domination of the whole earth. The "wild beast" tried to strengthen its position, determined to fight for the perpetuation of itself in power. The one who "can do battle" with this wild beast is God's archangel, Michael, whose name means "Who Is Like God?" But the people of earth raised the counter question, "Who is like the wild beast?" By their question they were begging for the "war of the great day of God the Almighty" at Armageddon.

ACTIVITY OF THE "WILD BEAST"

When on earth as a man, Jesus Christ, who is now the heavenly archangel Michael, said that Satan the Devil is the ruler of this world. (John 12:31; 14:30;

16:11) This ruler, who is the symbolic "dragon," is naturally the one that "gave the authority to the wild beast." The apostle Paul also called him "the god of this system of things." (2 Corinthians 4:4) So he is the "god" of the symbolic "wild beast." Unavoidably, then, the worship of the "wild beast" means also the worshiping of its "god," the symbolic "dragon," Satan the Devil. The "wild beast" promotes Devil worship. It is against the worship of the true God, Jehovah the Almighty. So John says of the "wild beast":

"And a mouth speaking great things and blasphemies was given it, and authority to act forty-two months was given it. And it opened its mouth in blasphemies against God, to blaspheme his name and his residence, even those residing in heaven. And there was granted it to wage war with the holy ones and conquer them, and authority was given it over every tribe and people and tongue and nation. And all those who dwell on the earth will worship it; the name of not one of them stands written in the scroll of life of the Lamb who was slaughtered, from the founding of the world."—Revelation 13:5-8.

The "wild beast," that ascended from the abyss of the sea, has seven heads, hence seven mouths, and yet it is said that "a mouth speaking great things and blasphemies was given it." This means that the opportunity to mouth great things and blasphemies would be allowed to it and that all seven heads would combine to speak these things, doing so as with one mouth.

Of course, Satan the Devil, the "dragon" that gave power, throne and authority to this "wild beast," would prompt it to speak these "great things," these loud boasts and big claims that ignored Jehovah God regarding world domination. The dragon would move this political "wild beast" to speak "blasphemies" against the true God, the Universal Sovereign. This would especially be true when the fulfillment of the prophecy of Daniel 7:8, 11, 20, 24, 25 went into action concerning the small horn that came up out of the beast's head and that had a "mouth speaking grandiose things," speaking "even words against the Most High." The improper use of the "mouth" of the wild beast would be made worse after the Son of God, Jesus Christ, came to earth and started Christianity.

A notable time period in the life and activity of this "wild beast" is made prominent in the statement: "And authority to act forty-two months was given it." (Revelation 13:5) This is the same length of time as that which is said to be given to the Gentile nations to "trample the holy city underfoot." In fact, it is the same period, for during that same period God's "two witnesses" prophesy for "a thousand two hundred and sixty days dressed in sackcloth." (Revelation 11:2, 3) Also, in Daniel 7:25 concerning the small horn on the beast it is said that "the holy ones themselves of the Supreme One" were to "be given into his hand for a time, and times and half a time." According to Daniel 12:7, this was to be the last time that the small "horn" of the beast would succeed in "the dashing of the power of the holy people to pieces."

Here the "forty-two months," the "thousand two hundred and sixty days," and the "time, and times and half a time" all measure the same amount of time, namely, from Tishri 15 of the year 1914 to Nisan 14 of the year 1918,* or from October 4/5, 1914, to March 26/27, 1918.

As an instance in which the "wild beast" out of the sea "opened its mouth in blasphemies against God, to blaspheme his name and his residence, even those residing in heaven," the words of the king of ancient Babylon are quite bold: "To the heavens I shall go up. Above the stars of God I shall lift up my throne, and I shall sit down upon the mountain of meeting, in the remotest parts of the north. I shall go up above the high places of the clouds; I

---

* See the explanation of this in chapter 19, pages 261-264.

shall make myself resemble the Most High." (Isaiah 14:3, 4, 13, 14) In a figurative way the king of Babylon did this in the year 607 B.C.E., when he destroyed Jerusalem on its mountains and looted and wrecked its temple, its holy meeting place. The spirit creature whom the king of Babylon represented, namely, Satan the Devil, repeated this blasphemous action in the year 1918 C.E. In that year he began to dash the power of the holy ones of the Most High God Jehovah to the ground to stop their witnessing.—Daniel 12:7.

From the very start of its existence after the Flood the political "wild beast" has been hostile toward those to whom Jehovah God has shown his favor and who have been looking and preparing for the coming of the Seed of God's "woman" who would bruise the symbolic Serpent and its wicked seed. (Genesis 3:15) But that "wild beast" is especially hostile to Jehovah's "holy ones," the ones actually associated with that Seed of God's "woman," the anointed followers of Jesus Christ.

The "wild beast" is not satisfied that these obey God's command to "be in subjection to the superior authorities" that represent the "wild beast." (Romans 13:1) Because these "holy ones" are "ambassadors" for the Messianic kingdom of God and preach it everywhere, the symbolic "wild beast" hates them. (2 Corinthians 5:20) For a test of them, to prove their unbreakable loyalty to God's Messianic kingdom, Jehovah God the Almighty has let the "wild beast" carry on war, even violently, against such "holy ones." This has been true particularly after the Gentile Times ended in 1914. As in the case of Jesus Christ himself, the "wild beast" could do nothing against them unless this was granted from God.—John 19:11.

So the apostle John correctly worded it when he wrote concerning the "wild beast": "And there was granted it to wage war with the holy ones and conquer them, and authority was given it over every tribe and people and tongue and nation." (Revelation

13:7) World War I was a very convenient time for the "wild beast" to wage this warfare with God's holy ones. This it did under the pretext of waging war against those who were seditious and obstructive to war operations and military victory. But the beastly conquest of the "wild beast" over God's holy ones near the close of World War I in 1918 was only short-lived. God's "two witnesses," his "two prophets" who had prophesied "dressed in sackcloth," lay dead in public disgrace for, as it were, only "three and a half days." Amazingly, in 1919, Jehovah God raised his symbolic "two witnesses" to life again and exalted them, heaven-high as it were, in his Kingdom service. —Revelation 11:11, 12.

But how did the rest of mankind fare under the paws of the "wild beast"? Over them it wielded world-wide dominion: "authority was given it over every tribe and people and tongue and nation." With what result?

The "wild beast" demands and gets the worship of the patriotic politically minded people: "And all those who dwell on the earth will worship it; the name of not one of them stands written in the scroll of life of the Lamb who was slaughtered, from the founding of the world." (Revelation 13:8) By "all those who dwell on the earth" the choice must be made between the "wild beast" and God's "Lamb who was slaughtered." That symbolic "Lamb," namely, Jesus Christ, was "slaughtered" in the year 33 C.E. for the sake of God's Messianic kingdom. He was also "slaughtered" sacrificially as the "Lamb of God that takes away the sin of the world." (John 1:29, 36) Those who are not for him are against him and against salvation by him. Logically, then, earth's dwellers who are not for him "will worship" the political "wild beast." How could the names of such worshipers stand "written in the scroll of life of the Lamb" as deserving of everlasting life within God's Messianic kingdom? From the time of the founding of the world of mankind in the days of Adam and Eve the names of those who are against God's "Lamb" were not meant to get into his "scroll of life."—Genesis 3:15; Revelation 21:27.

NEED FOR ENDURANCE AND FAITH

Since worship of the political state was to become world wide, and since Jehovah God had purposed to let the political "wild beast" go to such lengths in exercising world domination, God's "holy ones" would be severely tested. Hence Revelation 13:9, 10 fittingly follows up the account of the blasphemous, God-defying conduct of the "wild beast" by saying: "If anyone has an ear, let him hear. If anyone is meant for captivity, he goes away into captivity. If anyone will kill with the sword, he must be killed with the sword. Here is where it means the endurance and faith of the holy ones."*

2 Consequently, when in the throes of World War I the political "wild beast" took the remnant of Jehovah's anointed witnesses into captivity, banning their literature, denying them freedom of worship in public meeting places, throwing them into prison or military detention places, it was hard for them to be submissive and to endure. Under such circumstances as permitted by Almighty God whom they worshiped, it was not the proper thing for them as dedicated Christians to offer armed resistance against being taken into such "captivity" at the hands of the "superior authorities" (the symbolic "wild beast"). With a hearing ear they had to heed the warning: "If anyone will kill with the sword, he must be killed with the sword."

3 This meant not just one's refusing to take a direct or indirect part in the killing of humans on either side in World War I. It meant, rather, one's not taking up the steel sword in violent armed revolt against being unwillingly taken into "captivity" by the mili-

---

* See Revelation 13:10 in both its interlinear reading and its right-hand column reading in *The Kingdom Interlinear Translation of the Greek Scriptures,* published in 1969.

tarized "wild beast." Jesus in the garden of Gethsemane had warned against such unchristian action. (Matthew 26:52) Consequently, God's "holy ones" proved themselves peaceful, law-abiding.

There, amid World War I, as well as amid similar situations since then, it has called for the "endurance and faith of the holy ones." It was good for them to be thus forewarned. Of course, they used proper legal provisions for their defense and protection. But apart from that, the anointed "holy ones" yielded themselves unresistingly as their Exemplar Jesus Christ did. This afforded the "wild beast" no true grounds for killing them with the sword of the State for offering armed resistance with the sword. Accepting what Almighty God permitted, they endured the "captivity," at the same time being strong in the "faith" that in his own way and at his own time God would release them from such "captivity." How grandly their "endurance and faith" were rewarded in 1919 C.E.! This has strengthened them for their further tests till now.

THE SECOND "WILD BEAST"—OUT OF THE EARTH

By means of its sixth head (the Roman World Power) the political "wild beast" out of the sea had taken the aged apostle John into "captivity," imprisoning him on the Isle of Patmos, there to share with fellow Christians "in the tribulation and kingdom and endurance in company with Jesus." (Revelation 1:9) The seventh 'head' of the "wild beast" was then a sort of mystery head, for, in an indirect way, Revelation 17:9, 10 says to John concerning it: "The other has not yet arrived, but when he does arrive he must remain a short while." So this seventh 'head' would be a more modern political world power among the heads of the symbolic "wild beast." This seventh world power takes on the role of a political prophet and a promoter of political State worship. For this reason it is also portrayed as having a separate status and entity; while at the same time it still belongs to the "wild beast" as its seventh head. In Revelation 13:11-13 John tells how it appears:

1 "And I saw another wild beast ascending out of the earth, and it had two horns like a lamb, but it began speaking as a dragon. And it exercises all the authority of the first wild beast in its sight. And it makes the earth and those who dwell in it worship the first wild beast, whose death-stroke got healed. And it performs great signs, so that it should even make fire come down out of heaven to the earth in the sight of mankind."

2 This second wild beast could not be an eighth world power, for the "first wild beast," which pictures Satan's entire worldwide political organization is limited to only seven political "heads." It is merely another representation of the seventh head of the first wild beast, in order that a more detailed description of the historical role of this seventh 'head' of the first wild beast may be given. Because this second wild beast, which ascends out of the earth, has "two horns like a lamb," it would symbolize a dual political combination, hence a dual world power. This Seventh World Power, as referred to in the prophecies of the Holy Bible, is the Anglo-American World Power, which emerged quite recently upon the world stage of action, and which successfully held its world domination down to the end of the Gentile Times in 1914, and still does.

3 This two-horned wild beast ascended out of the symbolic "earth," the earth being more stable than the sea out of which the "first wild beast" ascended. When it emerged, in the *Annus Mirabilis* of 1763 C.E., two centuries ago, the "earth" or peoples in the general area in which the sea beast had dominated had become rather stabilized under strong, definitely constituted governments. How so?

4 Well, by then the countries of Europe had settled their religious status as either Roman Catholic or Protestant. Also, great European empires had then been formed, the French Empire, the Austrian Em-

pire, the Dutch (Netherlands) Empire, the Spanish Empire and the Portuguese Empire. The French Empire then embraced large land areas in the North American continent, but the British Empire also had its colonies there. The British Empire had its foundation laid, when, on December 31, 1600, Queen Elizabeth I incorporated the English East India Company by royal decree. But already in 1583 England had taken possession of Newfoundland in North America. Later came the establishment of the thirteen colonies south of the Saint Lawrence River.

By the Revolutionary War of 1775-1783 the thirteen American colonies gained their independence of Great Britain to form the United States of America. But this was after Great Britain had, in 1763, established itself as the "foremost commercial and colonial power in the world." By reason of her gains through the Seven Years' War that ended in that year in America and India and on the seas, as another historian said, "the kingdom of Great Britain had become the British Empire."

The United States of America and the British Empire had much in common, such as the same language, their being largely Protestant nations, many common traditions, and their being democratic types of nations. After a time of readjustment they found it in the common interest to have good diplomatic and trade relations. So strong was the attachment to Great Britain that, in World War I of 1914-1918, the United States of America joined Great Britain in its fight against the Central Powers, the Teutonic Alliance. Also, in World War II of 1939-1945, after giving aid to the British, the United States of America was plunged into the war, again on the side of Great Britain. Thus throughout modern history the British Empire and the United States of America have acted together as a dual world power, the Seventh World Power, as pictured by the two-horned wild beast out of the earth.

In agreement with the foregoing is the special dispatch to the New York *Times* and datelined "Washington, January 14," in which a report is made concerning the British ambassador to the United States of America Sir Patrick Dean, just two weeks before his ending eight years of service in the United States. According to this dispatch

> Sir Patrick is convinced that a "special relationship" between Britain and the United States still exists, though in a form considerably altered by changes in the world of international politics. It is no longer a relationship calling for high-level political consultations at major turning points, as existed between President Roosevelt and Prime Minister Churchill or, to a lesser extent, between President Eisenhower and Prime Minister Macmillan. But it is more than just a sentimental attachment deriving from common language and heritage, in the outgoing Ambassador's view. It shows up most in working-level consultations, comparing of notes and analyses of strategic matters among diplomats of the two countries, at the level of the ambassador and Secretary of State Dean Rusk as well as the lower levels in both capitals.—New York *Times*, page 17, as of January 15, 1969.

2 Gradually through the centuries the British Empire came to be the greatest empire of world history, eventually controlling one-fourth of the earth's surface and one-fourth of earth's peoples, and dominating the seas. The sympathy and cooperation of the United States added to its strength. In this manner the two-horned earth beast "exercises all the authority of the first wild beast in its sight."

3 Because it really belongs to the "first wild beast" of which it is the symbolic seventh 'head,' it was but logical for it to fulfill the prophetic picture: "It makes the earth and those who dwell in it worship the first wild beast, whose death-stroke got healed." (Revelation 13:12) Worshiping the "first wild beast" would mean worshiping the worldwide political organization of the dragon, Satan the Devil. This would include the worshiping of the seventh 'head' of the "first wild beast," namely, the Seventh World Power, the Anglo-American dual world power, which is also pictured by the two-horned second beast. As regards

worshiping political institutions, Jesus Christ did not engage in any political action against the Sixth World Power, the Roman Empire of his day, and neither have his faithful followers down till today meddled in the politics of the sixth world power and of the seventh world power. They are seeking God's kingdom first.—Matthew 6:33; John 17:14, 16.

How, though, was it that the two-horned earth beast performed "great signs, so that it should even make fire come down out of heaven to the earth in the sight of mankind"? (Revelation 13:13) Calling down fire from heaven reminds us of the prophet Elijah of the tenth century B.C.E. In his contest with the 450 prophets of Baal on Mount Carmel the prophet Elijah followed up the disgraceful failure on the part of Baal's prophets by building an altar to the true God Jehovah and then having his prayer to Jehovah answered by the descent of fire from heaven that consumed the sacrifice on the water-drenched altar. Later, when the new king of the ten-tribe kingdom of Israel sent bands of soldiers to capture Elijah for predicting the king's death, Elijah was protected as a "man of God" by the descent of fire from heaven twice that consumed two companies of fifty-one soldiers each.—1 Kings 18:17-40; 2 Kings 1:2-12.

By such feats Elijah proved not only that Jehovah was the only living and true God but also that he himself was a true "man of God," the true prophet of Jehovah God. For a corresponding reason, the two-horned earth beast made symbolic fire come down out of heaven to the earth to command respect for itself, especially in the prophetic role that it would assume and in the priestly role that it took by promoting idolatry. From a worldly standpoint, this dual world power offered evidence that it had heaven's approval and backing. Otherwise, how would it have attained to the top place politically and militarily on the earth? Its tremendous expansion and its military and naval victories to maintain itself in the top position were like fire from the superhuman heavens that supported the rightfulness of its position on earth. Moreover, this Anglo-American dual world power claimed to be Christian from its very start, from its very ascent out of the "earth." The royal monarch of the British Empire claims to rule by the grace of God and acts as religious head of the Anglican state church.

So this symbolic beast "had two horns like a lamb," pretending to be the political representative of the Lamb of God Jesus Christ. It pretended to be harmless, inoffensive, nonaggressive like a lamb, not intending to injure or defraud anybody. In reality, however, "it began speaking as a dragon." Just as the "great dragon," Satan the Devil, challenged Jehovah God and laid claim to the domination of all mankind, so the two-horned earth beast claimed the right to dominate the whole earth and the seven seas by right of its imperial, military and naval strength. It swallowed up like a dragon large portions of the earth and their peoples, colonizing them for commercial exploitation and naval bases. Correctly it came to be said that "the sun never sets on the British Empire." Complementary to this the United States of North America came to dominate all the Americas. Thus the two lamblike horns of the earthly "wild beast" were very deceptive in the impression that they made.

The diademed seventh head of the "great dragon" was invisibly controlling this dual world power, the greatest of all the seven world powers, and this at a time when, apparently, the dragon needed its strongest world power as a foe of "the mystery of God."

CHAPTER 23

"The Image of the Wild Beast"

IMAGES have long been used for carrying on idolatry. The "first wild beast," that is, Satan's worldwide organization of politics, likes to be idolized. It recommends, really demands, that it be idolized, by means of an image. It makes this recommendation by means of its seventh head. In the Revelation vision to the apostle John the idolatrous proposal is pictured as being made by "another wild beast," the two-horned one that ascends out of the earth. However, when we remember that this two-horned earth beast is identical with the seventh head of the "first wild beast" out of the sea, we are amused at discerning how the "first wild beast" itself makes the idolatrous proposal for itself to be worshiped, but does so by means of its own seventh head. Notice, please, in Revelation 13:14, 15, how John describes this:

"And it misleads those who dwell on the earth, because of the signs that were granted it to perform in the sight of the wild beast, while it tells those who dwell on the earth to make an image to the wild beast that had the sword-stroke and yet revived. And there was granted it to give breath to the image of the wild beast, so that the image of the wild beast should both speak and cause to be killed all those who would not in any way worship the image of the wild beast."

The "great dragon," Satan the Devil, has always favored idolatry. Imitatively, then, the two-horned earth beast in further "speaking as a dragon," makes an idolatrous proposal at a very crucial time in human history. In this it further misleads "those who dwell on the earth." Since the time of its ascent out of the earth as the seventh world power, it has misled mankind away from God and his Messianic kingdom "because of the signs that were granted it to perform in the sight of the [first] wild beast." Why should it not mislead earth's dwellers? Those very "signs" that it performed identify it as being the same one as "the false prophet" out of whose mouth comes one of the "three unclean inspired expressions that looked like frogs" and that gather the "kings of the entire inhabited earth" and their armies to the disastrous war against Jehovah God at Har–Magedon. —Revelation 16:13-16.

The identifying clue for showing that this "false prophet" is the same as the two-horned earth beast is found in the account of the war at Har–Magedon, in which, at Revelation 19:20, the capture of the "first wild beast" is described. Who is captured along with it? "Along with it the false prophet that performed in front of it the signs with which he misled those who received the mark of the wild beast and those who render worship to its image."

At the critical time the two-horned earth beast, as "the false prophet," "tells those who dwell on the earth to make an image to the wild beast that had the sword-stroke and yet revived." (Revelation 13: 14) At this time the "first wild beast" has received the "sword-stroke" that symbolizes costly defeat in World War I of 1914-1918 C.E. So the advice to build the "image to the wild beast" must come after World War I, that ended by the signing of an Armistice, November 11, 1918. The advice came at the Paris Peace Conference. Responsive to this advice, what did the people make that was an idolatrous "image"?

A man-made "image" for worship is forbidden by Jehovah God's law, for it turns men away from worshiping the one living and true God and from trusting in His Messianic kingdom. The idolatrous image was patterned after the "first wild beast" that came up out of the sea, not down from heaven as the New Jerusalem does. To that "first wild beast" the dragon, Satan the Devil, had given "its power and its throne and great authority." That "first wild beast" must therefore symbolize Satan's visible all-inclusive world political organization. (Revelation 13:1, 2; 20:1, 2, 10) Hence to be an "image of the wild beast" the man-made idol would also have to be a political organization and to have a worldwide scope or coverage. This is what the League of Nations and its successor, the United Nations, have proved to be. This international political organization for world peace and security is the modern "image of the wild beast."

THE MAKING OF THE "IMAGE"

The historical facts prove that two-horned earth beast did tell the people to make this symbolic "image of the [first] wild beast." One of the most prominent members of the Peace Conference in 1919 was the then British Prime Minister, David Lloyd George. Reminding his countrymen of what he had done in the interest of peace, Mr. Lloyd George, in a speech in Britain toward the beginning of 1931, said, with reference to himself:

"It was the member who was elected in this town forty years ago who proposed the first resolution in the gathering of the principal Allied statesmen in Paris in 1919 upon which the Covenant of the League of Nations was afterwards based. The cabinet of which I was the head was the only government in the world that had, before the conference met, and even before the Armistice was signed, prepared carefully thought-out plans for putting the principle of that resolution into operation. Even during the most anxious moments of the war there were committees of that cabinet sitting to frame a scheme for setting up an association of nations for ensuring peace on earth."*

* See letter by A. J. West, from Denmark, as published in *The Watch Tower* as of January 15, 1931. Also see pages 11 and 12, paragraphs under the subheading "Moulding the Image," of the *Watch Tower* issue of January 1, 1921, as to Britain's part.

Confirming the above, Mr. Lloyd George said, in chapter 28 of his *Memoirs:*

"It was found at the Peace Conference that the British Government alone had taken measures to work out a practical scheme for the constitution of a League of Peace. President Wilson had not gone beyond the vague idea and the striking phrase. He had not attempted to develop his thoughts into any concrete plan." —See *The Golden Age,* No. 402, as of February 13, 1935, page 311.

At the Paris Peace Conference in early 1919 T. Woodrow Wilson, president of the American ally of Great Britain in World War I, advocated the League of Nations. He won acceptance of the League of Nations Covenant as part of the proposed peace treaty, enlisting the support of such Great Powers leaders as Georges B. E. Clemenceau, "The Tiger," France's Premier who was made Permanent Chairman of the Paris Peace Conference. However, after the Treaty was adopted with the League of Nations Covenant as an integral part thereof, the American Senate refused to ratify the Treaty, and later (on August 25, 1921) a separate peace was concluded with defeated Germany. On the other hand, the Federal Council of Churches of Christ in America (Protestant) did favor the League, saying in its message to President Wilson at the Peace Conference:

"Such a League is not a mere political expedient; it is rather the political expression of the Kingdom of God on earth. . . . The Church can give a spirit of good-will, without which no League of Nations can endure. . . . The League of Nations is rooted in the Gospel. Like the Gospel, its objective is 'peace on earth, good-will toward men.'"

But later in that same year, on Sunday, September 7, in his public address the president of the Watch Tower Bible & Tract Society stated to an audience of 7,000 that "the Lord's displeasure is certain to be visited upon the League, however, because the clergy —Catholic and Protestant—claiming to be God's representatives, have abandoned his plan and endorsed the League of Nations, hailing it as a political expression of Christ's kingdom on earth."—The *Star-*

Journal of Sandusky, Ohio, under date of September 8, 1919.

The League of Nations did not begin officially until January 10, 1920, the day when ratifications of the Treaty of Versailles were exchanged in Paris, France. In 1919 Geneva, Switzerland, had been agreed on as the city of the League's headquarters, and the first assembly of the nations convened in that city on November 15, 1920. As history went on to show, the purpose of the League of Nations was frustrated by the outbreak of World War II in 1939, and the formal dissolution of the League took place on April 18, 1946, and its assets were transferred to the newly formed United Nations, its successor.

The League of Nations appointed a committee of experts to draft a scheme for the organization of a World Court of Justice. The Secretary-General of the League pointed out that the World Court was to be the "most essential part of the League of Nations." The League and the Court were considered to be complementary to each other. The Court was meant to be the judicial arm, the judicial tribunal, of the League. In course of time the United States of America did join this World Court, and for this it was accused of actually joining the League of Nations. As time went on the American share in the work of the League of Nations grew steadily. In this way the symbolic "two horns like a lamb" on the head of the second wild beast lent their power to the making and maintaining of the "image of the [first] wild beast."

It is thus historically correct to say that to the two-horned earth beast the permission was granted "to give breath to the image of the [first] wild beast" and make it live, function. (Revelation 13:15, *NW; NEB; AS; RS; Mo*) That first wild beast had seven heads and ten horns. Its "image" would have those same features, although its body would not necessarily have the same color. In Revelation 17:3-17 there is described for us the breathing "image of the wild beast." There it is the "scarlet-colored wild beast that was full of blasphemous names and that had seven heads and ten horns." In Revelation 17:11 we read that this scarlet-colored wild beast "is also itself an eighth king, but springs from the seven [heads]," thus indicating that the political "image of the wild beast" is, as a whole, an eighth world power in effect. But it owes its existence to the seven symbolic "heads," particularly the seventh 'head' that gives breath to it. It was given breath to function on January 10, 1920.

What was the purpose of giving breath of life to the "image of the [first] wild beast"? Revelation 13: 15 goes on to say: "So that the image of the wild beast should both speak and cause to be killed all those who would not in any way worship the image of the wild beast." The "image of the wild beast" was meant to speak, not idly, but with authority. Especially through its World Court it has done so. The "image" was meant to be worshiped. It was even empowered to command worship from dwellers on the earth through their governments, inasmuch as the people are represented by their national governments who were members of this international political organization. Those who would not worship it were "to be killed." According to the Constitution of the League, known as the Covenant, any nation violating its pledge to submit its disputes to arbitration instead of directly going to war "is automatically in a state of outlawry with the other nations, which are bound to sever all economic and political relations with the defaulting member." (*The Encyclopedia Americana,* Volume 17 [1929 edition], page 176) Eventually, feeling the need to worship the "image of the wild beast," sixty-three nations at one time or another were members of the League of Nations.

According to the way that the "image of the wild beast" spoke, and also according to the way that its promoters spoke, the very life of every person on earth depended on the worship of this international political "image." Without it in existence and functioning world war could not be prevented; another world war would wreck all civilization. Everybody would "be killed." In one's own interest it was a case of one's worshiping the "image" or being killed by the consequences. After the political "image of the wild beast" was proved to be ineffective in its then form by the outbreak of World War II, a successor to the League of Nations in the new form of the United Nations organization was provided in 1945 after the world war. This very act was a most dramatic act of worshiping the "image of the wild beast." The belief was international that without it the world could not exist in the newly introduced atomic age. An "image of the wild beast" must exist and be worshiped in order for the "wild beast" itself to continue existing on earth.

The dire need for the "image of the wild beast" to live and function effectively as a "third force" was recently pointed up after the "lightning invasion" of Czechoslovakia made by troops of the Soviet Union and four satellite states on August 21, 1968. At this the then Secretary General of the United Nations, U Thant, expressed himself because the balance of power between the two most powerful members of the United Nations was so precarious.

Speaking at a luncheon on September 19, 1968, held in support of a Fund that was established in honor of the late Dag Hammerskjold, former Secretary General of the United Nations, U Thant said that there was need for "a vigorous and articulate third force" to voice "the conscience of mankind." There was need for such a third force that would press "upon all member states the imperative of relying more and more on the machinery of the United Nations if we are to keep the peace of the world." The member states numbered at that time 124, including the United States of America, its strongest supporter from the start. All were worshipers of the "image of the wild beast."—New York *Times,* under date of September 20, 1968.

According to an earlier report in the New York

Times, under date of July 10, 1967, even the then Russian Premier Aleksei N. Kosygin enhanced the importance of the United Nations. Datelined Moscow, July 9, the United Press International dispatch said: "Premier Aleksei N. Kosygin said today that the international situation was 'very grave' and that the United States and the Soviet Union could not resolve world problems by themselves. He said settlements must be made by the United Nations. . . . 'It is an error to believe that all international problems can be resolved by the two great powers. These must be regulated by all the countries. That is why we do not believe in an agreement between the two great powers on world problems. We believe in the United Nations, where all countries, large and small, are represented. The international situation is now very grave.' "

MARK, NAME AND NUMBER OF THE WILD BEAST

Just as King Nebuchadnezzar of the ancient Babylonian Empire (the third "head") ordered the ruling officials of all parts of his empire to bow down to an image in united worship, in order to unify his empire, so now, since 1920, pressure is put upon all humankind to worship the "image of the wild beast," in order to hold together or perpetuate the political "wild beast" itself. The worshiping of the "image of the wild beast" is, in effect, the worshiping of the "wild beast" itself; the "image" of the real thing receives only "relative worship," not the principal worship. The modern-day effort to make all of earth's inhabitants identify themselves as worshipers of the political "wild beast" was foreseen prophetically by the apostle John, who writes:

"And it puts under compulsion all persons, the small and the great, and the rich and the poor, and the free and the slaves, that they should give these a mark in their right hand or upon their forehead, and that nobody might be able to buy or sell except a person having the mark, the name of the wild beast or the number of its name. Here is where wisdom comes in: Let the one that has intelligence calculate the number of the wild beast, for it is a man's number; and its number is six hundred and sixty-six [χξϛ′]."—Revelation 13:16-18.

Since "all persons" are involved, "the small and the great, and the rich and the poor, and the free and the slaves," it is vital for each one of us today to find out whether he has the identifying "mark" or not. The "mark" (kháragma, Greek) was either a seal applied for authentication of something or a brand mark that was burned into the skin of a slave or of an animal. It is therefore a "mark" of identification to show to whom or to what a person belongs or to which god a person is rendering religious devotion and service.

The idolatrous "image of the wild beast" causes its worshipers to receive this mark "in their right hand or upon their forehead." They receive the "mark," not of the "image of the wild beast," but of the "wild beast" itself. So, then, if you worship the "image of the wild beast," it automatically causes you to procure the "mark" of the "wild beast." It stamps you as a worshiper of the political "wild beast" and as being owned by it, like a branded slave. The forehead is generally exposed to everyone a person meets, so that the mark on the forehead betrays openly who is one's owner, one's master.

Except in the case of left-handed persons, the "right hand" is the one most generally used. Certainly if a person worships the "wild beast," which symbolizes Satan's visible worldwide political organization, he will lend a hand of assistance and cooperation to that political organization. He will actively take part in its political controversies, campaigns, elections and nationalistic plans and projects. By doing this he receives the symbolic "mark" in his "right hand." By this course of action, also, he reveals what sort of political personality he is, just as openly as if there were a political stamp upon his forehead. He betrays thereby that he is not for God's Messianic kingdom, but is for Satan's worldwide political organization in its various phases, pictured by the "seven heads" of the "wild beast." He openly shows that he is a "part of the world," in sharp contrast with Christ's true followers. These "are no part of the world" just as Jesus Christ himself was "no part of the world." (John 17:14, 16; 15:19) They "had not received the mark upon their forehead and upon their hand." —Revelation 20:4.

Those not worshiping the "image of the wild beast" were to "be killed." It appears that the killing was a threat and meant inescapable death in a world catastrophe that would come if there were no international organization for world peace and security. Worshiping the "image" meant also worshiping the "wild beast," and yet a person could worship the "wild beast" without worshiping its "image," as in the case of nations that existed before the building of the "image." So the scheme was that every dweller on earth should be forced to worship the "wild beast," whether directly or indirectly through the "image of the wild beast." Action was to be taken to make it practically impossible for the nonworshipers to live. This was to be brought about by a form of boycott: "that nobody might be able to buy or sell except a person having the mark, the name of the wild beast or the number of its name."—Revelation 13:15, 17.

Speaking of its member nations (not individual persons) the Charter of the League of Nations ruled that any member state breaking the laws of the Covenant would become an outlaw nation and the other member states would break off economic and political relations with that outlawed state. But what about individual citizens? In totalitarian or authoritarian political states citizens who have refused to join or give support to the ruling element in the one-party state have been boycotted, denied free rights of proper buying and selling. This is done to make it impossible for them to subsist. So if now a person feels unable to live, he must under such compulsion submit to accepting the "mark" of the political "wild beast."

The underlying principle of this compulsory procedure is this: that, if you desire the political "wild beast" to do business with you to your prospering and getting ahead in this world, you must do business with the "wild beast." You must lend your best hand to its aid and maintenance and make an open-face appearance, plainly detectable in your personality, to show that you belong to it as your owner and master. With national pride you must belong to the political state. Those who put their trust in only the political state yield to such compulsion and get marked in their "right hand" and upon their "forehead" of public profession. The faithful genuine Christian defies all such compulsion. He refuses to commit worldly idolatry and to be marked as such an idolater. He puts his trust in Jehovah's Messianic kingdom, which was "finished" as a mystery in the year 1914 C.E. He lends his hand to its service and support and does not meddle in worldly politics, although still being law-abiding.—Romans 13:1-7.

From the standpoint of the true God, "whose name is Jehovah," it is a disgraceful, unchristian thing for a person to have the "mark" of the wild beast in the right hand and forehead. Patriotic-minded people may object to that fact, but to Jehovah God the thing that such people worship as a most beautiful, noble, respectable, worthy, inspiring thing is like a hideous blasphemous "wild beast" that came up out of the sea. (Revelation 13:1) The idolaters would consider the object of their patriotic, nationalistic adoration as deserving of the name the symbolic value of which amounts to the number 777, the symbol of perfection up to the third degree $(7 + 70 + 700)$. If that were the case, then one's being marked with "the name of the wild beast or the number of its name" would seem to the idolaters as being an honor. But, as a shock to the patriotic sensibilities of the idolaters, Jehovah God gives an inferior numerical rating to the "wild beast." It takes wisdom to appreciate this, not worldly wisdom of men under the influence of the "dragon," Satan the Devil, but heavenly wisdom from God. Says Revelation 13:18:

"Here is where wisdom comes in: Let the one that has intelligence calculate the number of the wild beast, for it is a man's number; and its number is six hundred and sixty-six [χξϛ′]."

This numerical value of the name is the number 6 up to the third degree, namely, $6 + 60 + 600$. It is "a man's number," hence a human number. But for these past six thousand years humanity has been marked by imperfection, just as the number six comes short of the number seven, the symbol of perfection that is repeatedly used in the book of Revelation. Furthermore the number six has been associated with men who defied Jehovah God. For instance, the Philistine giant Goliath, who taunted Jehovah much to the indignation of the Israelite shepherd, David of Bethlehem, likely had six digits on each hand and foot. (1 Chronicles 20:5-7) Nebuchadnezzar the king of Babylon erected a tall national image of gold, sixty cubits high and six cubits broad, and he had the three Hebrew friends of the prophet Daniel thrown into a fiery furnace for refusing to break Jehovah's law and worship the golden image. (Daniel 3:1-23) In view of such connections the number six would stand for something man-made, something imperfect, sinful, like man in his rebellion against God, something that could be defiant and opposed to Jehovah God, hence something disapproved by Him.

Moreover, since doing something three times makes it emphatic, the compounding of the number six to the third degree, namely, six + six times ten + six times a hundred, would signify something emphatically imperfect, bad, disapproved by God, something falling far short of perfection. So this is what heavenly wisdom, as imparted by the inspired Word of God, calculates "the name of the wild beast" or "the number of the wild beast" to be. Human history since the days of the mighty hunter Nimrod, the founder of ancient Babylon, shows that this number of human imperfection and of inadequacy stamps the Devil's visible, worldwide political organization as symbolized by the wild beast. Is any man-made thing, that bears such a distinguishing number, deserving of being worshiped in defiance of God's law? Each person must answer for himself before God.

The number 666 stands as a warning to all people in this time particularly, when extreme efforts are being made to have all humans branded "in their right hand or upon their forehead" with the identifying "name of the wild beast or the number of its name." Faithful worshipers of the one living and true God Jehovah refuse at all costs to be marked with the wild beast's number. The very next verse after Revelation 13:18, which reveals the number 666, pictures the 144,000 triumphant anointed followers of the Lamb Jesus Christ as having something different "written on their foreheads." What? The name of the Lamb and the name of his heavenly Father. (Revelation 13:18; 14:1) Also, at Revelation 7:2-8, these 144,000 spiritual Israelites are said to be sealed as slaves of God "in their foreheads" with the "seal of the living God."

Immediately after that vision, the international "great crowd" are brought to view as having palms in their hands and as worshiping, not the "wild beast," but Jehovah God "in his temple." (Revelation 7:9-15) What a glorious "great crowd" to be among today! In order for us to enjoy their favored standing before Jehovah God and his Lamb Jesus Christ, one needs to shun getting the mark, the number of the political "wild beast," the beastly foe of "the mystery of God."

NOTE: For a verse-for-verse explanation of the remainder of the Revelation to John, namely, Revelation 14:1 to 22:21, please see the 704-page book *"Babylon the Great Has Fallen!" God's Kingdom Rules!*, chapter 21 (page 454) to the conclusion of chapter 31. This book was published in 1963 by the Watch Tower Bible & Tract Society of Pennsylvania, 124 Columbia Heights, Brooklyn, N.Y. 11201.

The Finished
"Mystery of God"
and You

THE FINISHED "mystery of God" stands revealed today! The all-wise God who formulated the mystery almost six thousand years ago has now solved it for us. That mystery, couched in language that breathed the only hope for all mankind, is the enthroned kingdom of God as exercised through the royal "seed" of God's "woman," that is, the kingdom of God by means of his Messiah, his Christ or Anointed One. (Genesis 3:15; Revelation 12:1, 2, 5-10) According to his own will and purpose God announced the mystery at the first crisis in human history; and, nearly six thousand years later, the same ever-living God finished it, in the world-shaking year of 1914 C.E.

In that year, when those long-lasting "times of the nations" that allowed for uninterrupted rule of the earth by the political "wild beast" ended, the glorious moment had arrived for Jehovah God the Almighty to finish his "mystery." He finished it by bringing to birth and enthroning his Messianic kingdom in the heavens. He did this by installing his self-sacrificing lamblike Son in the Messianic throne in the heavens. In such a way this one was authorized to serve as the reigning Messiah or Christ and to rid mankind on earth of all their enemies.—Revelation 10:7; 11:15-18; Psalms 2:1-9; 110:1-6; Luke 21:24.

You, the reader, stand to benefit everlastingly from this finished "mystery of God." We all stand to benefit everlastingly from the finished "mystery of God."

Will we peacefully, gratefully accept the benefits of it? It is well to do so, for the operations of this finished "mystery of God" extend to the four corners of the earth; they touch upon your life, our life, and the life of every human creature on earth. You cannot, we cannot, escape its marvelous operations. We are simply obliged to reckon henceforth with this finished "mystery of God." For us to do so in a right way means benefits unending for us. The former less responsible state of the world of mankind is gone forever! We are living in a changed situation in the "time of the end," the urgent time for making right resolves. We cannot move time backward to the easygoing past. Nor can we stop time from moving forward closer and closer to the disastrous end of all enemies of both God and man and then to the glorious realization of God's further purposes respecting his Messianic kingdom. For the soothing blessings from that perfect, righteous Messianic government over mankind our troubled hearts yearn, do they not?

Already the finished "mystery of God" has performed magnificent exploits, to its own credit and to the vindication of Jehovah God as Sovereign Ruler over all. In the year 1914 its crowned king, Jesus the Messiah, "went forth conquering and to complete his conquest." (Revelation 6:1, 2) Under his heavenly title, Michael the archangel, he led his holy angels in victorious warfare against the "great dragon," Satan the Devil, and his demon angels. Down he hurled them to this earth, where then the "heads" and the diademed "horns" of the symbolic "wild beast" were fighting for world domination in World War I of 1914-1918 C.E. That abasement of the "dragon" and his angels—what a victorious salvation it meant for all those who were on the side of Jehovah God and his reigning Messiah, Jesus!—Revelation 12:7-12; 6:3-6; 13:3.

Now we are in that "short period of time" during which the abased "dragon" and his angels are restrained to the neighborhood of our earth until they are removed from our vicinity to that prisonlike "abyss" of deathlike impotency and inactivity. Meantime, the victorious Messianic King has been gathering the remaining ones of the 144,000 spiritual Israelites that they may be sealed in their foreheads with the "seal of the living God" as his special possession. (Revelation 7:1-8; Matthew 24:31) But besides this remnant who are to be joint heirs with him in the heavenly Messianic kingdom, he has, even since before World War II broke out in the year 1939, been gathering also earthly subjects to the side of his Messianic kingdom.—John 10:16.

Already, despite all the "woe" that the abased "dragon" is angrily bringing upon both earth and sea, these earthly subjects have steadily increased in number to the point of becoming a "great crowd" made up of hundreds of thousands of dedicated, baptized disciples of the Messianic King, Jesus Christ. He promises to bring them miraculously out of "the great tribulation" into a new order on earth, free from trouble.—Revelation 7:9-17; 12:12.

The gathered remnant and the increasing "great crowd" all stand forth as a visible living evidence to all the world that the "mystery of God" has been finished and is irresistibly in action for carrying out its Messianic role. That is why they, although being "in the world," are different, for they are "no part of the world." (John 15:19; 17:14, 16) In this world of growing discontent and rebelliousness, persons are heard to say: "The words that I hate most are 'You must!'" But we are not here telling anyone, 'You must do this,' or, 'You must not do that.' It is other things that are putting all the peoples under compulsion, obliging them unwillingly to do something, even under sheer force of circumstances. It is the invisible "dragon," Satan the Devil, with his demons, who is exercising superhuman influence and saying to all people, 'You *must!*' These malicious intelligent spirit personalities are using the political "wild beast" to say, 'You *must!* if you are to survive under my rule.'

Look all around you! How many persons are there whom you find displaying the "mark of the wild beast" in their "right hand" or upon their "forehead"? They cannot deny whose slaves they are or who is their owner and master that says to them, 'You *must!*' The telltale "mark, the name of the wild beast or the number of its name," betrays those having it beyond all denial by them. (Revelation 13:16-18) If anyone because of his spiritual blindness does not discern the "mark," Almighty God does! Are these 'marked' worshipers of the political "wild beast" happy? Are they secure? Do they have peace of heart and mind? Do they have a promising future before them at the paws of the "wild beast," the Devil's visible worldwide organization of politics? No! And consider just why not.

Of what benefit is it for any human to bear the "mark" as a worshiper of the "wild beast" and of the "image of the wild beast"? Like it or not, such a worshiper now finds himself drinking a bitter potion, "the wine of the anger of God" from the "cup of his wrath." Along with that, he is "tormented with fire and sulphur in the sight of the holy angels and in the sight of the Lamb," even now before the utter destruction of all false worshipers in the not distant future. (Revelation 14:9-12) Also, today there are other things to consider, the "seven bowls of the anger of God" that are being poured out into all the earth by God's unseen "seven angels." The first "bowl" poured out affects the "men that had the mark of the wild beast and that were worshiping its image." Upon them there comes what corresponds to a "hurtful and malignant ulcer," a certain token that their idolatrous worship is leading to a painful, unpleasant death.—Revelation 16:1, 2.

Things of that kind that are pictured under such painful symbols in the Revelation could never stand for anything but something disagreeable from the hand of the living and true God, Jehovah the Almighty. It is very evident that he is not well pleased with those people that have the loathsome "mark." This brings up a serious question that deserves our consideration now, and that is, Where will all these 'marked' people be when the "war of the great day of God the Almighty" bursts forth at the approaching world situation that is significantly called Har-Magedon (Armageddon)? It is well for us to reflect that such people could be nowhere else but on the wrong side of the battlefield.

For years now the people have been greatly affected by what has been going forth from sources visible and invisible. One visible source has been the political "wild beast," which the people bearing the "mark" are worshiping, so patriotically. The other visible source has been the political "false prophet," making impressive predictions in favor of the "image of the wild beast." Still another source, the invisible one, has been the "great dragon," Satan the Devil, who is the mighty spirit creature that gave to the "wild beast" its worldly power, its throne and its authority over all mankind. What goes forth from these three sources is propaganda, talk, decrees, "inspired expressions," but not expressions inspired by the spirit of Jehovah God.

God's inspired Word pictures those "inspired expressions" as being unclean "frogs" hopping out of the mouths of the symbolic dragon, wild beast and false prophet. To whom, though, is it that those "unclean inspired expressions" are directed? To the political rulers that govern you, the reader! What can you do about this? Will you do as the people do? Today the rulers lead; the people follow. Such lead-taking rulers are being gathered by the three "unclean inspired expressions" to—where? To a final war against God the Almighty at the battlefield of Har-Magedon.—Revelation 16:13-16.

BATTLE LINES FORMING

How close are we to Har–Magedon? The march of the nations thither has been going on now for some time. The world situation that must finally be reached will call for divine action. That situation spells Har–Magedon (Armageddon)! Do not grow impatient. It will at last be here and we shall be there!

In view of the way that you, the reader, are living your life today, on which side are you logically bound to be at that battlefield? There will be only the two sides, and our course in life now bears us undeviatingly along to the one side or to the other side. Where do we desire to be—then? Will you be where you had never thought you would be—against "God the Almighty"? Has prejudice against his name, Jehovah or Yahweh, affected you? Whose name is better, God's name or the "name of the wild beast"?

Those bearing the "mark" symbolically branded in their right hand or on their forehead will find themselves where their present-day choosing will have brought them, onto the side of the symbolic dragon, wild beast and false prophet, hence against God the Almighty and his finished "mystery." Religious Babylon the Great will be of no spiritual aid to them then. That worldly empire of false Babylonish religion will already have been wiped out immediately preceding the "war of the great day of God the Almighty," her surprise destruction coming at the hands of her own former friendly political patrons. (Revelation 17:1 to 18:24) Religious hypocrisy, including that of Christendom, will have been openly exposed. No religious front will be a safe disguise then.

At the world situation of Har–Magedon the symbolic wild beast and false prophet will be fighting in battle array against the finished "mystery of God," God's empowered Messianic kingdom. That is against what the "dragon," Satan the Devil, wants them to fight, that he may boast before Almighty God of having the majority of the race of mankind on his side. The slogan of Satan the Devil is, Rule or ruin!

If he himself cannot rule them after his "short period of time" is up, he will ruin them. (Revelation 12:12) No person on earth should ever think that maybe the political "wild beast" whom he is now worshiping under the encouragement of the "false prophet" can win or fight to a stalemate. There is no chance of this! There can be only one outcome to the "war" at Har–Magedon, namely, that described under divine inspiration at Revelation 19:20, as follows:

"And the wild beast was caught, and along with it the false prophet that performed in front of it the signs with which he misled those who received the mark of the wild beast and those who render worship to its image. While still alive, they both were hurled into the fiery lake that burns with sulphur."

No gradual dying process for the "wild beast" and the "false prophet"! While "still alive," as functioning political organizations, they will speedily be plunged into everlasting destruction, as in fire and sulphur. But what about the individual political rulers and their armies and subjects who support the "wild beast" and "false prophet" to the last in a fight for their perpetuation? God the Almighty, then victorious, will not swerve from what he foretold as to the disposal of these individuals:

"But the rest were killed off with the long sword of the one seated on the horse, which sword proceeded out of his mouth. And all the birds were filled from the fleshy parts of them."—Revelation 19:21.

No decent burial, no burial with military honors, for those slain at Har–Magedon at the command that projects like a sharp long sword of execution out of the mouth of the victorious Warrior, Jesus Christ, the King of kings. Despised, their carcasses lie exposed on the ground for unclean carrion birds, on which carcasses they can gorge themselves as "the great evening meal of God," in response to the invitation issued by the glorious angel:

"Come here, be gathered together . . . that you may eat the fleshy parts of kings and the fleshy parts of military commanders and the fleshy parts of strong men and the fleshy parts of horses and of those seated upon them, and the fleshy parts of all, of freemen as well as of slaves and of small ones and great." —Revelation 19:17, 18.

At that time where is the benefit that today comes from worshiping in a patriotic, nationalistic manner the "wild beast" and its "image" at the urging of the political "false prophet"? Yes, at that time what about the badge of honor, of respectability and of public spiritedness that people think it is today to bear the "mark," that is, "the name of the wild beast or the number of its name," six hundred and sixty-six? Ah, then such present-day glamorous things prove to be all in vain!

During the "short period of time" before that disaster, the symbolic "great dragon" and its demon angels have great anger because of having lost the war in heaven and having been hurled down to the earth's vicinity. During this same "short period of time" the "dragon" has crowded in a lot of "woe" for all mankind dwelling on sea and on land; but shortly, at Armageddon, he counts on realizing his malicious intention of bringing upon the vast majority of humankind their greatest "woe"—their utter destruction at Almighty God's hands. O what satisfaction he will have at the fact that he will have brought down in irreparable ruin all these human creatures rather than let any other spirit person rule over them! But he and his demon angels are not given much time in which to gloat over the human wreckage that they have caused. For down from the holy heavens comes Jehovah's angel who is stronger than the "great dragon" and his demon angels, those wicked spirits in the heavenly places that have long wielded invisible power and might over all misguided humankind. The dreaded moment promptly arrives, the moment that they have long been awaiting—the solemn time when they are to be plunged into the abyss of total restraint!—Luke 8:29-31.

Who is Jehovah's angel that, unaided, comes down to perform the superhuman task? He is Jehovah's Key Keeper, "the angel of the abyss," the starlike one who has the "key of the pit of the abyss." (Revelation 9:1, 11) He is the one who, when on earth as a perfect man, had a personal experience in the "abyss." (Romans 10:7) He is the Principal One embraced in the millenniums-old "mystery of God," that is, the Principal One of the "seed" of God's "woman," who was foretold to be the Bruiser of the serpent in the head. (Genesis 3:15; Romans 16:20) Resistance to this mighty executive angel of Jehovah God is all for naught. "The dragon, the original serpent, who is the Devil and Satan," is seized, together with all his demon angels, and they are bound with an unbreakable "great chain" and hurled into the abyss, all exit out of which is locked with the "key" and then officially sealed shut. For how long? "For a thousand years."

Their being released at the end of those thousand years will be that they may have just one more brief try at again corrupting earth's inhabitants. After that malicious effort they will be eternally destroyed. —Revelation 20:1, 2, 7-10.

NEW HEAVENS AND A NEW EARTH

After the abyssing of Satan the Devil, what beautiful heavens there will be to smile down benignly upon the jubilant survivors of the "war of the great day of God the Almighty" at Har–Magedon! What a beautiful "earth" will then be ushered in for the Edenic pleasure of mankind! The old "heavens" and the old "earth" will have been put to flight into oblivion, never again to appear before the face of the Creator of heaven and earth, Jehovah God. (Revelation 20: 11) First to be put to flight will be the old "earth" by the divine destruction of all wicked human society at Armageddon or Har–Magedon. This will wipe out the man-made political, religious, social system of things that has held human society captive since

shortly after the earth-wide deluge of the prophet
Noah's day. To the happy satisfaction of the Creator
the ground will have been cleared down here for the
bringing in of the long-awaited new system of things,
ideally suited for a "new earth."—2 Peter 3:13.

Amid loud Hallelujahs ringing through all creation
under radiant azure skies the "new earth" starts off
with the divinely protected survivors of the "great
tribulation," an "earth" that will never be replaced
in mankind's future history. (Revelation 7:15; Matthew 24:21, 22) Theocratic organization reigns supreme upon all this terrestrial globe. Imprisoned in
the securely locked abyss, the "great dragon," "the
original serpent," cannot interfere with the theocratic
arrangement for humankind. No longer does the "wild
beast" out of the sea stalk through the earth, thrusting its seven heads of imperial world powers into
human affairs. It is no longer necessary to render
to Caesar the things that are Caesar's, but all things
must now be paid to God, the Great Theocrat. (Matthew 22:21) Worshiping of the "wild beast" and worshiping of the "great dragon" indirectly through the
"wild beast" are stamped out, forbidden, shunned. All
the ground is sanctified as the place for the worship
of Jehovah God alone. His name is sanctified; his
will is done on earth as it is fully done in heaven.
—Matthew 6:9, 10.

Brought to ruin are those of today who are "ruining the earth." (Revelation 11:18) The debris resulting from the "war of the great day of God the
Almighty" at Har–Magedon must be removed. The
time has come for beautification of the whole earthly
sphere as a paradise, of which the Garden of Eden
of six thousand years ago was the original God-given
model. (Genesis 1:26-31; 2:7-14) Mankind, redeemed
with the sin-atoning blood of the Lamb of God, deserves to have a perfect garden home in which to
enjoy life and the service and praise of Jehovah God
forever. The soil beneath man's feet must be made
productive to sustain human life in perfect health

and in ageless bloom for all time to come. The "new earth" of organized human society must flourish amid a true terrestrial paradise. Vibrant with inexpressible joy and eagerness, the Har–Magedon survivors set themselves to the challenging task, taking the lead for all mankind. They need to get things ready for the arrival of other redeemed ones. There is no time to lose!

Listen now! The precisely exact time clock of the purpose of Jehovah God strikes the wondrous hour! It is the hour for all those in the memorial tombs to begin hearing the voice of the Son of God and to come forth from the dead. (John 5:28, 29) The Son of God uses the "keys of death and of Ha'des." Look! Death and Ha'des begin giving up the dead that are in them, to continue doing so until Ha'des, mankind's common grave, gives up the last redeemed one found in it. Even the sea gives up the dead in its watery depths. (Revelation 20:12-14) Can we believe our eyes? There is the first martyr, Abel! There too is Enoch, yes, and Noah, Abraham, Sarah, Isaac, Rebekah, Jacob, Rachel, Moses, David, Daniel, Malachi, John the Baptist, O "so great a cloud of witnesses," all of whom preceded Jehovah's greatest witness of all, his beloved Son Jesus Christ. (Hebrews 11:1 to 12:2) And there— O how delightful to the Har–Magedon survivors— there are many of the "other sheep" whom Jehovah's "fine Shepherd" began gathering into his earthly flock in this "time of the end." With clear powers of identification the Har–Magedon survivors recognize them, and with these they proceed to renew their united service to the Most High God!—John 10:16.

When, in the "new earth," you see the dead raised out of their death sleep in Ha'des to life in the terrestrial paradise, how do you think you will feel? Really, how could you feel differently from those of the people who saw the Lord Jesus Christ raise the son of the poor widow of Nain in Galilee to life and restore him alive to his mother? Awesome fear should seize you as it did those resurrection witnesses! But more than that! "They began to glorify God, saying: 'A great prophet has been raised up among us,' and, 'God has turned his attention to his people.'" (Luke 7:16) More intimately than that, when you become witness to the resurrection of the first one of your own earthly relatives, how could the emotional effect of this upon you be otherwise than that upon the parents who saw the same Lord Jesus Christ restore their twelve-year-old daughter alive to their yearning arms? "At once they were beside themselves with great ecstasy." (Mark 5:42) Ah, indeed, unspeakable joy will be yours at the resurrection of the dead from Ha′des and the sea. Heartfelt comfort will be yours! O what a glorious tomorrow that will soon be here!

In view of that approaching hour of resurrection of the redeemed earthly dead, what loving preparations the Har–Magedon survivors will make toward receiving back all these who are in line for a resurrection through the redemptive perfect human sacrifice of the Lamb of God, Jesus Christ! How diligently they will cultivate the ground for the extending of the terrestrial paradise in which to provide living room for the resurrected ones! What preparations they will make to be faithful witnesses of Jehovah God and of his Lamb regarding all the words and works of God of which the restored dead will be ignorant! What a life-giving educational work they will carry forward in behalf of the returning dead ones, that they may live in an earth filled with the knowledge of Jehovah as the waters cover the sea basin! (Isaiah 11:9; Habakkuk 2:14) Serving as guidance, information and textbooks in this worldwide educational work will be the messages and decrees from God, concerning which Revelation 20:12 says:

"And scrolls were opened. . . . And the dead were judged out of those things written in the scrolls according to their deeds."

GOVERNMENT DESERVING OF MAN'S CONFIDENCE

Back to our ears come now the words of the announcement made after the blowing of the trumpet by the seventh angel: "the appointed time for the dead to be judged, and to give their reward to your slaves the prophets and to the holy ones and to those fearing your name, the small and the great." (Revelation 11:15-18) Perfect confidence is what you and the resurrected dead can have that this judgment, rendered according to one's deeds in the "new earth," will be fair, just, unprejudiced, flawless! Why so? Because over the Eden-like "new earth" there will reign the "new heavens." No longer is it necessary to wrestle with the invisible "great dragon" and his demon angels, "the world rulers of this darkness," "the wicked spirit forces in the heavenly places," these perverters of justice. Those old 'former heavens' have been consigned to the abyss. (Ephesians 6:12; Revelation 21:1) They have been replaced with the God-given "new heavens," the finished "mystery of God."

What a personnel that heavenly government will have, to inspire the full confidence of the Har–Magedon survivors and of those resurrected from the dead! Chief One in that celestial capital organization is the Lamb of God, the resurrected, glorified Jesus Christ, the one who is "called Faithful and True," and who "judges and carries on war in righteousness." (Revelation 19:11) He is the principal or essential one of the "seed" of God's wifelike heavenly organization, for bruising the Serpent in the head, that thus he might "bring to nothing the one having the means to cause death, that is, the Devil." (Genesis 3:15; Hebrews 2:14) Associated with the righteous Lamb of God in the heavenly capital organization are the 144,000 faithful anointed followers as "priests of God and of the Christ," who are to reign with Christ for a thousand years. This "little flock" of sheeplike followers are married to him and are lovelily spoken of as "the bride, the Lamb's wife." (Luke 12:32; Revelation 21:9) Inasmuch as that heavenly government will have as its officers the life-giving Bridegroom and his beloved Bride, it will be a paternal government caring for its subjects like its own children.

The Bride class is just as deserving of the confidence of all people on earth as is the Bridegroom, the King Jesus Christ. She is likened to an eye-entrancing city of beauty and is called "the holy city, New Jerusalem." In her all membership is debarred to "the cowards and those without faith and those who are disgusting in their filth and murderers and fornicators and those practicing spiritism and idolaters and all the liars." Indeed, "anything not sacred and anyone that carries on a disgusting thing and a lie will in no way enter into it; only those written in the Lamb's scroll of life will." (Revelation 21:8, 27) Nothing else but a clean, righteous, godly rule can be expected from such a government, one so carefully prepared by Jehovah God, the Holy One.

The "glory of God" lights up the citylike government, and the Lamb of God is as its "lamp." All earth beneath this citylike government will be lighted up, knowing the way to go in the paradise earth to gain the brilliant prize of everlasting life and happiness, with glowing perfect health. With proper confidence regarding this, Revelation 21:24 says: "The nations will walk by means of its light."

How heartwarming is the change that the "new heavens" bring to our earth! When the Satanic 'former heavens' were cast down from the holy realm of God's faithful angels and thus the "great dragon" and its angels came down to the vicinity of our earth, it was to mean "woe for the earth and for the sea!" And this has been so. (Revelation 12:7-12) But when the New Jerusalem comes down out of heaven from God in a beauty like that of a radiant bride adorned for her husband on her wedding day, it will be a time for blessing upon all the redeemed ones of mankind, the Har–Magedon survivors and the dead who are to be resurrected.

God's protection is spread over earth's inhabitants

like a tent, and by means of the Messianic government that he puts in power over them God resides
with mankind. "And he will wipe out every tear from
their eyes, and death will be no more, neither will
mourning nor outcry nor pain be any more. The former things have passed away." The death that we
all inherited from Adam after his fall into sin and
condemnation will be wiped out by the "life-giving
spirit," the self-sacrificing Lamb of God. (Romans
5:12; 1 Corinthians 15:24, 25, 45) All the bad effects
of the reign of sin and death will be undone forever!
—Revelation 21:1-4.

Refreshingly new—that is what everything on earth
will then be for redeemed mankind who were never
inside the paradise garden of Eden where human life
started out in beautiful perfection! And yet this new-
ness is absolutely certain to be, for Jehovah God on
his heavenly throne has unchangeably said: "Look!
I am making all things new." And to the apostle John
he said: "Write, because these words are faithful
and true." (Revelation 21:5) God does not lie. God
cannot possibly lie, either in spoken word or in inspired writings of his Holy Bible. His kingdom by
means of his Messianic King, Jesus Christ, will bring
to amazing reality all the divine promises.

CONSOLATIONS FROM THE FINISHED "MYSTERY OF GOD"

The "throne of God and of the Lamb" is established in the heavens since the year of change,
1914 C.E. The "throne of God and of the Lamb"
stands as the symbol of the installed Messianic kingdom of God, the finished and finally realized "mystery
of God." Out from that heavenly throne through the
"holy city, New Jerusalem," will flow to the "new
earth" the divine provisions for redeemed mankind
to partake of for everlasting life. Like an irresistible,
never-exhausted river of water of life, "clear as
crystal," those life provisions will flow to humankind
on the cleansed earth.—Revelation 22:1, 2.

Poor afflicted humankind of today! For almost sixty centuries you have suffered outside the lost Paradise of Eden. Bitter have been the tears that have streamed burning down your cheeks at the loss of loved ones in death. Piercing has been your irrepressible outcry at all the pain that has racked your body because of sickness, disease, decrepitude and crippling accidents. Anguished has been your sobbing at all the brutality and havoc of ungodly wars between your own members, brother men. Deep has been your mourning over all the religious hypocrisy and the perversion of truth and righteousness, resulting in the misrepresentation and reproach of the one living and true God, man's loving Creator. "How long, O God, how long?" you have moaned. How long will this divine permission of wickedness continue on among earth's inhabitants? Yet now lift up your drooping head. Let your tear-bedimmed eyes see all the evidences in world events and conditions that the end of the permission of diabolical wickedness is immediately upon you!

Turn your ears away from all the noisy tumult of clashing parties of men and open them wide to hear the cheering news that tells how we are living in the "time of the end" of this doomed system of things. Give ear to the joyful sound, "this good news of the kingdom." Can you not hear it? O you must be hearing it, for this consoling news is now being preached by the Christian witnesses of Jehovah God in "all the inhabited earth for a witness to all the nations." (Daniel 12:4; Matthew 24:14) Let the Lamb of God, like a Fine Shepherd, guide you to "fountains of waters of life," as he has already done in the case of the international "great crowd" of his "other sheep" all this earth around, in order that from now onward God may "wipe out every tear from [your] eyes." —Revelation 7:9-17.

Even now, as a foretaste of the fullness of God's provisions for everlasting life in the "new earth," soul-satisfying "water of life" is made available for you. The Lamb's Bride, of whom a faithful remnant are yet preaching on the earth, is joining with the spirit of divine prophecy in calling out: "Come!" You are athirst for the life that is real life, are you not? You wish to come, do you not? Ah, then, come and "take life's water free," for the invitation is extended to "anyone thirsting" and to "anyone that wishes." And do not be one who hears and comes mindful only of oneself, but follow the unselfish request: "Let anyone hearing say: 'Come!'" (Revelation 22:17) Lovingly point out to others the way to the "water of life" and spread the heavenly invitation to others. Drink and live—forever!

Make no secret of these things long ago foretold but now being marvelously fulfilled, "for the appointed time is near." (Revelation 22:10) Share the blessed information with others. These are the days in which the seventh angel of God has sounded the trumpet. Blessed are your ears in hearing the meaningful sound, for thereby you know and understand that the Messianic kingdom of God has been established in the heavens and is gloriously fulfilling the grand prophecies about it. With heartfelt devotion take your stand openly for this reigning kingdom of God by his Christ for the eternal blessing of all mankind. Hail this finished "mystery of God"!—Revelation 10:7; 11:15-17.

Subject Index

knowledge Universal Sovereign, 22
enthroned, 11-14
foreshadowed, 12, 14
symbol, 199
symbolic, praise Jehovah, 287
"Two olive trees," symbol, 265
"Two prophets," raised from death state, 314
2,520 years, explained, 315
seven symbolic "times," 284
"Two witnesses," 264-268
class, active in service, 280
killing and reviving, 268-272
resurrection, 273-279
warred on by "wild beast," 269-272

U

United Nations, appeared in 1945, 51, 237
membership, 51
United States of America, military conscription instituted, 123
persecution of Witnesses, 122, 123

W

War in heaven, 305-309
Watch Tower Society, headquarters transferred, 274

moved its printery, 246
officials arrested, 270, 271
Watch Tower Society officials, admitted to bail, 277
conviction reversed, 278
released from prison, 315
released on bail, 170, 171, 277
"Watchtower, The," in 1935, published information concerning "great crowd," 199-201
semimonthly printing, 1969, 279
White garments, walking in, 162-164
White robe, given, 67
"Wild beast," activity, 330-335
symbolic, existence, 324, 325
wars on remnant, 269-272
"Woman," Dragon's attempt to engulf, 317-322
identified, 297-300
influence, in modern-day Christian congregation, 144-148
World War I, 79
ended 1918 C.E., 51, 64
remnant had no "pull" with politicians after, 169
ride of four horsemen evident by, 80, 81
World War II, outbreak in 1939, 51, 171

Did Man Get Here by Evolution or by Creation?

Were our ancestors apelike men? How old is man? Why do so many persons believe evolution? The answers are available in the 192-page book **Did Man Get Here by Evolution or by Creation?** The evidence can be examined and the reader can see for himself which is most reasonable —a popular theory or the Bible's account of man's origin and his future. In less than two years this book has reached a circulation of 4½ million copies. Generously illustrated, it contains hundreds of references to scientific and scholarly works. Hardbound, sent anywhere, postpaid, for only 25c.

Is the Bible Really the Word of God?

This pocket-sized book clearly answers such questions as: Is the Genesis account of creation fact or fiction? Was there an earth-wide Flood? Can you always expect secular history to agree with the Bible? Is its record about early Christianity sound? Are the miracles of the Bible true? Does the Bible contradict itself? Are the Bible's moral standards consistent? Is the Bible practical for our day? Amazing Bible prophecies that you have seen fulfilled add to the evidence presented in this 192-page book. Hardbound, sent postpaid, for 25c a copy.

The Truth That Leads to Eternal Life

Here is a brief, easy-to-understand explanation of the Bible's basic teachings. This book presents an outstanding Bible-study course for all members of your family, young and old. It answers questions facing all kinds of people, such as: Where are the dead? Why has God permitted wickedness till now? How can we identify the true religion? It shows how many modern-day practices, such as ESP, astrology and the use of Ouija boards, stand in the light of Bible truth. In its first year, more than 15 million copies were printed in many languages to meet public demand. Only 25c a copy.

To order, see addresses on the last page.

WHETHER YOU KNOW GREEK OR NOT—

You will be delighted with the insight that the **Kingdom Interlinear Translation of the Greek Scriptures** gives you into the meaning of the Scriptures. Comparatively few persons today have been able to delve directly into the basic thoughts of the original written text. But now you can do just that without knowing Greek. Note the illustration below from 2 Timothy 3:1-4:

Greek interlinear	New World Translation
3 Τοῦτο δὲ γίνωσκε ὅτι ἐν ἐσχάταις This but be you knowing that in last ἡμέραις ἐνστήσονται καιροὶ days will be standing in appointed times χαλεποί· **2** Ἔσονται γὰρ οἱ ἄνθρωποι fierce; will be for the men φίλαυτοι, φιλάργυροι, ἀλαζόνες, fond of selves, fond of silver, self-assuming, ὑπερήφανοι, βλάσφημοι, γονεῦσιν superior appearing, blasphemers, to parents ἀπειθεῖς, ἀχάριστοι, ἀνόσιοι, disobedient, unthankful, disloyal, **3** ἄστοργοι, ἄσπονδοι, διάβολοι, without natural affection, truceless, devils, ἀκρατεῖς, ἀνήμεροι, without (self-) control, untamed, ἀφιλάγαθοι, **4** προδόται, προπετεῖς, not fond of goodness, betrayers, forward-falling, τετυφωμένοι, φιλήδονοι having been made to smoke up, fond of pleasures	**3** But know this, that in the last days critical times hard to deal with will be here. 2 For men will be lovers of themselves, lovers of money, self-assuming, haughty, blasphemers, disobedient to parents, unthankful, disloyal, 3 having no natural affection, not open to any agreement, slanderers, without self-control, fierce, without love of goodness, 4 betrayers, headstrong, puffed up [with

The left-hand column contains the original Greek text as revised by the Greek scholars Westcott and Hort. Between the lines of the Greek text will be found the word-for-word English translation.

In the right-hand parallel column one finds the modern-language rendering of the **New World Translation of the Holy Scriptures**, Matthew through Revelation, in its latest revision.

This excellent work will be sent anywhere, postpaid, for $2 a copy.

Also available is the regular edition of the **New World Translation of the Holy Scriptures**, from Genesis through Revelation, in English, for only $1.

To order, see addresses on the last page.

Aid to Bible Understanding

God's message for mankind, contained in the Bible, was meant to be understood.

Would you like an excellent aid in acquiring understanding of the Bible? Then you will profit from having and consulting the new publication **Aid to Bible Understanding**. When you read or study the Bible and come upon an unfamiliar term, it is easy to look it up in this helpful new volume. Articles are arranged alphabetically. The best scholarship, including the results of the most recent research, is brought to bear on such features in the Bible as:

✔ **PEOPLE:** What people of many races and nations said and did; their customs, emotions and their right or wrong worship.

✔ **PLACES:** Including lands, cities and villages, mountains, rivers, with their native trees and plants, birds and animals; the latest in archaeological investigations in such lands as Egypt, Palestine, Syria, Assyria, Babylon and Persia.

✔ **NOTABLE EVENTS:** The rise and fall of empires and kingdoms, political conspiracies and major battles.

✔ **RECORD OF GOD'S DEALINGS WITH MEN:** His mercy and miraculous saving acts, judgments, promises and prophecies.

✔ **FIGURATIVE EXPRESSIONS IN THE BIBLE:** These are made clear by means of a study of the context, related texts and surrounding circumstances.

All these things and many more are found in the Bible record. They all have significance, and the more we know about them the clearer God's purpose toward man can become to us. The aim of this publication is to enhance your understanding of the Bible.

Hardbound, more than 500 pages (including subjects in the letters A-E), helpful charts and illustrations.

You may obtain your copy of this volume of **Aid to Bible Understanding** by remitting $2.50 to WATCHTOWER, using the nearest address on the next page.

CHIEF OFFICE AND OFFICIAL ADDRESS OF
Watch Tower Bible & Tract Society of Pennsylvania
Watchtower Bible and Tract Society of New York, Inc.
International Bible Students Association
124 Columbia Heights, Brooklyn, New York 11201, U.S.A.

ADDRESSES OF BRANCH OFFICES:

ALASKA 99501: 1438 Medfra Street, Anchorage. ARGENTINA: Calle Honduras 5646-48, Buenos Aires 14. AUSTRALIA: 11 Beresford Road, Strathfield, N.S.W. 2135. AUSTRIA: Gallgasse 44, A-1130 Vienna. BAHAMAS: Box 1247, Nassau, N.P. BARBADOS, W.I.: Fontabelle Rd., Bridgetown. BELGIUM: 60, rue d'Argile, Kraainem, Bt. BOLIVIA: Casilla No. 1440, La Paz. BRAZIL: Rua Guaíra 216, Jardim da Saúde, São Paulo-8, SP. BRITISH HONDURAS: Box 257, Belize. BURMA: P.O. Box 62, Rangoon. CAMEROUN, REP. FED. DU: B.P. 5.428, Douala-Akwa. CANADA: 150 Bridgeland Ave., Toronto 390, Ontario. CENTRAL AFRICAN REPUBLIC: B.P. 662, Bangui. CEYLON: 7 Alfred House Rd., Colombo 3. CHILE: Casilla 261-V, Correo 15, Santiago. COLOMBIA: Apartado Aéreo 2587, Barranquilla. CONGO, REPUBLIC OF THE: B.P. 634, Kinshasa, Limete. CONGO REPUBLIC: B.P. 2.114, Brazzaville. COSTA RICA: Apartado 2043, San José. CUBA: Avenida 15 Núm. 4608, Almendares, Marianao, Havana. CYPRUS: P.O. Box 1590, Nicosia. DAHOMEY: B.P. 874, Cotonou. DENMARK: Kongevejen 207, 2830 Virum. DOMINICAN REPUBLIC: Avenida Francia 33, Santo Domingo. ECUADOR: Casilla 4512, Guayaquil. EL SALVADOR: Apartado 401, San Salvador. ENGLAND: Watch Tower House, The Ridgeway, London N.W. 7. FIJI: Box 23, Suva. FINLAND: Kuismatie 58, Tikkurila. FRANCE: 81, rue du Point-du-Jour, 92 - Boulogne-Billancourt (Hauts de Seine). GERMANY (WESTERN): Am Kohlheck, Postfach 13025, (62) Wiesbaden-Dotzheim. GHANA: Box 760, Accra. GREECE: No. 4 Kartali St., Athens 611. GUADELOUPE: B.P. 239, Pointe-à-Pitre. GUATEMALA: 11 Avenida 5-67, Guatemala 1. GUYANA: 50 Brickdam, Georgetown 11. HAITI: Post Box 185, Port-au-Prince. HAWAII 96814: 1228 Pensacola St., Honolulu. HONDURAS: Apartado 147, Tegucigalpa. HONG KONG: 312 Prince Edward Rd., Second Floor, Kowloon. ICELAND: P.O. Box 251, Reykjavik. INDIA: South Avenue, Santa Cruz, Bombay 54. INDONESIA: Djalan Batutjeper 25, Djakarta. IRELAND: 86 Lindsay Rd., Glasnevin, Dublin 9. ISRAEL: P.O. Box 44520, Haifa. ITALY: Via Monte Maloia 32, 00141 Rome. JAMAICA, W.I.: 41 Trafalgar Rd., Kingston 10. JAPAN: 5-5-8 Mita Minato-Ku, Tokyo, 108. KENYA: Box 7788, Nairobi. KOREA: P.O. Box 7, Sodaemun-ku P.O., Seoul. LEBANON: P.O. Box 1122, Beirut. LEEWARD ISLANDS, W.I.: Box 119, St. Johns, Antigua. LIBERIA: P.O. Box 171, Monrovia. LUXEMBOURG: 15, rue de l'Egalite, Luxembourg-Bonnevoie, G.D. MALAGASY REPUBLIC: II M 78 A Antsakaviro, Tananarive. MAURITIUS: 12 Lebrun Street, Rose Hill. MEXICO: Calzada Melchor Ocampo 71, Mexico 4, D.F. NETHERLANDS: Voorburgstraat 250, Amsterdam 17. NETHERLANDS ANTILLES: Oosterbeekstraat 11, Willemstad, Curaçao. NEWFOUNDLAND, CANADA: 239 Pennywell Rd., St. John's. NEW ZEALAND: 621 New North Rd., Auckland 3. NICARAGUA: Apartado 183, Managua, D.N. NIGERIA: P.O. Box 194, Yaba, Colony. NORWAY: Inkognitogaten 28 B., Oslo 2. OKINAWA, RYUKYU IS.: Higashi P.O. Box 2004, 91 Asato, Naha City. PAKISTAN: 8-E Habibullah Rd., Lahore. PANAMA: Apartado 1386, Panama 1. PAPUA: Box 113, Port Moresby. PARAGUAY: Casilla de Correo 482, Asunción. PERU: Gervasio Santillana 370, Miraflores, Lima. PHILIPPINE REPUBLIC: 186 Roosevelt Ave., San Francisco del Monte, Quezon City D-503. PUERTO RICO 00927: Calle Onix 23, Urb. Bucaré, Río Piedras. RHODESIA: P.O. Box 1462, Salisbury. SENEGAL: B.P. 3107, Dakar. SIERRA LEONE: Box 136, Freetown. SINGAPORE: 11 Jalan Sejarah, Singapore 11. SOUTH AFRICA: Private Bag 2, P.O. Elandsfontein, Transvaal. SURINAM: Box 49, Wicherstr. 8, Paramaribo. SWEDEN: Folkungavagen 8, Jakobsberg. SWITZERLAND: Allmendstrasse 39, 3000 Berne 22. TAIWAN (REPUBLIC OF CHINA): No. 5 Lane 99, Yun-Ho St., Taipei. THAILAND: 69/1 Soi 2, Sukhumwit Rd., Bangkok 11. TOGO REPUBLIC: B.P. 1237, Lomé. TRINIDAD, W.I.: 21 Taylor St., Woodbrook, Port of Spain. UNITED STATES OF AMERICA: 117 Adams St., Brooklyn, N.Y. 11201. URUGUAY: Francisco Bauza 3372, Montevideo. VENEZUELA: Avda. Honduras, Quinta Luz, Urb. Las Acacias, Caracas, D.F. ZAMBIA: Box 1598, Kitwe.